Balancing Liberty and Security

Crime Prevention and Security Management

Series Editor: Martin Gill

Titles include:

Mark Button
DOING SECURITY
Critical Reflections and an Agenda for Change

Paul Ekblom
CRIME PREVENTION, SECURITY AND COMMUNITY SAFETY USING
THE 5IS FRAMEWORK

Bob Hoogenboom
THE GOVERNANCE OF POLICING AND SECURITY
Ironies, Myths and Paradoxes

Kate Moss
BALANCING LIBERTY AND SECURITY
Human Rights, Human Wrongs

Kate Moss
SECURITY AND LIBERTY
Restriction by Stealth

Adam White
THE POLITICS OF PRIVATE SECURITY
Regulation, Reform and Re-Legitimation

Forthcoming:

Joshua Bamfield
SHOPPING AND CRIME

Crime Prevention and Security Management
Series Standing Order ISBN 978–0–230–01355–1 hardback
                             978–0–230–01356–8 paperback
(outside North America only)

You can receive future titles in this series as they are published by placing a standing order. Please contact your bookseller or, in case of difficulty, write to us at the address below with your name and address, the title of the series and one of the ISBNs quoted above.

Customer Services Department, Macmillan Distribution Ltd, Houndmills, Basingstoke, Hampshire RG21 6XS, England

Balancing Liberty and Security

Human Rights, Human Wrongs

Kate Moss
Wolverhampton University, UK

First published 2011 by
PALGRAVE MACMILLAN

Palgrave Macmillan in the UK is an imprint of Macmillan Publishers Limited, registered in England, company number 785998, of Houndmills, Basingstoke, Hampshire RG21 6XS.

Palgrave Macmillan in the US is a division of St Martin's Press LLC, 175 Fifth Avenue, New York, NY 10010.

Palgrave Macmillan is the global academic imprint of the above companies and has companies and representatives throughout the world.

Palgrave® and Macmillan® are registered trademarks in the United States, the United Kingdom, Europe and other countries.

ISBN: 978–0–230–23029–3

This book is printed on paper suitable for recycling and made from fully managed and sustained forest sources. Logging, pulping and manufacturing processes are expected to conform to the environmental regulations of the country of origin.

A catalogue record for this book is available from the British Library.

Library of Congress Cataloging-in-Publication Data

Moss, Kate, 1965–
    Balancing liberty and security : human rights, human wrongs / Kate Moss.
        p. cm.
    Includes bibliographical references and index.
    ISBN-13: 978–0–230–23029–3 (hardback : alk. paper)
    ISBN-10: 0–230–23029–6 (hardback)
        1. Human rights – Great Britain. 2. Civil rights – Great Britain. 3. Human rights – Europe. I. Title.

KD4080.M67 2011
341.4′8—dc22   2011013813

10 9 8 7 6 5 4 3 2 1
20 19 18 17 16 15 14 13 12 11

Printed and bound in the United States of America

*For all individuals in the world whose lives have been,
or are, touched by injustice*

Contents

Acknowledgements

With many thanks to Professor Ken Pease and Professor Herschel Prins for acting as critical readers and for their continued encouragement, which is greatly appreciated.

Special thanks to Michael Mansfield QC for agreeing to write the foreword for this book and for taking the time, in a very busy schedule, to read the manuscript.

Thanks also to the School of Law, Social Science and Communications, Wolverhampton University, for helping to facilitate this work.

Series Editor's Preface

Books which examine the role of law as a crime prevention tool are relatively rare, and Kate's latest book fills this important gap. She notes that over 400 forms of behaviour that were legal prior to the last Labour Government are illegal now, and, adding fuel to the fire, notes that much legislation works in the interest of offenders, including those who commit serious offences.

This is Kate's second book in this series. In the first, *Security and Liberty: Restriction by Stealth* (2009), she tackled the balance of national security needs with the protection of civil liberties, which included a critique of the emphasis placed by New Labour on using legislation as a form of crime prevention. A central premise of her work was that Government was taking too much account of perceived risks rather than real ones, with outcomes that have been counterproductive. Moreover, Kate chided criminologists for neglecting this important area of study, noting that critiquing the role of the State attracts little research funding.

In this book she further examines the erosion of people's democratic rights. She warns of the potential catastrophic dangers of neglecting this topic, citing genocides in various European and African countries, the segregation of blacks and whites in America and the McCarthy communist witch hunts as illustrative examples of what can happen when civil liberties are neglected. Her central theme is the endemic dangers of the enlarged power of the State and the central role of Government in undermining personal freedoms, which she feels go largely unchallenged or only mildly so. She outlines how 'the use of state force in the name of the protection of security is a common theme in the avoidance, ignoring or sidestepping of many civil liberties issues'. But the commercial sector too comes under scrutiny by, for example, trading in equipment that is used in torture.

As Kate says, in this book she is 'tracing the compromises, fudges and accommodations by which the protection of human rights is now beset'. This includes the inadequacy of laws in the way they have been drafted; the role of judicial decision making in effectively undermining what was intended by Convention and law; and political manoeuvring to appeal to higher principles than law, namely grave risks. The problem for Kate is that laws such as the Human Rights Act 1998 have 'facilitated behaviour in relation to terrorism which erodes civil liberties and undermines the basic principles of those essential rights which are supposed to be held so dear'.

She traces the origins of habeas corpus and the doctrine of 'innocent until proven guilty' from 1215 and the signing of the Magna Carta; assesses deviations from what otherwise might be considered legitimate practice epitomised in the Diplock courts in Northern Ireland in the 1970s, and the unlawful interrogation at Guantánamo Bay; and highlights specific individual abuses such as those of Baha Mousa, who died in 2003 after sustaining 93 injuries whilst in UK detention in Iraq. Indeed, the text is littered with examples which enable her to assess the ineffectiveness of the supposed legal safeguards that are derived from legislation such as the European Convention on Human Rights and the UK Human Rights Act 1998. She completes the book by critiquing the impact of the EU's new five-year strategy for justice and home affairs and security policy for 2009–2014, including the 'shadowy Future Group'.

The issues and the balances are difficult and complex; indeed Kate herself admits to both changing her views and to not being able to 'entirely reconcile myself to one overarching view which covers all situations'. In clarifying some important issues about personal freedoms and the protection of them, and in examining the powers of states in this regard, she is able to highlight different ways forward and the potential dangers they represent. Perhaps though her main objective, completely fulfilled, is to draw attention to the subject area, the knowledge gaps that exist, and to generate debate on what is perhaps one of the main issues affecting the type of security we should be seeking in the future.

MARTIN GILL

Foreword

Two thousand and twenty-five years ago, a political commentator and historian who witnessed the birth of a major global enterprise headed by a president/chief executive with immense autocratic powers made the following perceptive observation: 'History is philosophy teaching by example'. The commentator was the Greek Dionysius of Halicarnassus, who was watching the turbulence, the internal constitutional wrangles and power brokering, the foreign wars and acquisitions of an emergent Roman Empire under Octavian, later known as Augustus. Much of what he saw, the aspirations, the avarice, the threats, the tensions, bears a clear resemblance to what is going on now and reverberates through the events of the 20th and 21st centuries.

Implicit in Dionysius's message was a recognition that the lessons of history have to be re-learnt by successive generations, infused with a sense of principle and practice. But this is far from what happens; memories are short, 'a week is a long time in politics' and exigency becomes the name of the game.

Not in this book, however, which sets a very different pace and agenda. The joy of this work is its passion. It carries you from page to page traversing a huge tapestry of compelling contemporary issues, through a maze of moral dilemmas and legal conundrums, which touch every corner of everyone's life however and wherever lived. It is about the very nature and quality of our existence expressed through the prism of rights and freedoms. It's clear, breathtakingly broad yet detailed, rooted in reality and, above all, humane.

This kind of analysis, especially from the academic world (save for the two recent books by Professor A.C. Grayling), has been in short supply and is long overdue. The advent of rapidly expanding and instantaneous information technology has transformed the communication marketplace and the forum of public debate. Whether it is mass media or parliamentary discourse, the dominant force has become the soundbite, the ready-made fact file, the easily digestible digi-comment, the quick flick e-link. Lateral and critical thinking have become conspicuous by their absence.

In contrast to this, Professor Kate Moss refreshingly rejuvenates the spirit and logic of enquiry. Had this pervaded the last three decades of public life, we might have avoided the political and legislative nightmare created by a raft of politicians on all sides who were either asleep, or more likely numbed into atrophy by the constant refrain of 'national security'. The repercussions of this anaesthesia have not been restricted to the erosion of fundamental freedoms within the UK (from civil surveillance and the Prevent agenda to indefinite detention without trial), but have led to disastrous and continuing incursions elsewhere in the world, most notably Iraq and Afghanistan.

Throughout this period, I have been a barrister working in the areas graphically described by Professor Moss, and my experience is a mirror image of the sentiments she expresses in each chapter. I have witnessed at first hand the steady and cavalier manner in which respect for the rule of law and civil rights has diminished. This has been marked by an arrogance of power and a striking lack of accountability. It is no coincidence that the resultant democratic bankruptcy and meltdown have been accompanied by a similar phenomenon in the economy and the environment.

The remarkable feature of the legal and political landscape, however, has been the indomitable and indefatigable spirit of ordinary people fighting back for the single purpose of restoring accountability and justice. The list is endless and many instances are chronicled in this book: Doreen and Neville Lawrence; the Finucanes; Eileen Dallaglio and the Marchioness families; de Menezes; Mubarek; Moussa; the Birmingham Six and the Guildford Four; Binjam Mohamed; service families who forced an Inquiry into the Iraq war; victims of 7/7 and their families; the Bloody Sunday families; and the G 20 Tomlinson family – whose inquest is set down for the spring of 2011. At all the hearings which have been completed, as well as those which are ongoing, crucial truths have been uncovered. Vital recommendations involving systemic change have been made and implemented. It is certain that nothing would have happened had it been left to the whims and fancies of the authorities.

The achievements are inspiring and tangible, accomplished more often than not through the medium of inquests and public judicial inquiries. Small wonder therefore that both have been seriously threatened, and the latter has been severely circumscribed by the Inquiries Act 2005. Such developments rarely excite headlines, let alone sensible discussion. Thankfully they receive careful exposure in Chapter 2, providing a rare and chilling insight into the shadows and curbs imposed on our essential 'need/right to know' by the proponents of political paralysis.

This struggle is not new, nor is it confined to the UK. Within the recent past it has erupted in Eastern Europe; the Balkans; the Philippines; Burma; China; South Africa; Thailand; Nepal; Venezuela and Argentina.

As I write, the French public are consuming in prodigious numbers a pamphlet, 'Indignez Vous!', published by an eminent 93-year-old human rights protagonist. Over Christmas it became a bestseller, with copies sold reaching nigh on 1 million. The reason is simple. Stephane Hessel, incarcerated in concentration camps during the Second World War, later becoming one of the architects of the Universal Declaration of Human Rights (UDHR) in 1948, has resurrected the spirit of resistance to the creeping inequalities and injustices being perpetrated throughout the world. One obvious arena is Palestine, where the Israeli state has consistently and flagrantly violated the norms and resolutions of international law. Once again it is ordinary citizens who are seeking to redress the situation by instituting the Russell Tribunal on Palestine in 2010/11 and by organising flotillas and convoys of humanitarian aid.

One of the most pernicious and powerful ways in which international human rights conventions, treaties and protocols are circumvented is by the collusion of global commercial syndicates with Government agencies. This often occurs through bodies that are unaccountable and unelected, and under the pretext of national and international security. In Chapter 7, Professor Moss pinpoints 'the shadowy Future Group' set up by the Council of the European Union to consider a five-year strategy for justice, home affairs and security, with powers to accumulate even more data on our daily lives. Another example is the Bilderberg Group, established in 1954 in a hotel of that name in Holland. Innumerable British prime ministers and politicians have gathered along with high-profile US personalities, representatives of the banking and financial world, royal dignitaries and media moguls. They meet in the midst of the tightest security imaginable and never reveal their discussions. A trifle odd, if it's all so innocent and they're only consuming tea and iced buns!

Professor Kate Moss has set out what she admits to be a modest objective of tipping the balance back towards civil rights and away from perceived, as opposed to real risks. She emphasises, on more than one occasion, that it is not her intention to proclaim 'a maximalist paradigm of civil liberties'. This is entirely reasonable and honourable but I would ask the reader to consider why it might be necessary to go the extra mile.

The reason for making this endeavour is to restore the content, context and impact of fundamental human rights and freedoms. Since 1948 they have been subjected to a steady, almost imperceptible dissolution and emasculation. The concept which has done the most damage is 'balance' – it is the idea that somehow there has to be a balance struck between, for example, rights and security. The Blair/Brown brotherhood embraced successive Home Secretaries (Jack Straw, John Reid, David Blunkett, Charles Clarke, Jacqui Smith, Alan Johnson), all of whom sold the public the line that in the new age of terror and cybercrime, we must expect a 'trade-off' between rights and the need for extraordinary powers to combat the 'hidden enemy'.

This is an extremely dangerous approach. It led the Bush administration to adopt the US Attorney General's dismissal of various human rights conventions, particularly those relating to war, as 'antiquated' and to violate the clear prohibition on torture, cruel, inhuman or degrading treatment (Article 5 UDHR and Article 3 ECHR). All kinds of devious and reprehensible methods of interrogation and imprisonment were devised, sometimes with British knowledge and collusion, in Guantánamo, Abu Graib and other sites of extraordinary rendition.

In my view, no balancing exercise should be contemplated. Either we mean what we say and hold dear our core values, or we throw everything to the winds.

The Universal Declaration as drafted by Hessel and others was clear, concise and unequivocal, for example:

Article 20

Everyone has the right to peaceful assembly and association.
No one may be compelled to belong to an association.

Unfortunately later conventions and protocols have drastically diluted the UDHR Articles with provisos, caveats and extensive exceptions.

Article 11 ECHR

Everyone has the right to freedom of peaceful assembly and to freedom of association with others including the right to form and to join trade unions for the protection of his interests.
No restrictions shall be placed on the exercise of these rights *other than* such as are prescribed by law and are necessary in a democratic society in the interests of national security or public safety, for the prevention of disorder or crime, for the protection of health or

morals or for the protection of the rights and freedoms of others. This Article shall not prevent the imposition of lawful restrictions on the exercise of these rights by members of the armed forces, of the police or of the administration of the state.

It's time to stand up for principle, set an example and make history, as Dionysius would have wanted!

MICHAEL MANSFIELD QC
Author of *Memoirs of a Radical Lawyer*
(Bloomsbury 2009)

1
Liberty versus Security

One of the major questions facing contemporary society in the areas of political theory and practice, law, philosophy and human rights is whether there is an acceptable balance between national security needs and the protection of civil liberties. This is an issue which I tackled in my book – *Security and Liberty: Restriction by Stealth* (2009) – in which I questioned the rights, responsibilities and expectations of individual citizens and the accountability of the organs of the State as well as the lack of interest of academe in becoming truly engaged in this debate. The preface to that book notes that when the writer became interested in crime in the 1970's, ideas then in the ascendant included the strict circumscription of behaviour properly criminalised, and the corresponding circumscription of properly exercised judicial discretion. Concerning the lengths to which those ideologies have changed (2009: x),

> If... anyone had predicted that a generation later Guantánamo Bay would be filled with untried people and flights of extraordinary rendition exported prisoners to places convenient for their torture, they would have been thought insane. That the UK Parliament is now haggling not about the principle of detention without trial but how many weeks and months such detention would be allowed to last, is breath-taking.

In *Security and Liberty: Restriction by Stealth* (2009) I dealt with a range of aspects of the creeping power of the executive, some less dramatic than others, but all of them important elements of what I consider to be burgeoning fear-driven law and practice. I questioned the heavy emphasis by New Labour on using legislation to facilitate crime control which has been passed with relatively little academic evaluation and the restrictions imposed on people by the criminalising of behaviour that in many cases has long been held to be reasonable. My point is that more laws do not make crime less likely, indeed they can make it more common. For me, crime control has lost direction; legislation has been based on perceived rather than real risks. As a consequence, what has emerged is a legislative framework that is heavy handed and dispropor-tionate. It is also counterproductive and beyond being unnecessary and an infringement of basic human rights, it will work in the interests of offenders, not least terrorists.

Since the events of September 2001 it seems to me that we are now living in a world that is characterised by fear and subsequently obsessed with security. The success of those attacks, beyond the immediate tragic loss of life, lies primarily in engendering a climate of 'risk aversion' in which whole groups of people are placed under suspicion, thus acceler-ating their alienation and possible radicalisation. A decade ago it might have been unthinkable for anyone involved in crime reduction within the democratic world to imagine that we could see the demise of some of our basic democratic principles. Who would have thought that the notion of habeas corpus – traceable to the 13th century – and the con-cept of 'innocent until proven guilty' would be so easily suspended and that people would be held without trial, sometimes for years both here in the UK and in the US – the self-proclaimed land of the free. More surprising perhaps is that fact that relatively few people appear to be speaking out about these developments, including academics who argu-ably ought to be interested in them. It is somewhat ironic that similar developments in other countries such as Iraq, Libya and Saudi Arabia have received huge comment, but arguably, when Britain and the US perpetrate similar behaviour in respect of innocent people, many seem to turn a blind eye or accept the justification which is often given for it; that it is part of the 'war against terror'.

It seems dangerous for any of us to turn a blind eye to these develop-ments, particularly those of us whose professional obligation ought to be speaking out against them. The systematic disintegration of various human rights and personal freedoms has happened before. We have only to remind ourselves of some of the genocides of the 20th century in Germany and Rwanda, and currently that in Darfur – to name but a few. Let's not forget also the segregation of blacks and whites in America and the McCarthy witch hunts. In all of these cases, certain groups of people were persistently attacked purely on the basis of their religious, ethnic or political beliefs. It is not as if we do not have experience of this historically, but to my thinking, it seems that the State's potential to repress is now much wider.

My concern with the enlarged power of the State is not new but there does not appear to be a great deal of contemporary academic comment. Is this due to complacency, are academics just not interested in this area of research or does something else drive it? I have written earlier (Moss 2006: 184) that one of the problems with some academic disciplines is that research interests are money and outcome driven. In relation to research concerning crime and its control, researchers often preach flexibility in dealing strategically with crime but this approach means that what drives the research is what the policy makers wish to fund. Thinking imaginatively about crime, and of course criticising the State's approach to crime, human rights and personal freedoms, is not therefore something which is likely to attract funding. Added to this, given that future research assessment exercises are likely to take a metric form, then the push to undertake greater amounts of funded research may well obscure other types of research which are arguably no less worthwhile, but which are less likely to attract funding from traditional sources.

Since completing *Security and Liberty* I am keenly aware that the examples I gave represent only a fraction of those that could have been discussed. In fact, writing the book has simply heightened my awareness that I have merely scratched the surface of this important area and that more attention should be drawn to these and other related issues by academics, and the general public; many citizens are only too well aware, from personal experience, how ill-thought-through and knee-jerk legal measures can indict the innocent. It is also pertinent to point out that the role the Government has played in all of this should not be underestimated. Arguably one of the factors on which an effective Government ought to be judged is its commitment to civil liberties. The Blair–Brown administration was the longest serving 'Labour' Government in history. During its tenure in office, more legislation reached the statute books than was the case for any other Government. It is paradoxical that a European and more recently a UK benchmark for human rights have been developed at a time when concerns about terrorism and subversion have undermined the mindset which gave these ideals birth. In this book I want to further these ideas by tracing the compromises, fudges and accommodations by which the protection of human rights is now beset, and place this in its historical context. Given the questions currently being raised regarding the role and accountability of the organs of the State, this book seems both timely and necessary.

However, lest the reader gains the impression that the aim of this book is to promote some maximalist paradigm of civil liberties, I would like to state very clearly that this is not my intention. The subject matter of this book will clearly raise strength of feeling about issues that are of interest to many people, many of whom may have extreme views. I can appreciate that the tenor of this book may give the impression that my 'take' on this is one sided, but that is far from my intention. For this reason I think it is prudent to explicitly acknowledge the human rights critics. For example, Waddington's (2005) 'Slippery slopes and Civil Libertarian Pessimism' essay immediately springs to mind. Jim does not accept the case that the law (in books or elsewhere) has markedly changed the freedoms we have to protest. I've no doubt that he would cite the case of the Tibetans and Brian Haw's previous occupancy of Parliament Square saying that in some respects people now have more freedom to protest than previously. Readers should note that before his death in June 2011, peace campaigner Brain Haw faced being evicted from an area of grass in Parliament Square after losing an appeal against a possession order instigated by the Lord Mayor of London, Boris Johnson.

There are also a growing number of scholars who contest the whole notion of human rights as non-enforceable; some have even questioned the whole concept, alleging that it is based on the 'nonsense of a social contract'. I don't agree with this obviously (and it's more exciting that I don't), but it is important not to dismiss these critiques.

Turning to specifics, there was a case, a few years ago, concerning a major drug dealer in the north west of England, who was tried and sentenced in Holland. The police freely admitted that he could have been tried in England, but Dutch law was more accommodating in admitting tape recorded phone conversations as evidence. There is also Doreen McBarnet's (1991 & 2004) work on white collar crime, in which she points to how business people go 'opinion shopping' when formulating a dodgy deal. Penny Green and Tony Ward (2005) point to a similar process when it comes to locating business premises using equipment, materials, and so on. that would be disallowed in the UK. Everybody is at it in a globalised world. Critics have also, for example, pointed out to me recently that the prohibition against the use of torture was made under a UN Convention that the UK has ratified so that *must* mean people cannot be tortured. Whilst this is correct in the sense that there is a legal prohibition, it fails to acknowledge the case law on this matter. For example, in one case, the use of hooding, white noise and standing on tip toes and finger tips against a wall for long periods of time, was held by a court not to amount to torture. More on this later.

My intention in this book therefore is to demonstrate specifically this issue, namely that although something may be outlawed by the UN Convention (or any other law for that matter) it is judicial decision making which actually decides what behaviour amounts to torture. What I am trying to demonstrate is that whilst the laws may exist, there are three very specific problems with laws. First, they may not necessarily be well drafted in the first place. This can lead to confusion and disagreement about what Parliament intended by passing a given law. Second, they rely on judicial interpretation for their enforcement and this is often where further problems lie. Finally, it is possible – and I shall come back to this point specifically later in this chapter, with reference to Tony Blair's evidence to the Chilcot Enquiry – for politicians to sidestep legal obligations or prohibitions if they can persuade us that the 'risk' of harm to the majority is significant.

I would also like to think that this book has a novel approach – this being that my approach to this subject will in part come from the process of combining my two central expertises – law and crime reduction. Whilst this will not be easy I believe that it will allow greater thought regarding the lightest touch by which protection can be achieved and which will hence alienate the fewest people. I believe that this expertise (currently lacking from the literature in this subject area) is a necessary base for understanding subtler and less intrusive ways of achieving security without compromising liberty, in contrast to the crudities I rail against. What I would like to do now is to contextualise these issues by looking back at the origins of our civil liberties in the UK, at the relevance of the rule of law and issues of law and morality. My intention then will be to give an overview of some of the more contemporary developments in relation to the suppression of civil liberties and the rise of surveillance currently in the UK. My explanation for this is based on what I see as political attempts to enhance unquantifiable issues of risk to the extent that this facilitates indiscriminate and ill-judged law making and decision making – even in relation to legal powers to wage war.

The origins of civil liberties

Some analysis of the historical evolution of civil liberties in the UK is pertinent to this discussion. So too is the relevance of the Rule of Law – according to legal scholars such as Dicey (1915) and more recently, Raz

(1977) – and the notion of law and morality in achieving a balance between security and civil liberties.

It has frequently been said that Magna Carta is an unlikely benchmark for democracy. Often referred to as (and some would say more properly 'called') the Great Charter of Liberty, it was June 15, 1215, at Runnymede when 'Bad' King John was persuaded to accede to a number of demands made by a powerful group of his barons. Destined to be short-lived, it was swiftly declared null and void by Pope Innocent III (urged on, it has to be said, by John himself) although this was perhaps not unreasonable, because it was in reality procured through blackmail and extortion. In spite of this, however, and seven hundred years later it is still recognised as the cornerstone of British (and American) democracy. It is one of those rare pieces of legislation, if not perhaps unique, which has been reaffirmed on numerous occasions in the centuries since John's death being reissued three times by John's son, Henry III, and entered on the Parliament Rolls by Edward I on March 28, 1297. It has retained its statutory force ever since, although its application has been severely curtailed by a number of amending statutes. Only chapters 1, 9 and 29 remain in force. Of those three sections chapter 29 (which were chapters 39 and 40 in the 1215 version) is the one that resonates today. Take for example the decision by David Davies, MP, to stand down from Parliament and fight a by-election on the issue of 42-day detention. For him, as for so many people in Britain and around the world, Magna Carta, and chapter 29 in particular, remains an enduring symbol of freedom; of the fundamental rights that lie at the very heart of our open and democratic societies as they have developed over the long centuries from Runnymede. So what makes it important?

Chapter 29 originally stated:

> No freeman is to be taken or imprisoned or disseised of his free tenement or of his liberties or free customs, or outlawed or exiled or in any way ruined, nor will we go against such a man or send against him save by lawful judgment of his peers or by the law of the land. To no one will we sell or deny or delay right or justice.

This was subsequently amended in 1354 by Edward III as follows:

> no man of what estate or condition that he be, shall be put out of land or tenement, nor taken, nor imprisoned, nor disinherited, nor put to death, without being brought in answer by due process of law.

These statements demonstrate the origins of the commitment to the right to fair trial and the rule of law. In placing his seal on Magna Carta, the real significance for King John (and more so for his subjects perhaps) was that he was no longer above the law. This of course was also highly significant in the newly formed United States of America when it was given legal sanctity within the 5th and 14th Amendments to the US Constitution. Most recently, it has undoubtedly lain at the heart of the drafting of the European Convention on Human Rights, most specifically in Article 6. However, its significance is bigger even than this since the same principles can be found within the constitutional framework of many countries throughout the world. It ought to continue to resonate in the current political climate if Governments are to continue to seek to strike the right balance between issues of security, individual rights, the rule of law and the principles of justice that lie at the foundation of society. Michael Zander QC, Emeritus Professor of Law at the London School of Economics, has commented that:

> Habeas corpus has a mythical status in the country's psyche. In reality it is no longer of great practical significance as there are today very few habeas corpus applications, but it still represents the fundamental principle that unlawful detention can be challenged by immediate access to a judge – even by telephone in the middle of the night. It no longer plays a role in regard to detention by the police as it has been superseded by the much more detailed and workable provisions of the Police and Criminal Evidence Act 1984, which lays down precise rules about the length of pre-charge detention. But there have been occasions when the British Parliament has suspended it, usually in times of social unrest.[1]

So the good news is that given its influence, and its centrality to the rule of law, it seems doubtful that any truly democratic society could attempt to completely abrogate the principle to which it gives expression. However, the reality of this is perhaps not quite so simple or straightforward given the complications of competing rights to security (with which I do not disagree) and the politicking and power struggles which will continue throughout the world, especially in the light of heightened security fears connected with terrorism.

The relevance of the rule of law

Also relevant to this discussion is the paradigm of the rule of law – considered to be one of the fundamental doctrines of the UK constitution.

The doctrine is an important concept in all western liberal democracies but has particular resonance in the UK where there is no written (or perhaps more correctly, we might say 'codified') constitution. Having said this, the concept is difficult to define. At one level it means Government according to law but at another, Allan (2001) has noted that the term rule of law seems to mean primarily a corpus of basic principles and values, which together lend some stability and coherence to the legal order. The expectation arising from this is that Governments should act politically within an ideological framework that takes account of rights, justice and fairness.

Wade has commented (2004: 21) that:

> The rule that the courts obey Parliament...is above and beyond the reach of statute... because it is itself the source of the authority of statute. This puts it into a class by itself among rules of the common law... The rule of judicial obedience is in one sense a rule of common law, but in another sense – which applies to no other rule of common law – it is the ultimate political fact upon which the system of legislation hangs.

Dicey (1915) describes sovereignty as meaning that Parliament has the right to make or unmake any law whatsoever: and further, that no person or body is recognised by the law of England as having a right to override or set aside the legislation of Parliament. Implicit in this view of sovereignty is the idea that Parliament has unlimited legislative authority. In the absence of a written constitution that authority is dependent upon the courts recognising this to be the case. Judicial obedience to Acts of Parliament was established by the 19th century. In the case of *ex parte Canon Selwyn* (1872), the issue concerned the validity of the Crown's assent to the Irish Church Act 1869 on the grounds that the Act was contrary to the Queen's Coronation Oath under the Act of Settlement. Cockburn CJ stated; 'There is no judicial body in the country by which the validity of an act of parliament could be questioned. An act of the legislature is superior in authority to any court of law'. The more recent cases of *Madzimbamuto v Lardner Burke (1969)* and *Manuel v AG (1982)* underline this view. What therefore is the likelihood of the Government seeking to repeal the Human Rights Act 1998 or the European Communities Act 1972? Does this mean that Parliament has effectively bound its successors? Does any of this rhetoric really matter if Government chooses which statues, treaties or charters to comply with or to ignore, depending on what happens to be politically expedient at the time?

Law and morality

The debate about reconciling issues of law and morality is also of ongoing interest to academics, practitioners and ordinary people, whose lives may become inextricably entwined, through the legal process, with these issues. Law and the social structures in which it operates are variables which by necessity must interact. Neither can be understood in isolation from the other, and most legal systems are both discretionary and idiosyncratic of the particular society in which they operate. The discretionary element of legal systems has often been criticised for a number of reasons, not least the possibility of unfairness and inconsistency in judicial decision making. There are also those who have emphasised the advantages that a discretionary legal system offers. For example, Hay (1975) argued that such discretion was an essential expression of the power of paternalism and that it could affect issues such as the ability to grant or deny mercy. Whilst there are those who would both agree and disagree with these sentiments, the long, often impassioned and certainly unconcluded debate about law and morality has continued. Whether one agrees or disagrees with Hay it is certain that no one interested in the relationship between law and morality can dismiss three of Hay's particular insights. Namely that;

- law enforcement can only be understood by placing it within an historically specific social and political context;
- an understanding of the functions of legal authority is necessary to any evaluation of the legal system and;
- legal power and particularly the power of discretionary authority can be routinely manipulated to support those privileged by position.

Added to this, Moss (2006 & 2009) has emphasised that criminality itself is a flexible and rapidly changing concept. For example, if we ask the question 'what is a crime?' we could answer this by saying perhaps that it is an action prohibited by law or behaviour prohibited by a criminal code. If we ask a further question 'what is a criminal?' we might say a person who breaks the law or a person who has been convicted of a crime. (Although this conveniently shuffles off anyone outside of the convicted population – so would this be a fair definition?) However, we could also highlight what is wrong with these definitions.

First, what is defined as crime or criminal can change over time (and does). For example, law relating to homosexuality, to prohibition in the US and also rape laws. Second (and which fits in with Hay's ideologies) what is defined as a crime is arguably more to do with a reflection of the interests of the powerful of the time and not necessarily to do with what is moral/immoral. Third, there are different perceptions of crime. For example, those crimes we could collectively refer to as 'not so bad' and those we could say were 'really bad'. For example, and generally speaking, most people (whether justifiably or not) might view tax fraud or speeding as not particularly serious (or perhaps victimless) crimes. Conversely crimes such as murder, rape or genocide are generally thought of as very serious. The result of this is that definitions of crime and criminals become very slippery because they change over time depending on changes in society. Accordingly, in most societies crime is viewed as a relative concept, and criminality neither a wholly objective nor subjective phenomenon but rather a subjective interpretation of objective acts. Law enforcement and the definition of criminality can therefore never be never neutral because they emanate from Governments and thus they logically express the concerns of those pre-eminent in the social structure. Weber (1978) regarded the political systems of modern Western societies as forms of 'legal domination' with their legitimacy based upon a belief in the legality of their exercise of political power. Weber's was a positivistic concept of law – meaning that law is precisely what the political legislator (whether democratic or undemocratic) enacts as law as long as it accords with legally institutionalised procedures. As such, Weber (ibid.) suggested that the law cannot legitimise itself by claiming that it has an alliance between law and morality. Rather, he suggested that law possesses its own rationality, independent of morality and that any assimilation of law and morality threatens the rationality of law and thus the legitimate basis of legal domination. So how does the law currently reconcile issues of law and morality and what do judicial decisions in these matters demonstrate to us about judicial understanding, its approach and its consistency?

Reconciling issues of law and morality

One of the difficulties of reconciling issues of law and morality was highlighted by the Hart–Devlin debate which surrounded the legalisation of homosexuality between consenting male adults and which questions whether there is a role for law at all in matters of morality. Patton (1993: 8) suggests that:

> in all communities that reach a certain stage of development there springs up a social machinery which we call law.... In each society

there is an interaction between the abstract rules, the institutional machinery existing for their application, and the life of the people.

McTeer (1995: 895) also suggests that:

> Throughout history, law has played an important role in the defini-tion and protection of certain relationships, systems and institutions and in the control of individual and collective human behaviour. Through the use of normative and prescriptive rules, supported by varying degrees of sanctions, law has been used to create a climate of social order, the usual justification of which has been that it benefits members of society.

It is certainly the case that historically the law was seen as being inex-tricably linked with issues of morality since medieval law makers were seen to derive their authority directly from God as a 'Divine Right'. In this context laws were respected because they were seen to be con-nected in a fundamental way, with issues of morality. With the passage of time, the development of science and technology and other such significant changes in society such as a greater degree of secularity, the connection between law, religion and consequently morals has dimin-ished. Today, there appears to be a more general acceptance that whilst there is not necessarily an interdependence between law and morality, it is still most people's perception that the law should work in such a way as to protect society including certain moral aspects, although the morality of society is of course not a static notion.

As such, as society's moral outlook changes, so the law must change with it. The problem with this is how far should the law intervene in matters of morality or personal conscience before it becomes inappro-priate? Where should the line be drawn between the legitimate role of the law in such matters – perhaps where it is deemed necessary to protect the public interest – and where issues should be left to an indi-vidual's own conscience? This is a particularly difficult question if one accepts that what might have been deemed an acceptable role for the law historically, would not, in the modern world, perhaps be thought of as such. Thus, the debate itself is not a static one. In the UK, the Wolfenden Report (1957) was particularly influential in raising the pro-file of this debate more than 50 years ago. The Report suggested that the law, which previously made consensual homosexual relations in private an offence, should be changed, primarily because the suggestion was that the law had no part to play in decisions about morality. This was no doubt also influenced by the Montagu case of 1954 in which Lord Montagu, the [then] youngest peer in the House of Lords, was one of three men convicted of 'consensual homosexual offences'. The trial provoked a wave of public sympathy and doubtless influenced the British legal system. Subsequent to this, both Lord Patrick Devlin and Professor Herbert Hart engaged in the debate which has been discussed since by other authors such as George (1996) and Hittinger (1990). In 1957 a Government committee recommended that homosexual acts between consenting adults in private should be legalised. These recommendations were made law in 1967.

The relevance of this is rooted in the issue of the enforcement of morality and what the basis of decisions should be in circumstances where there is a conflict between individual moral freedom and social control. Specifically within this debate, Lord Devlin addressed himself to two particular issues. First, he asked, has society the right to pass judgement on matters of morals and second, if society has this right, does it also have the right to use the law to enforce it? Devlin's view was that the law *should* be able to intervene in matters of morality, in order to preserve what he called 'society's constitutive morality'. In relation to the Wolfenden Report, Devlin claimed that homosexuality was a threat to society and, as such, it fell within the domain of public morality, on which the law should pass judgement to preserve social cohesion. Devlin claimed that in order to decide which rules of morality should be enforced, a 'feelings test' should be applied in order to determine the potential for harm to an individual. Hart agreed with Devlin that if a threat existed, which was sufficient to challenge social cohesion, then the law ought to be able to intervene. He did not agree that homosexuality was an example of this and was clear about his view that in order to prove what constituted true threats to society, empirical evidence was required. What appears to be the case with these respective positions is that both Devlin and Hart have inherently different values and this then informs each of their arguments in a different way as regards the enforcement of morals. This is precisely why the question of law and morality is so difficult since it must be attached to the current social condition, and the expectations and values of society, but social conditions are not constant. Thus, we have a potentially continuous debate about the balance between law, morality, freedom and social control. Whichever position one takes in such matters, there will no doubt be some intellectual philosophy which will support it and in this sense, perhaps this dilemma can never be resolved by reason. For what might be one man's reason may well be another's unreason. Moreover, and in line with the birth of the positivist paradigm within criminology, who should decide what is rational and for whom and in what circumstances?

Contemporary developments

In the light of contemporary developments in relation to the competing rights to security and liberty, all of these issues seem not less but increasingly important. Scanning the horizon for the latest developments in security, surveillance and technology there is some evidence to suggest that we should remain mindful of these basic paradigms of essential civil liberties, the rule of law and morality in the face of current trends. A brief overview now follows.

Since the first Information Commissioners' Office report in 2006, border control in the UK is clearly moving to a mass dataveillance system. Biometric passports are now the norm (and are likely to become de facto ID cards) and IRIS (eye recognition) systems have been introduced at Manchester and other airports. This biometric 'wall' is buttressed by a deep and arguably disproportionate amount of dataveillance. Advanced Passenger Information (API) and other pre-flight information collection systems in Europe and North America seek more and more information on passengers, and have been commented on both by Moran (2010) and Moss (2009). There are two drivers for this unprecedented system of data collection: the new post-9/11 measures implemented by the European Union and the new and ever more intrusive systems implemented by the US with which other countries must agree if they want to continue travel relationships with the US. Importantly in Europe, the UK (particularly under Tony Blair and former Home Secretaries David Blunkett and Charles Clarke) led the way in pushing for these measures but the trend has continued and deepened since then. Thus we might speak of the UK as being the 'Trojan Horse of surveillance' in a Europe which, since the Second World War, has been historically suspicious of data collection and sharing. In March 2007 a new Home Office Document 'Securing the UK Border: Our Vision and Strategy for the Future' was produced in which the Government and the Foreign and Commonwealth Office set out their aims for the future security of the UK's borders. This document sets out what the Government sees as 'the exponential growth in global movement' which creates new challenges which demand a new doctrine for the national border. Added to this cases such as *R (on the application of Hoverspeed Ltd) v HM Customs and Excise* [2002] EWHC 1630 have demonstrated worrying trends in the reversal of the burden of proof in relation to the stop and search powers of customs personnel. Importantly these measures are being instituted with little or no accountability. Arguably this merits a more serious examination of the ways in which non-transparent transnational procedures are increasing the web of dataveillance across the European continent. Recent trends in relation to overall State surveillance and to some of the more unique ways in which this is taking place are also important. For example, the manner in which, since 2005, children are becoming the latest and expanding target surveillance category. Children are treated as both citizens to be protected and as citizens who may pose a future risk. The subject of surveillance on children is a particularly appropriate means for examining the mindset and justifications for dataveillance generally and the way in which it changes the relationship between the individual and the State. For example, Parton's (2008) 'The Change for Children Programme in England: Towards the Preventive Surveillance State', *Journal of Law and Society* 35(1). 166–187 and *The Times* 2008 report; 'Children of 11 to be finger printed' outline Home Office plans to take and store fingerprints on a secret database when children apply for a passport. Documents leaked from Whitehall indicated that the scheme would start in 2010. Thus far this has not yet been implemented in the UK. The relationship between surveillance and discipline is also worth comment, since in 2009 the Government announced plans to place CCTV in the homes of an estimated 20,000 'problem families'.[2] There has been much concern about the civil liberties of those groups and individuals placed under surveillance and an argument to suggest that surveillance is increasingly being used by the State as a surrogate form of punishment.

In line with the idea that the tide of surveillance is 'washing out' to previously uncovered areas of society there is now also a trend in relation to the way in which universities, formerly a buttress of civil society with an independent or arms length relationship to the State are being drawn into the surveillance web. Following the 7/7 attacks the State has encouraged universities to identify and report radicalism on campuses. Two reports have identified certain universities as being at risk of radicalism. These moves have been resisted by management, staff and student unions but Special Branch has increased its activity in universities. For example, see Copeland's (2008) article 'Academic Freedom: Are there Limits?' Furedi (2005)[3] has also commented on this trend:

> In July [2005] the heads of universities were told that they had to sign up to the crusade against terrorism by clamping down on extremist

campus groups that promote terrorism. Bill Rammell, the Higher Education Minister, informed vice-chancellors that they had to do their bit to challenge the 'evil ideology' responsible for the recent bombings in London. Rammell claimed that free speech was important but added that 'we also have a responsibility to tackle extremism on campus'. Unfortunately, experience indicates that coupling free speech with the demand to 'tackle extremism' restricts discussion.

Hitherto, within universities there has been an assumption that there is the opportunity to raise and discuss freely all points of view. However, recent moves to restrict certain ideas, perhaps labelled as objectionable in some quarters, represent a worrying trend. I have written before (Moss 2009) about the right to offend which seems to have been undermined through numerous new laws and codes of conduct. Similar attacks on academic freedom are untenable. The question is, does anyone care? I have also commented before (ibid.) that academics currently appear unmotivated to resists these attempts. Furedi (ibid.) suggests that perhaps free speech has ceased to be fashionable:

> Loss of belief in the creative dimension of academic freedom co-exists with a powerful current of cynicism towards it. No one argues that they are against academic freedom. In principle, everyone is prepared to embrace it. But in practice, academic freedom is not something that academics are very bothered about. We rarely notice when it is tested and many claim it is not always worth the hassle to defend it.

As well as these new areas of surveillance contestation the controversial debate about the DNA database trundles inexorably on. One of the most important judgements of the European Court stated that the UK's system of DNA collection, which included the collection of samples from individuals who had not been charged or convicted of any crime, was not appropriate. Whilst this seemed like a victory against the rolling waves of DNA database, the Government responded with a new policy of DNA collection which adhered to the letter but not the spirit of the ECHR judgement. The Government, the public and sections of the mainstream media remain in favour of the expansion of the DNA database and it remains to be seen whether the Conservative and Liberal coalition will adhere to the policy of adopting the Scottish model in the face of populist calls for a wide database and dramatic case studies of 'DNA justice'. DNA is clearly one of the most problematic areas with regard to dataveillance since the arguments in its favour seem so powerful. There are of course shifting coalitions both for and against DNA databases. Whilst not in favour of such a database, I think it is important to explicitly acknowledge the arguments both for and against this potential development.

Take, for example, Mark Dixie's conviction for the murder of Sally Anne Bowman which sparked a debate about the desirability of a national database containing everyone's DNA. The Senior Investigating Officer in the case, Stuart Cundy, said that had a national database existed, Dixie would have been arrested within twenty-four hours rather than the nine months which it actually took. When dealing with possible serial killers, delay can of course cost lives. The Yorkshire Ripper investigation was thrown off track by the tapes sent by 'Wearside Jack' claiming responsibility for the murders, leading to police concentration on men with Wearside accents. This rendered the death of the Ripper's latest victims more certain. Identification of Wearside Jack was made by DNA taken as a result of a *later* offence. So under present arrangements, the fate of the Ripper's later victims would not have been avoided. However, had current DNA technology and a national DNA database been in place, the Ripper's later victims may have been saved, as would the later victims of any serial rapist or killer leaving DNA at the scene of the first crime in the series.

There are a number of liberal crime reduction specialists who have been inclined in favour of a national DNA database, not merely because of its role in detection, but also because of its use in identifying the victims of accidents and atrocities. There are three substantial objections to the universal national database, and these are now taken in turn. First, there is David Davies' assertion that it would turn us into a 'nation of suspects'. The first forensic use of DNA analysis served to exonerate the prime suspect of two brutal murders, only later being used to identify the real murderer, Colin Pitchfork. This is especially remarkable because the impressionable 17-year-old who had been the suspect confessed to one of the murders. He was saved by DNA from a terrible injustice. So its proponents would argue that instead of turning us into suspects, the database would serve to reduce suspicion of all those whose DNA is not found at a crime scene. In the US, the Innocence Project, by bringing DNA evidence to bear, has led to over two hundred murder convictions being quashed, some thirteen of those exonerated having spent time on Death Row. As was true in the Pitchfork case, the Innocence Project noted that:

> Since 1989, there have been tens of thousands of cases where prime suspects were identified and pursued – until DNA testing (prior to conviction) proved that they were wrongly accused.[4]

The second criticism is that people with a grudge will plant the DNA of others at crime scenes, as a means of revenge. This is likely to happen, much more in the use of DNA than in the case of fingerprints, since all that is needed is a hair, a drop of blood or a cigarette stub. The police already emphasise that DNA analysis must go along with traditional police work for detection to occur.

The third criticism of a national database is that the Government's record of keeping sensitive data safe is poor, and we cannot, or perhaps should not trust it with our DNA. Again proponents of DNA would doubtless ask, is this criticism relevant? No doubt they would also say that these problems are not DNA specific. For example, if your bank account details get lost, you are vulnerable to identity theft. Those who support a national DNA database ('the innocent have nothing to fear' argument) also oppose the collection of children's DNA. Similarly some groups historically associated with the left/liberal political spectrum and the advancement of civil society such as women's rights groups have recently advocated the collection of the DNA of men accused of partner abuse. Thus, not only are we witnessing the expansion of DNA use, the conditions which may make its further expansion possible remain important. So too does the expansion of other areas of surveillance such as Home Office plans to ask communications firms to monitor all Internet use[5] and the widened use of cameras to track mobile phone users and non-seatbelt wearers through the wider application of automatic number plate recognition (ANPR).[6]

Inevitably there have been rapid developments in surveillance technology. These include issues such as biometrics – particularly with regard to airline passengers and the justifications behind them – as well as developments in improving CCTV images. This is particularly relevant in relation to the use of such images in legal proceedings where they need to be clear to provide quality evidence. Developments in tracing and monitoring people through mobile phone calls, the use of 'Oyster' travel cards and the electronic scanning of work emails are becoming the norm. So too is the normalisation of having personal details verified over the telephone by, for example, credit card companies – who in turn make profits by selling information that they acquire when we purchase goods. Information gained from consumption patterns is now such a sophisticated process that it is an academic discipline with its own name – geodemographics. More recently developments in relation to CCTV include 'CCTV in the sky' and police plans to use military-style spy drones.[7] Dorward (2010) recently reported that there are now at least 500,000 EU computers with the potential to access private

British data. The Schengen Information System (or SIS) holds information regarding immigration status, arrest warrants, entries on the police national computer and a multitude of personal details and is currently causing some concern about the security of data. Statewatch has said it is already aware that in one case in Belgium, personal information from this system was sold by an official to an organised criminal gang. Commenting on this in the 2010 (ibid.) report Statewatch said:

> It is well known that the greater the points of access, the greater the number of people who have access and the greater the chance that data will be misplaced, lost or illegally accessed. The idea that mass databases can be totally secure and that privacy can be guaranteed is a fallacy.

A further recent development is the Digital Economy Bill which has been introduced to update the regulation of the communications sector. The recent House of Lords and Commons Joint Committee on Human Rights reported on a number of aspects of this Bill including illegal file-sharing, the right to a fair hearing and the reserve powers contained in clause 17. Specifically they examined the mechanism whereby under the Act, holders of copyright will be able to issue a 'copyright infringement report' to an ISP where it appears that the service has been used by an account holder to infringe copyright. Although the Committee considered it unlikely that this proposal alone would lead to a significant risk of a breach of individual Internet users' right to respect for privacy, their right to freedom of expression or their right to respect for their property rights (Articles 8, 10, Article 1, Protocol 1 ECHR) they were still keen for the Government to provide a further explanation of why they considered their proposals to be proportionate. In relation to the right to a fair hearing, although the Bill provides such a right, the Committee expressed concern about the lack of detail in relation to this and commented that a statutory provision for a right to appeal to an independent body would be a human rights enhancing measure. They have asked for further information about the quality of evidence to be provided and the standard of proof to be applied to be provided. Finally in relation to clause 17, the Bill provides the Secretary of State with the power to amend the Copyright, Designs and Patents Act 1988 by secondary legislation. The broad nature of this power has been the subject of much criticism and remains overly broad. Parliamentary scrutiny may remain inadequate, and the Committee recommended a series of clarifications to address these concerns.

In other parts of Europe it appears that uneasiness about increased technological surveillance may not be as acute. Reuters[8] recently reported that a Polish priest had installed an electronic reader in his church for schoolchildren to leave their fingerprints in order to monitor their attendance at Catholic mass. Apparently the pupils will mark their fingerprints every time they go to church over three years and if they attend 200 masses they will be freed from the obligation of having to pass an exam prior to their confirmation. The report comments that the pupils in the southern town of Gryfow Slaski told the daily press that they liked the idea and also the priest, Grzegorz Sowa, who invented it:

> This is comfortable. We don't have to stand in a line to get the priest's signature (confirming our presence at the mass) in our confirmation notebooks.

Poland is probably the most devoutly Roman Catholic country in Europe today and churches are well attended. However, this type of technological authentication of attendance (especially in relation to children) has raised concerns among Polish state agencies responsible for protecting personal data and civil liberties. The General Office for Data Protection and the Polish Ombudsman's Office have both stated that they will take all the necessary action to check the legality of this very unusual procedure.

It is worthy of note in this section which relates to the technological, another unusual development somewhat closer to home. Part of the widely debated Climate Change Bill has proposed what is known as 'bin and chip' technology. This will give Local Authorities the power to charge for refuse collection and disposal. As part of this move they could have microchips installed in occupiers bins which would measure and then report to a central point how much rubbish a household has. Presumably, if you are producing too much rubbish, you will be charged more. But again, who decides what is too much, and do we really need this type of technology and invasion of privacy in relation even to our waste disposal services?

There is arguably also an increasing need to focus on ascertaining how and where the Governments' proposals have encouraged informing by one citizen on another. The Government has, for example, encouraged informing on benefit cheats. Local police forces have encouraged the public to inform on people who live a 'lavish lifestyle' and thus may have gained money from crime. Police anti-terrorist hotlines are another example and the advertisements by the Metropolitan Police are a stark example of the extremely low level of suspicion now asked for by the State before someone is expected to contact the authorities. The 'child protection industry' (Furedi, ibid.) encourages informing on a similar basis and there are numerous reports of individuals baselessly being accused of child cruelty whose details are nevertheless retained by the authorities. The NHS is encouraging similar styles of reporting although in this case it is the staff that are encouraged to inform, recording more and more intrusive information about those who use its services. Recent cases include individuals incorrectly being noted as having alcohol or mental health problems by NHS staff.

According to the Home Office, over 400 forms of behaviour that were legal when the Labour Government came to power are now outlawed. The context in which this propensity for legislating has arisen is at least in part due to the Government's manifesto commitment in 1997 to be 'tough on crime, tough on the causes of crime'. Legislation has been a key part of the Home Office's approach but the question is, does more law reduce more crime or does this represent a new form of social control? One of the key questions in relation to this is whether current parliamentary safeguards in relation to legislating are adequate and to assess developments in data protection legislation. For example, the most recent Terrorism Act which came into force in April 2006 making 'glorification of terrorism' an offence doubled the length of detention to 28 days. It has also recently been announced by the Government that a new Police and Justice Bill will allow police to fit electronic tags on suspects for an unlimited period without reference to a Judge. Proposed new Licensing Laws announced on 19th Jan 2010 suggest a Government ban may be imposed on the sale of cheap alcohol and so-called 'happy hours'. Plans to do away with courts for petty crime and trial by jury for some crimes have also been discussed. In November 2007, the Government was again considering the penalties for speeding with suggestions being made for tougher penalties and the possibility of banning drivers after they incur only 6 points rather than 12, as well as the potential for speed cameras to identify motorists who then may be awarded 12 points in one 'go' rather than 3, depending on how fast they are going. They would also seek to include other developments such as the Regulation of Investigatory Powers Act, which has allowed local authorities to investigate dog fouling and underage smoking, fly tipping and rogue trading.[9]

In December 2009 reports of the expansion of the Government Child Protection agenda by the Department of Children Schools and Families were highlighted. Developments included the suggestion that schools should vet parents attending school concerts and that parents giving children lifts to and from school could be forced to get Criminal Records Bureau enhanced clearance or face a £5,000 fine. Such developments have been widely commented on (for example, by Furedi 2010) as being negative. Other recent policy developments include moves with regard to NHS patients with unhealthy lifestyles who may be penalised under a proposed NHS constitution being considered as part of Lord Darzi's review of the NHS, ahead of the National Health Service's 60th anniversary. Recent reports have indicated smokers and obese people could be refused treatment. In January 2008 it was reported that the Home Office Report, 'Tackling Violence Action Plan' suggested the installation of border-style security arch metal detectors in hundreds of schools in England, in an effort to reduce knife crime and deal with violent behaviour. In August 2008 a new Community Safety Accreditation Scheme allowed State and private sector employees to hand out fines, photograph fined people and stop vehicles to control traffic and allowed them to require personal details or to seize tobacco. By November 2009 the Government had announced new guidelines for local councils stating that only senior officers could authorise surveillance. At the same time the Government also announced proposals for Child Maintenance and Enforcement Commission staff to lose intrusive surveillance powers but to retain limited surveillance powers (for example, in relation to Internet and telephone records). The Government has also promised to require all social network and gaming sites to archive all information including conversations so that they can subsequently legislate to access it.

What about developments in accountability? The key question here is whether accountability for the UK's surveillance network remains either a) bureaucratic or b) in effect non-existent. In terms of bureaucratic accountability the system appears to be opaque. The main system of energetic accountability is the Information Commissioners' Office and informally the various media and academic organisations which campaign on surveillance issues specifically such as Privacy International, NO2ID, or as part of a wider remit, Liberty. The main problem here is that there are, as yet, no realistic studies which compare accountability for surveillance with that, for example, in other areas – such as police accountability.

A more recent development has been the move within civil society groups, Judges and others who have tried to resist surveillance. Some examples include the Privacy International campaign which was successful in getting intrusive biometric surveillance removed from

Heathrow (Moran 2010) and the media/public outcry after Devon Council (amongst others) was found using Regulation of Investigatory Powers Act 2000 powers to enact surveillance for minor cases. This led to new Government guidance to local authorities to hold back from using the Regulation of Investigatory Powers Act 2000 for surveillance purposes (Ford 2009). Could it be argued that a culture of counter surveillance is taking place (deriving from the criticisms from both left and right wing daily newspapers and films such as 'Taking Liberties' (2007), or does the UK continue to be culturally open to surveillance (as evidenced by the only mildly critical 2009 BBC2 series Who's Watching You?) Alternatively, are we speeding down the path towards a kind of 'surveillance porn' in which CCTV camera series, programmes such as 'Rude Tube' and others continue to portray covert filming as a source of late-modern voyeurism? As if this were not enough, research is now being carried out into noses. At the University of Bath six types of noses have apparently been scanned in 3D (Roman, Greek, Nubian, hawk, snub and turn up) with the intention of using this information for identification in covert surveillance. Although the researchers claim that noses have been overlooked in the developing field of biometrics, they would do well to be reminded of the work of Cesare Lombroso – the founding father of the Positivist School of Criminology and his (1876) thesis, 'L'Uomo Deliquente.[10]

Security and risk

How has all this been made possible? The basis on which much of the current political preoccupation with global security and mass surveillance appears to hinge (or so we are told) is the threat of risk post-9/11 and 7/7. It is pertinent to remind ourselves of a point I made a little earlier, namely, that Hay (ibid.) commented that legal power and particularly the power of discretionary authority can be routinely manipulated to support those privileged by position. Perhaps the best and most recent example of how the threat of risk can be used to orchestrate a manipulation of discretionary authority is that demonstrated by the debate about the legality of the war in Iraq and pertinently the evidence recently given by the former Prime Minister Tony Blair to the Chilcot Inquiry (2010). It is interesting to note that the issue of risk provided by Mr. Blair was the cornerstone of his justification for engaging in the war in Iraq – even though the risk was not at the time conclusively proven, has now been proven to be a fallacy (in terms of the existence of weapons of mass destruction) and despite the fact that such action did not comply with security council resolutions governing the declaration of war. (This is a point to which I shall return in more detail in a later chapter.)

In the face of all of this, what can we predict for the future and should we be worried about a possible imbalance between security and liberty? Certainly, when all of this becomes a part of history in due course, the late 20th and early 21st centuries will doubtless be marked by two things. First, the huge advances in technology and the impact that these have had (either positive or negative) upon society. Every aspect of our lives has been touched by technology. The way we work, where we work, the way businesses and Governments operate and moreover the entire way in which we now communicate has been altered unrecognisably. There are of course positive aspects to this, but we should not be misled completely by them. There is another, darker side to the technological age – the surveillance society. Not only the Government but also private organisations now have the potential to monitor almost everything about us including our communications, our physical movements (by way of CCTV) our mobile phone signals and our habits and preferences by a sophisticated and secret analysis of our Internet traffic. Let us not be fooled by this, surveillance and the information society in which we now live require careful and continuous examination. There continues to be a need to identify the key issues that society faces in dealing with the spread of surveillance and information technology. Since the Thomas-Walport Report (2008) and the Lords Select Committee Report, *Surveillance: Citizens and the State* (2009) how well has the Government done in addressing the concerns raised by these reports, and how can the process of addressing these challenging issues be pushed forward? There are clearly legal and political shortcomings in relation to the current regime; further discussion about the best way to regulate the system in terms of issues such as the retention of DNA data, the growth of database collection and profiling and the legal regime surrounding the use of CCTV cameras is required. We should not be persuaded by the strenuous advocates of these developments that they do not entail some dangers – specifically perhaps that posed by State power in the hands of the security services. We should consider what mechanisms can be adopted to draw the line between necessary powers and those that cannot be justified by necessity. Within the UK, can the ICO alone oversee effectively the growth of surveillance powers in the secret sphere be it by State bodies or private security organisations? Where are the oversight bodies that exist to oversee surveillance, data collection and the work of the security services? Are they able to deliver on oversight, and how can individual freedoms and liberties be secured for the future?

The second issue here is that of risk, and how this concept has been used as the single most important justification for not only the increases in State surveillance, security technology and, in effect social control on a wider scale that has ever been known before, but also as the justification for engaging the UK, alongside the US in a 'war on terror'. This has resulted in tragic loss of life and frustratingly, strong evidence that the so-called 'risk' was not as portrayed. Barder (2010) comments,

> Tony Blair's six hours at the witness table of the Chilcot Iraq Inquiry gave us a bravura performance, allowing him to display all the old familiar dramatic and forensic skills that got him out of so many scrapes during his years at No. 10....The performance, which is exactly what it was, revealed all the old familiar weaknesses...the evasion of inconvenient detail by elevating the discussion to a grand, sweeping level of generality; the reduction of all issues to a Wagnerian conflict between Good and Evil, with Blair doughtily championing the former; above all, the constant justification by reference to his 'passionate belief' in his own unvarying rightness of every decision, however badly flawed by inattention to the facts, or failure to heed contrary advice or predictably disastrous consequences. Self-belief is his trade-mark, and what makes him appear strong and decisive. Challenged to defend his misrepresentation in the government dossier, and in the key house of commons debate on the eve of war, of the intelligence about Saddam's weapons of mass destruction as definite and beyond doubt (when it was neither), he counters that it was definite and beyond doubt in his own mind, which was all that mattered – to him, anyway. For Blair, as for Hamlet, 'There is nothing either good or bad, but thinking makes it so'.

Barder (ibid.) further emphasises an interesting aspect of Blair's evidence at the Inquiry. That is his personal attitude to risk. Clearly with this in mind Sir Roderic Lyne, one of the more probing of the Inquiry's members, asked why the Blair Government's perception of Saddam Hussein and his alleged weapons of mass destruction as posing a global threat, had not been shared by anyone else except the US. Blair (2010: 105) replied that:

> You are right in saying, 'If this and if that', but you see, for me, because of the change after September 11, I wasn't prepared to run

that risk. I really wasn't prepared to take the risk.... given Saddam's history, given his use of chemical weapons, given the over 1 million people whose deaths he had caused, given ten years of breaking UN Resolutions, could we take the risk of this man reconstituting his weapons programmes, or is that a risk it would be irresponsible to take? I formed the judgment, and it is a judgment in the end. It is a decision. I had to take the decision, and I believed, and in the end so did the Cabinet, so did Parliament incidentally, that we were right not to run that risk, but you are completely right, in the end, what this is all about are the risks.

Perhaps the most important issue that is demonstrated here (but not one we should be surprised by) is Mr. Blair's inability (or unwillingness) to accept that there was little or no thought given to balancing the actual risks that were in evidence at the time, against the possible consequences that going to war in Iraq would inevitably have. The argument he puts forward to the Inquiry appears to hinge on a number of what Mr. Blair see as 'givens', namely, the Iraqi non-cooperation with the weapons inspectors; the fact that the Government felt this constituted a 'material breach' sufficient to justify the invasion and occupation of the country; Saddam Hussein's failure to allow the interview of Iraqi scientists by UN inspectors and the vileness (Mr. Blair's terminology) of a regime responsible for murdering thousands of its own citizens. Whilst all of these things are true and indeed unacceptable to most right thinking individuals, the question still remains, did this constitute a big enough risk to global peace and democracy to merit going to war? Perhaps there is another explanation; that our security services, Government ministers and others were afraid that if they did not act, or if they were not seen to be acting in the face of the threat they had been continually stating was a grave and serious one, then they would be blamed for having done nothing to avert or pre-empt a risk which then materialises. So perhaps the option to invade Iraq, overthrow its Government and thus to prevent some possible but unquantifiable future risk was deemed to be a better course of action. With this in mind, and having spent at least the last nine years persuading the public at large that the global threat of terrorism is huge, it enables the Government to pass more laws enabling them to lock up various types of people the Government have labelled as 'threats' or to ignore existing safeguards for civil liberties and free speech on the basis of that old chestnut 'national security' – the panacea for all ills.

These and other important questions need to form the basis for a continuous debate about the balance between security and liberty. In the next chapter I will trace some of the landmark historical and contemporary deviations from the essential principles of civil liberties in order to further this discussion.

Notes

1. Quoted from http://news.bbc.co.uk/go/pr/fr/-/1/hi/magazine/4329839.stm accessed 11 April 2011.
2. Announced as 'CCTV for problem families' in the September 2009 edition of *Camera Watch* (http://camerawatch.hostinguk.org/news/september-2009/cctv-for-problem-families.aspx) accessed 20 September 2010.
3. http://www.frankfuredi.com/index.php/site/article/66/ accessed 11 April 2011.
4. http://www.innocenceproject.org/ accessed 11 April 2011.
5. See for example www.news,bbc.co.uk/1/hi/uk_politics/8350660.stm accessed 11 April 2011.
6. *The Guardian* March 2007.
7. *Statewatch* January 27 2010.
8. *Reuters* Warsaw 2010.
9. Reported in *The Times* 15 August 2008 as '10,000 spy missions by councils last year' the issue of proportionality is key.
10. Lombroso used a scientific approach which included aspects of physiognomy, early eugenics and psychiatry to argue that criminality was inherited and that the 'born criminal' could be identified by physical defects. This particular idea of the 'atavistic' criminal is generally no longer considered valid, although the idea that certain factors may predispose individuals to commit crime continues to be foundational to some areas of study in criminology. A modern version is found in Lombroso, C. (2006) Criminal Man. NY: Duke University Press.

2
Historical and Contemporary Deviations from Essential Civil Liberties

> Nobody has an absolute right to freedom. Civilisation is the story of humans sacrificing freedom so as to live together in harmony. We do not need Hobbes to tell us that absolute freedom is for newborn savages. All else is compromise.[1]

In this chapter my aim is to trace some of the landmark historical deviations from the essential principles of civil liberties as established in Chapter 1. For example, those which occurred during World Wars I and II, the Northern Ireland issue and in particular the Pat Finucane case, the relevance of the Tribunal and Inquiries Act 2005 and the emergence of the Diplock courts. I also want to highlight certain contemporary civil liberties issues which have arisen in relation to a number of topical areas. For example, those demonstrated by the case of *Liberty and the ICCL (2008) a*nd the Al-Skeini case involving Baha Mousa. The interesting issue here for me is that historically it could be argued that prior to the Convention on Human Rights and of course the UK Human Rights Act 1998, safeguards for preserving the balance between security and civil liberties were somewhat less than they are today. Certainly Waddington (2005) amongst others would probably argue this. The natural result of this – one would guess – would be that contemporary deviations from civil liberties would thus occur less frequently, or when occurring, would give rise to legal cases in which the laws protecting such rights would be reaffirmed. However, I shall demonstrate that both historically and contemporaneously, the use of State force in the name of the protection of security is a common theme in the avoidance, ignoring or sidestepping of many civil liberties issues. In short, this chapter highlights examples of issues which are contributors to this erosion including the citizen-combatant blurring: from citizen army to insurgency; Northern Ireland as contributor to the erosion; recent outrages and the resulting political imperative to protect.

But first, something anecdotal. Since my interest in what a number of people have called 'woolly minded liberal issues' (how kind people are), I regularly receive comments by email from both supporters and critics of my work. As I began to write this chapter, three particular recent communications came to mind which read thus;

> Hardly a day goes by without you coming to mind. Today, for example, I note that the government wants to target the clients of prostitutes by holding them responsible for the any exploitation suffered by the girl they employ. A day or two ago it was whether chips in bins could be used to detect whether a welfare claimant had entertained a 'guest' for awhile. I keep thinking: civil liberties are being eroded from all quarters.

> Can you imagine working for a company that has a little more than 600 employees and has the following employee statistics? 29 have been accused of spouse abuse; 7 have been arrested for fraud; 9 have been accused of writing bad cheques; 17 have directly or indirectly bankrupted at least 2 businesses; 3 have done time for assault; 71 cannot get a credit card due to bad credit; 14 have been arrested on drug-related charges; 8 have been arrested for shoplifting; 21 are currently defendants in lawsuits; 84 have been arrested for drunk driving in the last year; 1 used the tax payers' money to have a floating duck island constructed on his pond; 1 used tax payers' money for pool cleaning. Which organisation is this? It's the 635 members of the House of Commons, the same group that cranks out hundreds of new laws each year designed to keep the rest of us in line.

> Giving the police the power to lock up anybody suspected of being a terrorist, who they don't have enough evidence to charge, effectively means they can lock up anyone they want. It means you, your granny, anyone at all. Mahatma Gandhi and Nelson Mandela were labeled terrorists and locked up. Mandela has been on the terrorist list in the USA up till this year. Even an 82-year old Labour party member was arrested under the Anti-Terrorism act in the UK for saying 'Nonsense!' at a Labour party speech.[2]

Such scandals and departures from human rights are of course not new and from these communications I am glad to see that I am not the only one who is keeping track of them.

However, Governments *do* have a duty to take steps to protect their citizens but this should never justify the sidestepping of democratic values. Since the Prevention of Terrorism Acts of the 1970's, for example, terrorism laws have done little to ensure that society is safe from terrorist attack, but much to infringe the human rights and civil liberties of those living in the US and UK. Rather they have satiated a political desire for a 'quick fix' in response to terrorism and arguably have undermined not only civil liberties and human rights but one of the cornerstones of western democracy, namely the presumption of innocence as a core value of once robust democracies. The concept of human rights was first expressed in the 1948 Universal Declaration of Human Rights, which, according to Davis (2003: 94) established 'the recognition of the inherent dignity and inalienable rights of all members of the human family.'

This theory of the fundamental rights which are associated with civil liberties and human rights is often linked to the notion of Locke's ideas on individual liberty. It can also be tied in to Rousseau's notion of the social contract where that contract exists between the State and the individual and each individual agrees to cede some power to the State and to obey its laws in return for the State being the guarantor of the fundamental rights of each of its citizens. Rawls (1999) takes this theory further by arguing that in order to enjoy a society that will provide each of us with the 'good life', it is necessary to live in a society that not only protects fundamental human rights but does so irrespective of a person's standing or class or other individual difference.

The use of State force in the protection of security

I have said in the previous chapter that it is absolutely necessary to acknowledge that there are two sides to any debate about the legality of State action and the basis upon which states act in the interest of the security and safety of their citizens. Sure, some cases are clearer cut than others. Ethnic cleansing can, for example, never be deemed to be carried out for lawful or moral reasons. On the other hand there are other situations which are more difficult. One of these is the issue of maintaining security in the light of terrorist threats. In particular the problem of the terrorist suicide bomber has brought to the forefront of discussion the issue of the amount of force which the police may use in arresting a suspected terrorist. The Metropolitan Police has previously been reported as adopting a shoot-to-kill policy (Waddington, 2005) and in relation to this, the killing of Jean Charles de Menezes, on 22nd July 2005 illustrated the problem to tragic effect. He was shot by members of the police as he sat on a tube train. He had apparently been suspected of being a suicide bomber. The legal position as to what the police may or may not do in such a situation is governed by one provision in a British statute and another in Article 2 of the European Convention on Human Rights. The statutory provision to note is section 117 of the Police and Criminal Evidence Act 1984. This empowers a police officer to use reasonable force in the exercise of any of the powers under the Act, including the power of arrest for any offence.

The question that immediately arises is 'what is reasonable?' and more specifically can it ever be reasonable to use *lethal* force? Stone et al. (2006) suggest that the answer to such a question must be no, because if an officer wishes to arrest someone, then the intention is to have a live suspect at the conclusion of this, rather than a dead one. At the same time he cautions that Article 2 of the European Convention on Human Rights (ECHR) must also be considered as well as any domestic provisions which are relevant because this article is specifically concerned with the right to life and is, of course, currently emphasised in the UK by the Human Rights Act 1998, which imposes an obligation on public authorities (including the police) to act compatibly with the Convention Rights. Article 2 states clearly that the force which can be used in such situations should be 'no more than absolutely necessary;' this is rather different from applying a more objective 'what is reasonable?' test. In October 2006, lawyers acting for the family of Jean Charles de Menezes tried to mount a legal challenge against the decision not to charge individual officers involved in the shooting, concluding that a review of available evidence 'justifies a prosecution for murder'. Lawyers at solicitors Birnberg Pierce sent the Crown Prosecution Service a letter raising serious misgivings over the decision to level health and safety charges at the Metropolitan Police over the shooting. The letter claimed that prosecutors should have considered murder, or at the very least, gross negligence manslaughter. In spite of this, however, in October 2007 the case proceeded but on Health and Safety grounds only.

This case can be compared to that of *Edwards v UK [2002]* which established that such a duty *was* violated when a prisoner was killed after being placed in a cell with another known dangerous and unstable prisoner. This had exposed the deceased to *'real and serious risk'* of loss of life. So we can deduce from this that if risk is known and quantifiable then Article 2 will be violated. Similarly in the case of *Jordan & Others v UK [2003]* it was stated that failure to properly investigate the lethal shooting of IRA suspects was also a breach of Article 2. Finally in *McCann, Farrell & Savage v UK [1996]* in the attempted arrest and shooting dead of 3 IRA suspects in Gibraltar the court held that it would not be a breach of Article 2 if you shot dead, people you thought were about to detonate a bomb. However, in this case they said a lack of proper planning meant that the officers had been unable to make a rational decision about when lethal force should be used and that consequently the level of violence used was disproportionate to the circumstances of the case.

Currently therefore, it might well be argued that the balance between maintaining adequate public protection, whilst at the same time preserving the rights of the individual, has not been achieved in the most fair way possible and that the numerous justifications which have been made for the manifold increases in restriction have outweighed any of the arguments for the retention of fundamental freedoms and civil liberties. However, as Garland (2001) points out, both the political and social climates of the last thirty years in the UK and the USA have facilitated such changes in ways that previously may have been thought impossible. There have certainly been a number of recent social developments which have impacted upon the State's response to human rights. One of these was the London bombings on 7 July 2005. Fifty-two people were killed and hundreds of others wounded as a result of four bomb attacks on London's transport system. Another series of serious security incidents took place on 21 July 2005. At least four people were subsequently charged with offences in connection with the 21 July events. On 5 August 2005 the former Prime Minister Tony Blair announced a 12-point plan concerning a 'comprehensive framework for action in dealing with the terrorist threat in Britain'. He declared: 'Let no one be in any doubt. The rules of the game are changing.' He said his proposals were 'necessary' and that administrative measures that did not need primary legislation would be put in place 'with immediate effect'. The Prime Minister's plan included:

- deporting people to countries where torture or other ill-treatment are known to be practised on the basis of 'diplomatic assurances';
- new grounds for deportation and exclusion;
- new offences criminalising 'indirect incitement of terrorism';
- automatic refusal of asylum to persons deemed to be associated with terrorism;
- significantly extending the maximum time limit of pre-charge detention of persons held under anti-terrorism legislation.

The result of these proposals was, of course, the Anti-Terrorism, Crime and Security Act 2001 (ATCSA). At the time, Amnesty International expressed concern that some of the proposals announced would threaten the independence of the Judiciary and undermine the rule of law and fundamental human rights in the UK. The organisation was also disturbed that the Prime Minister criticised the decisions of domestic courts to strike down deportation orders in cases where the individuals concerned faced expulsion to a country where there would be a real risk of torture or other ill-treatment. What these developments demonstrate quite clearly is the potential of the State's capacity to react to incidents such as this, even to the extent of legislating and the clear need for continued openness and debate about such issues. ATCSA 2005 is the fourth piece of anti-terrorism legislation passed in five years but felt by the Government to be necessary to combat terrorism. Amnesty International commented extensively on various drafts of the Bill and was concerned that it contained sweeping and vague provisions which, if enacted, could violate the human rights of people prosecuted under them, and would have a chilling effect for society at large on its exercise of the rights to freedom of expression and association. The Act included numerous provisions – for example, a new offence of publishing, processing or disseminating publications that indirectly incite terrorist acts or are likely to be useful to a person committing or preparing a terrorist act and the extension of pre-charge detention of people held under anti-terrorism legislation from 14 days to three months. This was later cut in a Parliamentary vote to 28 days creating a new offence of indirectly inciting terrorism and glorifying terrorist acts; proscribing groups that 'systematically' glorify terrorism and creating a new criminal offence of attending a 'terrorist training camp'.

In November 2005, Louise Arbour, the UN High Commissioner for Human Rights, wrote to the UK Government expressing concern about various aspects of the Terrorism Act. Her concerns included: the absence of a precise definition of terrorism upon which the new offences would be based and the broad and sweeping nature of some of these offences, raising questions as to how the principle of legality would be respected; the lack of the actual intent requirement in some offences; their questionable scope in light of Article 19 of the ECHR (on freedom of expression), resulting in a failure to strike a balance between national security interests and the fundamental right to freedom of expression and he overbroad reach of the provision concerning new grounds for proscription. Finally, in commenting on the period of pre-charge detention of up to 28 days for those held under anti-terrorism legislation the High Commissioner said that she remained gravely concerned about how the rights guaranteed by Articles 9 of the ICCPR and 5 of the ECHR (the right to liberty and freedom from arbitrary detention) would be protected.

For me, one of the most interesting issues emanating from this is the question of whether the Judiciary, in light of such developments, can retain and preserve their independent judicial powers particularly in respect of sweeping powers brought in the by Government in the form of anti-terrorism legislation. A particularly pertinent example of the capacity of the State to legislate and the effect that this can have on judicial independence can be demonstrated by the Inquiries Act 2005. For several years, Amnesty International has been concerned that the UK Government has successfully introduced legislation that curtails judicial powers. The 'anti-terrorism' measures described above are illustrative examples. In addition, in the field of determining asylum claims, legislative provisions have limited judicial discretion in finding facts favourable to asylum-seekers. Recently, Amnesty has said that the Inquiries Act 2005 has fundamentally compromised the role of Judges in upholding the rule of law and human rights for all by undermining the proper separation of powers between the Judiciary and the Executive in the UK. What do they mean by this?

Judicial Inquiries are supposed to be independent of the Government and used to find out what has really happened in cases where things have gone wrong with Government procedures. This Act introduced a new rule that Inquiries conducted under this law would largely be controlled by Government Ministers – and would therefore not actually be independent or objective any longer. The Act enables the executive to control inquiries initiated under it, effectively blocking public scrutiny of State actions. This means that the Government would have the power to:

- decide upon the inquiry and its terms of reference;
- to decide that there should be no independent parliamentary scrutiny of any decisions made;
- appoint each member of an inquiry panel, including the chair of the inquiry;
- dismiss any members of the inquiry if it wants to;
- impose restrictions on public access to the inquiry, including, for example, whether the inquiry or any individual hearings are held in public or private;
- impose restrictions on attendance by witnesses at the inquiry;
- decide whether the final report of the inquiry will be published;
- decide whether any evidence will be omitted from the report 'in the public interest',

In a democratic society, where we expect the Government to be acting in our best interests, and in many ways they are, there are still occasions when Government conduct is not all that it should be. State crime can be many things, from the violation of international laws to genocide, and it is important not to dismiss those actions at the thin end of the spectrum. What do these facts about the Inquiries Act 2005 tells us therefore? Basically that a judicial inquiry held under the Inquiries Act would fail to comply with the requirements identified by the European Court of Human Rights in its case law under Articles 2 and 3 of the ECHR. Such an Inquiry may also not comply with the requirement of 'an independent and impartial tribunal' under Article 6 of the ECHR. Lord Saville of Newdigate, the chair of the Bloody Sunday Tribunal of Inquiry, has expressed the view that the Inquiries Act 2005 made a very serious inroad into the independence of any inquiry and is likely to damage or destroy public confidence. He has also commented that he would not be prepared to be appointed as a member of such an inquiry. The Act does not therefore provide the foundation for effective, independent, impartial or thorough public judicial inquiries into allegations of serious human rights violations.

Interestingly the Government has stated its intention to hold just such an inquiry into the murder in Northern Ireland of Patrick Finucane, an outspoken human rights lawyer who was shot dead by loyalist paramilitaries on 12 February 1989 at his home in Belfast, Northern Ireland, in front of his wife and children. Substantial and credible allegations of State collusion began to emerge almost immediately after Patrick Finucane's death. Since then, evidence of criminal conduct by police and military intelligence officers acting in collusion with members of a loyalist paramilitary group in the killing has come to light. In addition, allegations of a subsequent cover-up have implicated Government agencies and authorities, including the police, the British Army, the UK security service (MI5) and the Office of the Director of Public Prosecutions in Northern Ireland. It has also been alleged that his killing was the result of State policy. His was just one among a number of killings in Northern Ireland alleged to have been carried out with the collusion of UK security forces. In the past, the Special Representative of the UN Secretary-General on human rights defenders and the UN Special Rapporteur on the independence of Judges and lawyers, as well as international and local human rights organisations, including Amnesty International, the International Federation for Human Rights, Human Rights Watch, the Committee on the Administration of Justice, British

Irish Right Watch and the Pat Finucane Centre have called on the UK Government to proceed to an independent inquiry without delay.

In May 2002, the UK and Irish Governments appointed Justice Peter Cory – a former Canadian Supreme Court Judge – to make recommendations as to whether public inquiries were warranted in a number of unlawful killings in which State officials were alleged to have colluded. In April 2003, the then Metropolitan Police Commissioner, Sir John Stevens, delivered his long-awaited report into collusion in Northern Ireland, only a short summary of which was published. Among other things, it confirmed widespread collusion between State agents and Loyalist paramilitaries, including State agents being involved in murder such as the killing of Patrick Finucane. It also confirmed the existence of the British Army's secret intelligence unit known as the Force Research Unit, which had actively colluded with Loyalist paramilitaries in targeting people (including Patrick Finucane) for assassination. In July 2003, the European Court of Human Rights found that the UK authorities had violated Patrick Finucane's right to life by failing to promptly investigate allegations of security personnel collusion in his murder. In October 2003, Justice Cory submitted his reports, but it was not until six months later that the UK authorities finally published them. As to the Finucane case, Justice Cory's conclusion was unequivocal: 'only a public inquiry will suffice'. He also added that '[t]his may be one of the rare situations where a public inquiry will be of greater benefit to a community than prosecutions.'

In September 2004, Kenneth Barrett, a former loyalist paramilitary, pleaded guilty to the murder of Patrick Finucane and was convicted. His was the only outstanding prosecution arising from the case. Kenneth Barrett's conviction removed any purported justification on the part of the UK authorities not to initiate a public inquiry into the allegations of collusion in Patrick Finucane's killing. Amnesty International and others observed the trial of Kenneth Barrett. As a result, the organisation was able to confirm that Kenneth Barrett's guilty plea led to no significant information about the circumstances surrounding the murder being made public. Shortly after the conviction of Kenneth Barrett, the UK Government finally announced that an inquiry into the killing of Patrick Finucane would be established. However, instead of announcing a *public* judicial inquiry under the Tribunal of Inquiry (Evidence) Act 1921 then in force, the UK authorities stated that the inquiry would be held on the basis of legislation that it *planned to introduce* to take account of 'the requirements of national security'.

Amnesty International expressed concern that the UK authorities were using 'national security' to curtail the ability of the inquiry to shed light on: State collusion in the killing of Patrick Finucane; allegations that his killing was the result of an official policy; and the role that different Government authorities played in the subsequent cover-up of collusion in his killing. The Inquiries Act was enacted in April 2005. The UK Government has repeatedly stated that it intends to hold an inquiry into the murder of Patrick Finucane under the Inquiries Act 2005. It has added that it was likely that a large proportion of the evidence would be considered in private since it involved issues 'at the heart of the national security infrastructure in Northern Ireland'. The Northern Ireland Office described this as 'genuinely the only way in which the inquiry can take place effectively... whilst taking into account the legitimate need to protect national security'. To date, the UK Government has yet to establish any such inquiry.

Patrick Finucane's widow, Geraldine Finucane, has called on senior Judges in England, Wales and Scotland not to serve on an inquiry into her husband's case under the Inquiries Act. Amnesty International supported her call. Since then, the organisation has urged those members of the Judiciary who may be approached by the UK authorities to sit on an inquiry into the Finucane case held under the Inquiries Act 2005 to decline to do so. Seventeen years after the killing of Patrick Finucane, his family are still awaiting a public independent judicial inquiry into his death. Justice Peter Cory (2005) has said:

> It seems to me that the proposed new Act would make a meaningful inquiry impossible. The Commissions would be working in an impossible situation. For example, the Minister, the actions of whose ministry was to be reviewed by the public inquiry would have the authority to thwart the efforts of the inquiry at every step. It really creates an intolerable Alice in Wonderland situation. There have been references in the press to an international judicial membership in the inquiry. If the new Act were to become law, I would advise all Canadian Judges to decline an appointment in light of the impossible situation they would be facing. In fact, I cannot contemplate any self-respecting Canadian Judge accepting an appointment to an inquiry constituted under the new proposed Act.[3]

Other senior Judges in the UK and abroad have also intimated that they would not be prepared to sit on a Finucane inquiry held under the Inquiries Act 2005. Recently, media reports attributed to Peter Hain

MP, Secretary of State for Northern Ireland, indicated that he had intimated that the Finucane inquiry would be held under the Inquiries Act or there would be 'none at all'. The Committee of Ministers of the Council of Europe, which supervises the implementation by member states of the judgments of the European Court of Human Rights, is continuing to consider whether a Finucane inquiry under the Inquiries Act 2005 would, as the UK Government claims, comply with the European Court of Human Rights judgment in the case. Amnesty International continues to call on the UK Government to establish without delay a truly independent public judicial inquiry into the Finucane case which fully complies with relevant domestic and international human rights standards. This example demonstrates therefore that it is certainly possible for the Government to legislate in particular ways in order to achieve particular things and in the current social climate, perhaps more possible than it has ever been. Lest the reader should imagine, however, that this is a totally new departure, let me disabuse you of that by looking back at some historical deviations from essential civil liberties.

Historical deviations from civil liberties

Following World War II the world recognised that international laws needed to be strengthened to prevent the inhuman way in which people had treated each other during this time; this led to the creation and strengthening of international institutions such as the United Nations Organisation, the NATO Alliance and the European Union. All these organisations have claimed a common objective of promoting peace and security and international laws have been developed since to deal with every aspect of human endeavour. One major development has been the establishment of criminal liability for individuals, States and their leaders for crimes against humanity which was embodied in the Nuremberg International Military Tribunal for the trial of major war criminals. The charter lays down the following principles:

> **Principles of International Law Recognized**
> **in the Charter of the Nürnberg Tribunal and**
> **in the Judgment of the Tribunal**
>
> **Principle I**
> Any person who commits an act which constitutes a crime under international law is responsible therefore and liable to punishment.

Principle II

The fact that internal law does not impose a penalty for an act which constitutes a crime under international law does not relieve the person who committed the act from responsibility under international law.

Principle III

The fact that a person who committed an act which constitutes a crime under international law acted as Head of State or responsible Government official does not relieve him from responsibility under international law.

Principle IV

The fact that a person acted pursuant to order of his Government or of a superior does not relieve him from responsibility under international law, provided a moral choice was in fact possible to him.

Principle V

Any person charged with a crime under international law has the right to a fair trial on the facts and law.

Principle VI

The crimes hereinafter set out are punishable as crimes under international law:

(a) Crimes against peace:
   (i) Planning, preparation, initiation or waging of a war of aggression or a war inviolation of international treaties, agreements or assurances; (ii) Participation in a common plan or conspiracy for the accomplishment of any of the acts mentioned under (i).

(b) War crimes:
   Violations of the laws or customs of war which include, but are not limited to, murder, ill-treatment or deportation to slave-labour or for any other purpose of civilian population of or in occupied territory; murder or ill-treatment of prisoners of war, of persons on the Seas, killing of hostages, plunder of public or private property, wanton destruction of cities, towns, or villages, or devastation not justified by military necessity.

(c) Crimes against humanity:
   Murder, extermination, enslavement, deportation and other inhuman acts done against any civilian population, or persecutions on political, racial or religious grounds, when

such acts are done or such persecutions are carried on in execution of or in connection with any crime against peace or any war crime.

Principle VII
Complicity in the commission of a crime against peace, a war crime, or a crime against humanity as set forth in Principle VI is a crime under international law.

In spite of this charter however, there continue to be war crimes and crimes committed against humanity. New measures have been brought in to respond to more recent genocides and grave crimes against humanity. Some examples are the ad hoc UN Tribunals of Rwanda and the former Yugoslavia, but they have proved somewhat inadequate. So what is going wrong and how is it that Governments can still act in ways clearly outlawed by numerous international laws and treaties?

The ideology of war

Warfare is a strange and contradictory idea. On the one hand, countries that go to war condone the killing of those considered to be enemies (for whatever reason) and in doing so, require soldiers to risk their lives for their country and the cause of war. On the other hand, they also seek to place some limits or boundaries on what can actually legally be done during a time of war. So it's acceptable to kill people in the cause of war, but it is not acceptable to do other things whilst you're at war, such as torture. Clearly trying to distinguish war from crime in this way is difficult at best and nonsensical at worst.

Any laws in relation to warfare actually legitimate the use of violence and thus license soldiers to carry and use weapons in the name of the State. It is conventional then that those who do not accept or fight against this can lawfully and legitimately be killed in the name of war, whilst those who do not – let's say civilians – can be left alone to go about their business. However, it is not that simple to distinguish between combatants and non-combatants in modern times when 'people wars' are fought increasingly by insurgents who lack proper uniforms and cannot easily be distinguished from general populations. In an effort to acknowledge this, international law in the form of the Geneva Convention states that, for example, guerrillas must carry their weapons openly during engagements. The Hague Convention 1907 codified the rules of warfare but this convention has been widely criticised for not enforcing any control at all. Writers have said that those countries who were involved in drawing up the convention purposefully allowed it to be too vague, and the result is that it does not control or regulate warfare at all, thus leaving it open for people to commit atrocities during times of war without actually being in breach of the convention. The treatment of conscientious objectors in the UK is one example of how such unacceptable behaviour has been perpetrated against individuals in the past and is worth mentioning.

Conscientious objectors were people who did not want to fight in World War I for religious or other reasons of conscience. Conscientious objectors became known as 'conscies' or C.O's. Battles such as Ypres and the Somme had cost Britain a vast number of casualties. By 1916, volunteers to join the British Army were starting to dry up. In response to this, the Government introduced conscription in 1916 – where the law stated that you had to serve your country in the military for a certain period of time. A 'conscience clause' was added whereby those who had a 'conscientious objection to bearing arms' were freed from military service. There were several types of conscientious objector.

1. Some were pacifists who were against war in general.
2. Some were political objectors who did not consider the Government of Germany to be their enemy.
3. Some were religious objectors who believed that war and fighting was against their religion. Groups in this section were the Quakers and Jehovah Witnesses.
4. Some were a combination of any of the above groups.

Some conscientious objectors did not want to fight but were keen to 'do their bit'. These people were willing to help in weapons factories and some went to the trenches to become stretcher bearers though not to fight. Other C.O's refused to do anything that involved the war – these were known as 'absolutists'. By the end of 1915, the British Army had lost almost 600,000 men killed, wounded or missing presumed dead. Volunteers had dried up, and conscription was introduced. The whole issue of conscription was a thorny issue even in the army. The British Army commander in South Africa – Lord Roberts (c1915) – wrote about conscription:

Compulsory service is, I believe, as distasteful to the nation as it is incompatible with the conditions of an Army like ours, which has such a large proportion of its units on Foreign Service. I hold moreover, that the man who voluntarily serves his country is more to be relied upon as a good fighting soldier than is he who is compelled to bear arms.

In 1916 the Military Service Act was introduced – this was soon nicknamed the 'Bachelor's Bill' as to start with conscription only included unmarried men between 18 and 41, but it was widened in May 1916 to include married men as well. By April 1918, it had been expanded to include men up to 51. However, the Act also included a 'conscience clause' which allowed people the right to refuse to join up if it went against their beliefs. Those who claimed to be conscientious objectors had to face a tribunal to argue their case as to why they should not be called up to join the army. However, even this clause was not enough for some who wanted the act withdrawn in full. The 'No-Conscription Fellowship' was founded as early as 1914 and it produced a leaflet entitled 'Repeal the Act.' This leaflet stated the following;

Fellow citizens:

Conscription is now law in this country of free traditions. Our hard-won liberties have been violated. Conscription means the desecration of principles that we have long held dear; it involves the subordination of civil liberties to military dictation; it imperils the freedom of individual conscience and establishes in our midst that militarism which menaces all social graces and divides the peoples of all nations. We re-affirm our determined resistance to all that is established by the Act. We cannot assist in warfare. War, which to us is wrong. War, which the peoples do not seek, will only be made impossible when men, who so believe, remain steadfast to their convictions. Conscience, it is true, has been recognised in the Act, but it has been placed at the mercy of tribunals. We are prepared to answer for our faith before any tribunal, but we cannot accept any exemption that would compel those who hate war to kill by proxy or set them to tasks which would help in the furtherance of war.

We strongly condemn the monstrous assumption by Parliament that a man is deemed to be bound by an oath that he has never taken and forced under an authority he will never acknowledge to perform acts which outrage his deepest convictions. It is true that the present act applies only to a small section of the community, but a great tradition has been sacrificed. Already there is a clamour for an extension of the act. Admit the principle, and who can stay the march of militarism? Repeal the Act. That is your only safeguard. If this be not done, militarism will fasten its iron grip upon our national life and institutions. There will be imposed upon us the very system which statesmen affirm that they set out to overthrow.

What shall it profit the nation if it shall win the war and lose its own soul?[4]

The No-Conscription Fellowship was an organisation made up of members of the Socialist Independent Labour Party and the Quakers. Although the law clearly stated that it was possible to be a conscientious objector, any men who signed the above leaflet were subsequently charged under the Defence of the Realm Act. They were all fined, and those who decided not to pay the fine were sent to prison. So although the 1916 Military Service Act allowed conscripts to opt out 'on the grounds of a conscientious objection to the undertaking of combatant service' it was not quite as simple as that.

The Army's Non-Combatant Corps was known as the Non-Courage Corps. The nation's women plucked pillows to provide white feathers to send in anonymous envelopes to refuseniks. Families were torn. Lieutenant-Colonel Maurice Hunter, big in the army in Belper in Derbyshire, never talked again to his sons John and Arthur when they resigned their commissions, appalled by what they saw on the Western Front. John, who refused an order to rejoin his men, was dismissed with dishonour and sentenced to a year's hard labour. Arthur emigrated. The local paper wrote sympathetically, not of John and Arthur, but of their father's shame.

Ronald Skirth turned conscientious objector whilst fighting. Skirth had gone to Ypres and in June 1917 was close to the infamous Lone Tree Crater near the Messines Ridge. 91,000 explosives were detonated which could be heard 100 miles away and within seconds there were over 10,000 German casualties. The battle carried on for hours and created total carnage. Skirth was sent into no man's land on reconnaissance and witnessed thousands of dead, mutilated bodies. He came across a young German soldier sitting upright as though alive but who was also dead. He would have been about the same age as Skirth – then 19. In his hand he held a photo of his girlfriend upon which she had written 'Mein Hans'. For the rest of the war, he felt a fraud and although he remained in the army he made a private pact with God to put 'no more young Hans's into the ground'. He refused to accept the military medal.

Bert Brocklesby was a Methodist minister who was incarcerated for being an absolutist – this means that he refused to serve with the non-combatants. His argument, delivered from the pulpit of his local church, was that you could not imagine Christ dressed in Army uniform or bayoneting a German soldier, but Christ carrying a dying man on a stretcher? Yes, he could visualise that. Brockelsby's notion of individual liberty was the inalienable right of every man to follow his conscience and not be bullied by Government. At that time, this was totally incompatible with military thinking. In spite of the exemption within the Military Service Act 1916, he was arrested for not joining the war effort and was imprisoned in Richmond Castle. Brocklesby held fast to his religious ideals of 'thou shalt not kill' and that he believed that people demonstrated their beliefs by what they did. During this time he and about fifty other CO's were taken to Bologna to stand trial before a military court (again, in spite of the Military Service Act 1916). All were found guilty and sentenced to death, and if you are asking how this could be the case when the law gave them the right to object to war – the explanation is that it was a sham. A piece of military theatre designed by the UK Government to try to frighten these men into signing up. A classic example of man's inhumanity to man and more than this, an example of a war crime. An MP at the time told the House of Commons that no one could deny that the conscientious objectors displayed the most difficult courage in the world, the courage of the individual against the crowd.

Historically therefore there have always been clear deviations from the essential principles of civil liberties, in spite of numerous charters, treaties or domestic statutes which purport to protect such beliefs and principles. This creates a worrying scenario in which we have to acknowledge that the reality is that such deviations will continue to occur whilst it remains possible for Governments to excuse their actions for a variety of reasons. Clearly this still occurs in current theatres of war where the commission of criminal activities is often justified in a number of different ways. War itself therefore can arguably be described as an organisational crime. Green and Ward (2005) analyse war crime on three levels in order to explain it. First, criminal wars they describe as being where the nature of the war itself is illegal or that in the war there are no incentives to behave legally – that is – within the terms of existing international conventions. For example, the Vietnam War was said to be illegal because the US was not at war with Vietnam but was fighting insurgents within the country. They did this with high technology weaponry which was said to be a violation of the general principles of customary international law because it led to massive levels of destruction in relation to civilian lives and property. This idea of a criminal war can also be demonstrated by the wars against Iraq in

1991, 2003 and currently. Here the war is between countries that have completely different technological capacities. Critics argue that in such wars, soldiers from the UK or the US are actually more likely to die in friendly fire incidents than anything else. In addition, this kind of warfare might lead in future to wars which take place only by one country sending deadly missiles to another without the need for soldiers at all.

Second, Green and Ward (ibid.) suggest that there can also be criminal armies, within which soldiers can commit criminal acts in two potential ways. First, their officers can direct them or permit them to commit criminal acts, or second, officers can adopt policies which then lead to criminal acts by their soldiers. One example of this is the secret bombing of Cambodia by the US in 1969. This had been specifically prohibited by US congressional legislation but was ignored by those on the ground and continued in 1972–1973 when the US and North Vietnam were on the brink of peace. Third, they suggest that there can also be criminal soldiers. Historically the most common form of crime committed by soldiers has been the killing of enemies or prisoners who are trying to surrender. There have often been conflicts between what the army wants – that is a live prisoner who might have important intelligence information – and what the soldier feels he has to deal with. Green and Ward (2005 155) cite a US marine in WWII who said of the Japanese:

> we had such intense hatred for [them] and they were so tricky. I mean they'd have their hands up like that, and then when you got close enough they spread their arms out and out popped two grenades.... so we just automatically shot them...

Soldiers can also commit acts like this out of a sense of revenge. Research has pointed to the fact that revenge can account for things like 'battlefield frenzy' which includes slaughtering civilians and mutilating the dead. Writers say that this type of revenge is provoked by feelings of shame or grief which are then converted into blind rage in which a soldier goes berserk. This is different from another explanation which is the phenomenon of 'righteous slaughter' in which the soldier who kills has a sense of power and a conviction that s/he is acting righteously and restoring the moral order which s/he thinks the victim has violated.

Again there are difficult contradictions to reconcile here because soldiers undergo military training, and part of that includes teaching them how to kill. This includes training which gets over those psychological barriers which people normally have to killing such as repeated realistic simulations of combat killing and the instilling of slogans such as 'ambushes are murder and murder is fun.' The military distinguish between legitimate and criminal killing and try to break down any humanitarian beliefs that soldiers might have as well as neutralising those beliefs which in effect free a person from behaving in a normal moral way. A good example of the interaction between all of these issues is that of the My Lai Massacre which took place on March 16, 1968 and involved the mass murder of approximately 500 unarmed men, women and children, by US Army forces. Many of the victims were sexually abused, beaten, tortured or maimed, and some of the bodies were found mutilated. Of the 26 US soldiers initially charged with criminal offences for their actions at My Lai, only one was convicted. He served three years of his life sentence. When the incident became public knowledge in 1969, it prompted widespread outrage around the world. The massacre also reduced US support at home for the Vietnam War. Three US servicemen who made an effort to halt the massacre and protect the wounded were denounced by US Congressmen, received hate mail, death threats and animals that had been mutilated on their doorsteps. Only 30 years after the event were their efforts honoured. One of these was helicopter pilot Hugh Thompson who attempted to stop the carnage and then reported it to his superior officers.

Closer to home, but no less important in terms of the question of preserving essential human rights and civil liberties (and more precisely where such rights have been abrogated or suspended and on what basis), a pertinent example is the Northern Ireland troubles of 1970's, the Diplock courts and the suspension of trial by jury. The Diplock courts were a type of court established by the UK Government in response to a report by Lord Diplock; this addressed the problem of dealing with paramilitary violence through means other than internment and to prevent jury intimidation during the conflict. The courts essentially suspended the right to a trial by jury for certain offences. In these cases a single Judge sitting alone heard the case. The Diplock report marked the beginnings of a policy known as *criminalisation*, in which the State removed any legal distinction between political violence and normal crime, with paramilitary prisoners treated in exactly the same way as common criminals. The report – which provided the basis for the Northern Ireland (Emergency Provisions) Act 1973 and, although later amended (with the Prevention of Terrorism (Temporary Provisions) Act 1974 and subsequent renewals) – has continued as the basis for counter-terrorist legislation in the UK. The number of cases heard in Diplock courts reached a peak of 329 a year in the mid-1980s. With the Northern

Ireland peace process that figure fell to 60 a year in the mid-2000s. On 1 August 2005, the Northern Ireland Office announced that the Diplock courts were to be phased out, and in August 2006 they announced that the courts were to be abolished from July 2007. This was achieved under the Justice and Security (Northern Ireland) Act 2007. Non-jury trials, however, may still be used in Northern Ireland, as elsewhere in the UK, but only in exceptional cases. In 2009, for example, it was decided to hold the trial of Londonderry-based solicitor Manmohan 'Johnny' Sandhu in Belfast as a Diplock court. Famous cases also heard by the Diplock courts include the trials of the Shankill Butchers, Sean Kelly and Christy Walsh.[5]

In spite of the fact that the Diplock courts represented a clear departure from the right to a fair trial these courts have not received a great deal of academic attention. One exception to this is Jackson and Doran's (1995a) analysis which observed twenty-six Diplock and seventeen jury trials of serious criminal cases in the Belfast Crown Court over a twelve-month period. Critics had feared that Diplock Judges would become 'case hardened,' or biased against the accused. To establish this, the authors chose to count and classify instances of 'judicial intervention' (that is, instances in which a Judge interrupted the proceedings to question witnesses and defendants). Jackson and Doran (ibid.) chose to study this aspect of the Diplock system because they felt it would be the best indicator of whether Diplock courts had shifted from an adversarial approach to a more inquisitorial approach. It is perhaps not surprising that they found that 'inquisitorial' questioning (in the form of cross-examination by the Judge) occurred almost exclusively in Diplock trials and not in 'ordinary' criminal trials. They also found that Diplock Judges were far more likely to question defendants, defence witnesses and experts than Judges in jury trials. One could argue, of course, that having two systems for defendants charged with essentially similar crimes, based on suspected political affiliation, is not necessarily unfair as long as the requirements of Article 6 of the European Convention are honoured. Whilst the right to jury trial is considered an important safeguard in the common law, dating back at least to 1215 and the Magna Carta, critics would also argue no doubt that it is not an international human right and the fact that a procedure appears to comply with the specific minimum standards enshrined in Article 6 does not necessarily mean that the procedure satisfies the standards of a fair trial. Unfortunately this was not something which Jackson and Doran (ibid.) applied themselves to. Likewise there has been little academic comment on other implications of the Diplock trials such as coerced confessions, 'supergrass' testimonies and anonymous witnesses, although Boyle (1982: 144) has noted that:

> The elimination of the jury...led to...an increase in the extent to which the judges themselves sought to take a direct role in the elucidation of the truth by questioning witnesses and counsel. The overall effect was...to emphasize the extent to which the trial process had become a 'closed-shop' in the hands of a small group of professional lawyers.

In spite of this, there has been little historical or legal academic analysis in relation to this hugely important piece of social history; so too, little about the trials of Bobby Sands or the Birmingham Six. In addition, little mention has been made about the fact that the Judge who sat on the Diplock court that tried the 'Black Supergrass'[6] case was Basil Kelly – a former Unionist Protestant member of Parliament and former Attorney General. In the face of all of these issues, the fact that the implications of the denial of a trial by jury are largely unexplored is unusual. In a subsequent article (1995b: 12) Jackson and Doran commented that:

> In the changing political climate, modifications to the legal process which were effected in response to the Troubles are being stripped of their original justification. As political violence loses its grip, much rethinking needs to be done on the entire legal strategy which was developed to counter its threat. If features of the legal process are in line for dismantling in the event of lasting peace, then surely the system of non-jury trial in the form of the Diplock courts must be at the front of the queue?

I am not suggesting that trial by jury is perfect because it isn't. It costs money, it is often very slow and sometimes there are mistakes. Some trials by jury fall apart but the question is, is it a system worth preserving? The answer to this must be yes – it may not be perfect but it's better than the alternatives and importantly symbolises public participation in the criminal justice system which is more important now than it has ever been. It represents an element of transparency which is arguably necessary within the criminal justice process and an important example of the power of judgment being passed to citizens rather than being kept exclusively in the hands of the Judiciary. There are good reasons why Russia and Spain reintroduced jury trial after the collapse of their totalitarian regimes and why other jurisdictions sometimes say they aspire to the UK model of jury trial. Perhaps they would agree with former master of the rolls Lord Devlin, who described it as the lamp that shows freedom lives.

Contemporary issues surrounding civil liberties

One of the most pertinent examples to use at this point is the ongoing debate about the legality of the war in Iraq. The circumstances leading up to that are relevant. On 8 November, 2002, the United Nations Security Council passed Resolution 1441 because it found that Iraq had been in breach of earlier resolutions throughout the 1990's following the first Gulf War relating to its programme for weapons of mass destruction. The Resolution required Iraq to allow weapons inspectors, led by Dr Hans Blix, into Iraq and if they did not comply, the issue would go back to the Security Council for further discussion.

The Resolution had included the phrase '*all necessary means*' and in international law and diplomacy this is well known to authorise the use of military force. The final version of the Resolution however did *not* contain this phrase and was not ever secured, but in spite of this in March 2003 Iraq was invaded. Many people have claimed that it was illegal under international law. Lord Steyn, a famous, and now retired law lord, said that the Government's attempt to find a legal justification for the invasion had been 'scraping the bottom of the legal barrel'. Kofi Annan, then Secretary-General of the UN, confirmed that in his view the invasion was illegal. All regarded it as contrary to Article 2 Paragraph 4 of the UN Charter which sets out the fundamental norms of international law against the use of force against another State.

In December 2002 CND – the Campaign for Nuclear Disarmament – took judicial review proceedings in the High Court in this country. It asked the Divisional Court to rule upon the meaning and effect of Resolution 1441 and in particular to declare that that Resolution did not authorise the use of force against Iraq. The Divisional Court rejected the claim for judicial review and gave three reasons for doing so. First they claimed that courts do not usually give 'advice.' Second, they stated that to give 'advice' in this case would damage international relations and would involve the courts in issues they did not want to be involved in (war); finally they stated that resolution 1441 was an unincorporated international instrument, so not part of domestic law and therefore the courts did not need to review it because it did not affect any person's rights or duties in the domestic legal system. So does this mean that the invasion of Iraq was legal? No court has ever had the opportunity to determine whether the invasion of Iraq was legal or not. Currently we must await the findings of the Chilcot Inquiry. It was vital, however, at the time of the decision making process regarding the possible invasion of Iraq, that in order to maintain the rule of law, the Attorney General gave his advice. This was eventually published by Government in 2005 and contained three suggestions why the use of force might be legal. First, could it be classed as self defence? The Attorney General rejected this, as well as the American notion of the right of pre-emptive self defence. So this was not the basis on which the UK went to war. Second, was it 'humanitarian intervention'? The Attorney General said there may, in certain cases, be a lawful authority to intervene in another State by force to avoid a humanitarian 'catastrophe' but he said this was not the case with Iraq. Finally, the Attorney General said that *lawful force* could be authorised by the United Nations Security Council itself. He did not say directly that Resolution 1441 had that effect but rather that it was an earlier resolution of the United Nations Security Council which had been revived in the light of subsequent events and in particular in the light of Resolution 1441. He was of course referring to resolution 678.

Resolution 678 had actually been passed in 1990 and its effect was to authorise members of the United Nations to use all necessary means to assist in expelling Iraq from Kuwait and to restore international peace and security in the region. That was the first Gulf War. It is fairly clear that Resolution 678 had therefore been passed in wholly different circumstances, in the context of another armed conflict, and had absolutely nothing to do with whether member states of the UN could unilaterally attack Iraq in March 2003, twelve years after the end of the first Gulf War, in wholly different circumstances. It is quite amazing that a resolution passed in 1990, in those circumstances, led to the invasion of 2003 and were used as an excuse for that – but it was. At the time of writing, we are in the middle of the Chilcot Inquiry which is seeking to establish more precisely the legality of the war in Iraq, but should we feel heartened by this? Will it in fact establish the truth? At the outset there have been criticisms that a formal inquiry was not established, but does this matter? Arguably formal inquiries with QCs and the numerous 'juniors' they use are not necessarily guaranteed to do a better job at establishing the truth than will Chilcot and of course lawyers cost far more. The Saville Inquiry in Northern Ireland is a good example of this and has cost approximately £300 million.

Interestingly also though, it is almost as if the public are being persuaded that the Chilcot Inquiry is a unique example of a Government being asked to account for its actions and as if we did not already know that such a thing as a 'crime of aggression' already existed. It was in fact the London Agreement of 8 August, 1945 which created the International Military Tribunal (IMT) and which conducted the trials at Nuremberg. Within the jurisdiction of the tribunal was 'initiation or waging of a war of aggression.' Twelve defendants were found guilty of this and the IMT argued that 'aggression' existed as a crime before 1945 and so the trials did not fall foul of the principle of law known as *nullum crimen sine lege* (no crime without law). There have been no trials for aggression since 1947. The House of Lords has also previously recognised that although the international crime of aggression existed – in the case of *R v Jones and others (2006)* – it did not exist in UK domestic law. It would therefore require an Act of Parliament to make it a domestic crime (such as is the case with torture under the Criminal Justice Act 1988). Interestingly, some countries do provide for aggression in their national criminal law – for example, the German Criminal Code. In 1974 the UN General Assembly adopted a resolution which contained a definition of aggression – (Resolution 3314 of 14/12/1974). However, there was no follow-up to this until the idea of the International Criminal Court re-emerged. As things transpired, the ICC statute recognises a crime of aggression but does *not* permit a trial for it until such time as a detailed definition is agreed. Against this background it must surely be the case that nobody could be lawfully impeached by Parliament for aggression The crime does not exist in English law: only in international law. Impeachment remains a theoretically possible form of trial for some matters but the whole process is antiquated and would fall foul in numerous ways of modern legal due process and human rights law. At the most fundamental level, such a 'trial would not, in modern times, be independent of the executive. I don't understand all the quotation marks on the words in this paragraph

There have been some allegations that UK soldiers have committed serious human rights violations in Iraq. The UK Government, however, has repeatedly asserted (in court proceedings) that neither the ECHR nor the HRA applies to the conduct of UK personnel in Iraq. Even the parliamentary Foreign Affairs Committee acknowledged that there have been abuses, concluding in its March 2005 report stating that some British personnel had committed grave violations of human rights of persons held in detention facilities in Iraq. One such example is the Al-Skeini case involving Baha Mousa.

On 14 September, 2003 in Basra, Iraq, Baha Mousa was among eight Iraqi citizens arrested and reportedly beaten in a hotel by members of the UK military. Baha Mousa was 26 years old. He worked as a receptionist at a hotel in Basrah City. In the early morning of 14, September, 2003, a unit from 1 QLR (Queen's Lancashire Regiment) raided the hotel. The troops were particularly concerned to ascertain the whereabouts of one of the partners who ran the hotel. Brigadier Moore himself took part in this operation and was up on the roof of the hotel when the troops were effecting arrests. It was in these circumstances that they rounded up a number of the men they found there, including Baha Mousa. Baha Mousa's father, Daoud Mousa, had been a police officer for 24 years and was by then a colonel in the Basrah police. He had called at the hotel that morning to pick up his son at the end of his shift, and he told the lieutenant in charge of the unit that he had seen three of his soldiers pocketing money from the safe. During this visit he also saw his son lying on the floor of the hotel lobby with six other hotel employees with their hands behind their heads. The lieutenant assured him that this was a routine investigation and that it would be over in a couple of hours. Colonel Mousa never saw his son alive again. Four days later he was invited by a military police unit to identify his son's dead body. It was covered in blood and bruises. His nose was badly broken, there was blood coming from his nose and mouth, and there were severe patches of bruising all over his body. Witnesses said there was a sustained campaign of ill-treatment of the men who were taken into custody, one of whom was very badly injured, and they suggested that Baha Mousa was picked out for particularly savage treatment because of the complaints his father had made.

The UK Government decided not to hold an independent inquiry into the deaths. The Ministry of Defence initially claimed that neither the ECHR nor the Human Rights Act 1998 was applicable in respect of the conduct of its military personnel in Iraq at the time of the deaths. They said this was because Iraq was outside Europe and was not a party to the ECHR. Subsequently three of the seven military personnel were charged with the inhuman treatment of Baha Mousa, and the Court of Appeal subsequently ruled that the ECHR and the HRA *did* apply to the case of Baha Mousa and that the authorities are required to ensure an independent, impartial investigation into this death. The Court also found that the system for investigating deaths at the hands of UK armed forces personnel was seriously deficient, including in its lack of independence from the commanding officer, and it needed to be scrutinised. This was commented on by Norton-Taylor & Dyer (2007) whose report in the Guardian confirms that British soldiers who imprison detainees during military campaigns abroad *are* bound by the Human Rights Act, which prohibits torture and inhuman or degrading treatment. By a four-to-one majority, the court ruled that the jurisdiction of the Human Rights Act applied overseas, including detention centres over which British troops had 'effective control'. Importantly this ruling potentially opens the way to an independent public inquiry into the Mousa killing and other alleged abuses of Iraqi civilians. It will now be up to the High Court to decide whether to demand such an inquiry. The European Convention on Human Rights, which the HRA 1998 enforces in British courts, obliges Governments to carry out independent, timely, open and effective investigations when someone dies allegedly at the hands of agents of the State. Importantly, however, this does not necessarily mean that the Government will set up an independent inquiry into how Baha Mousa died. The case would first have to go back to the High Court, where the Government could argue that the military police investigation and the court martial of seven soldiers fulfilled the State's obligations to conduct an independent investigation. The European Convention on Human Rights requires States to carry out an adequate and effective investigation where an individual protected by the convention has been killed as a result of the use of force. The House of Lords held in an earlier case that the investigation must deal with the events leading up to the death and make recommendations for the prevention of similar occurrences, making it hard to argue that a court martial fulfilled the requirements. It remains to be seen, therefore, what the outcome of this might be particularly in light of a recent decision in June 2010 by the Supreme Court. The case, brought by the mother of a soldier[7] who died of heatstroke in Iraq in June 2003, asked the court to decide whether troops were protected by Human Rights law when they were outside overseas bases. Although two lower courts had decided that they were, the Supreme Court ruled that the legislation could not be extended to cover situations outside of the bases because it would make command and control functions too difficult.

Generally speaking, expectations from independent inquiries and war crimes trials have been set too high. People have thought that they would be magical events which would demonstrably assist and aid peace. Of course, it is not as simple as that. No human institution can be only good or only useful and not have a cost, whether financial or human. Such institutions do not exist. It is relevant in this context to consider this issue further. Specifically, what for example was the effect of Nuremberg on War Crime?

The International Criminal Court was set up on 1 July, 2002. Prior to this there was no similar institution except for that which had existed at Nuremberg, before which there had been no such thing as an international criminal law. There had never before been any significant trial of individuals for war crimes. There were puny attempts after the First World War but they did not amount to very much. Nuremberg was good for a number of reasons: It was the first time there had been recognition of a rule of law in the international community and that the rule of law could be applied internationally. It was the first refusal by victorious powers just to execute enemy leaders (in this case, the Nazis). They were offered and given, certainly by the standards of the middle of the 20th century, a fair trial. It provided important official acknowledgement for the victims of the most appalling war crimes and a credible, recorded history of the criminal activities of the Nazi leaders. That is a very important benefit that comes from all forms of justice, not only official trials, but also Truth and Reconciliation Commissions. Whatever the form of justice, the official record of the history is very important because it makes fabricated denials of atrocities more difficult. The work of holocaust deniers, for example, would be a lot easier but for Nuremberg. The evidence was meticulously collected by the four prosecution teams. Seventy-five per cent of the Nuremberg record consists of Nazi documents. They were really condemned from their own documents. It also helped to avoid the attribution of collective guilt to the whole German nation. The identification of the criminality of the leaders who were responsible for the crimes is crucial.

In the immediate aftermath of the Nuremberg Trials and their successes, a permanent international criminal court should have been established. That was the intention. If one looks at the 1948 Genocide Convention one will see in Article 6 there is a reference to an international criminal court having jurisdiction. However, the Cold War intervened and the idea was placed on hold for almost half a century. The Soviet Union and China during the Cold War would certainly not have been willing to agree to any international criminal court. It was only in 1993, in the face of huge war crimes being committed in the former Yugoslavia that the United Nations Security Council, to the surprise of all lawyers and politicians, decided to set up the first-ever truly international criminal court for the former Yugoslavia. That was followed shortly after by the international criminal court for Rwanda.

Like Nuremberg, the UN tribunals brought acknowledgment to the victims, they provided a credible record of the war crimes committed by all sides in the former Yugoslavia and of the genocide in Rwanda.

All sides now have had to acknowledge and accept that they were all, to a greater or lesser extent, both perpetrators as well as victims. It has also put a stop to many of the fabricated denials which in themselves continue to be a problem. A noteworthy example of this is the case of Dragan Erdemovic and the Srebrenica massacre.

Erdemovic was a member of the Bosnian Serb army who had had a fall out with his commanding officer and decided to confess. He offered to meet with a news team from ABC and confessed to having shot and killed in excess of 70 men and boys outside Srebrenica. He said he was under considerable duress. His commanding officer had told him to form part of the firing squad. A mass grave had been dug, and these men were lined up in groups of about 20, facing the grave. They were shot in the back of their heads, and their bodies fell into the grave. Erdemovic drew a remarkably accurate map of where this mass grave was located. It turned out to be a mass grave not known to the NATO forces who were then in Bosnia. The journalists took the map to the US embassy in Belgrade. Then they made a mistake. One of the journalists called her London office and said that she had the video of Erdemovic's confession and she was bringing it out that evening on a flight from Belgrade to London. Her telephone conversation was tapped. At the airport she was arrested, the video tape was confiscated by the Belgrade police, and she was allowed to continue her trip. Her understandable fear was that Erdemovic would be murdered by the Serb security police once they saw the videotape. Fortunately she had friends in high places, and after a phone call, Serbia was ordered to deliver Erdemovic to the International Tribunal as a potential witness to what happened at Srebrenica. In the event, Serbia handed him over but denied the massacre at Srebrenica. It was said to be anti-Serb propaganda. It was denied that this mass grave would contain war dead from Srebrenica and that even if such a grave existed it would contain war dead from battles decades and decades before. The grave was subsequently found with the map that Erdemovic had given to the journalist. US intelligence corroborated the version with satellite photographs. Subsequently Madeleine Albright, the [then] US ambassador at the United Nations, handed the photographs to the media. The mass grave was exhumed and it was established that the people *were* killed in 1995. All of them were male; all of them had their hands tied behind their backs and the cause of death was a single bullet wound to the back of the head. That is not the way people die in battle, and that evidence put a stop to the denials.

In a sense we have become unsurprised by atrocities such as this, occurring in other countries in times of social disorganisation and as

Cohen (2002) so ably points out, the further away it is, the more we can divorce ourselves from its reality. The more we see these images in the media, the more we have become immune to them and hence the easier it is to deny them. However, we should be mindful of two further issues. First, such atrocities *are* still occurring in spite of various prohibitive legislations, conventions and treaties and despite Governments throughout the world (including our own) claiming to adhere to varying standards of civil liberties. Perpetrators do not often face trial when they are apprehended (which again is not often). When they do, we become witnesses to bizarre and very public denials – for example, the ongoing trial of Radavan Karadic. On the run for so long, disguised and living blatantly in society, he now claims in his defence that the massacres he is accused of were staged by his enemies. Second, these issues are no longer far away. We cannot continue divorcing ourselves from the reality of – for example – terrorism. For one thing, the Government continues to claim that it is a very real threat and it is on our doorstep and second, that because of this we must be ever vigilant and assist the Government to combat it wherever possible. Nowhere is this more aptly pertinent, from the authors' point of view, than within academe itself where we are currently being told we are at risk of terrorism by radicalised students and that we must help both research this concept and weed the perpetrators out. Garner (2007)[8] reports that both the US and UK Governments are funding research projects that will assist counter-terrorism operations in spite of the fact that many academics say they are unwilling agents of the State. As military strategies fail and more attention is focused on the 'battle for hearts and minds', a new programme is attracting academics' concern: Combating Terrorism by Countering Radicalisation, a £1.3m initiative run by the Economic and Social Research Council (ESRC). The original programme, a joint project with the Arts and Humanities Research Council and the Foreign and Commonwealth Office (FCO), was withdrawn in October after some academics said that it amounted to spying for the Government. It was revised and re-released earlier this year as New Security Challenges: 'Radicalisation' and Violence – A Critical Assessment. But academics say that it still fails to address their concerns about the need for academic research to be independent from Government.

The Economic and Social Research Council's (ESRC) tender document for this type of research bid – and which explicitly links the initiative to the Government's counter-terrorism strategy – is really inexcusable. The idea of encouraging British academics to become involved with the UK Government's counter-terrorism strategy is the stuff of fiction. In spite of some strong protests from the academic world, it is unlikely that an organisation like ESRC will back down. More important to them will be the potential to cooperate with the Government. No doubt ESRC would say that such research is merely in the spirit of intellectual enquiry; that research outputs will be in the public domain and that it is a good thing to collaborate with Government departments on important issues. However, this does not factor in the argument that research should be independent of Government – and seen to be so. What we are left with then is the fact that many academics feel that the ESRC programme tarnishes the reputation of British academics around the world. Added to this, in the US the Pat Robertson Intelligence Scholars Program offers science students $25,000 (£12,700) a year to work in intelligence-gathering after graduation. The American Anthropological Association has now set up a commission to examine the issues involved in anthropologists working with intelligence agencies. The crux of this issue is perhaps the need for transparency; any research – or decisions based on research – should be carried out in public and certainly should in no way involve secret interactions with these agencies.

It is worth mentioning by way of concluding this chapter, the important decision in the case of *Liberty and the Irish Council for Civil Liberties and British Irish Rights Watch v The United Kingdom* (application no. 582443/00) (2008). In this case the Irish Council for Civil Liberties (ICCL) took their case to Strasbourg because, over a seven-year period, all telephone, fax, email and data communications between the UK and Ireland, including legally privileged and confidential information, were intercepted and stored *en masse* by an Electronic Test Facility operated by the British Ministry of Defence. Previously the applicants had taken their complaints to the Interception of Communications Tribunal, the Director of Public Prosecutions and the Investigatory Powers Tribunal, on the basis of a challenge to the lawfulness of the alleged interception of their communications. However they were not successful as the domestic tribunals found that there was no contravention of the Interception of Communications Act 1985. The applicants argued that the interception of their communications *had* breached Articles 8 and 13 of the ECHR and as such they were entitled to a remedy.

At the European Court of Human Rights it was held unanimously that the right to respect for private and family life and correspondence, as guaranteed by Article 8 of the European Convention on Human Rights, had been violated. Specifically, in relation to Article 8 the Court recalled that it had previously found that the mere existence of legislation which allowed communications to be monitored secretly had entailed a surveillance threat for all those to whom the legislation might be applied. In the applicants' case, the Court therefore found that there had been an interference with their rights as guaranteed by Article 8. Further they commented that section 3(2) of the 1985 Act allowed the British authorities an extremely broad discretion to intercept communications between the UK and an external receiver, namely the interception of 'such external communications as described in the warrant'. Indeed, that discretion was virtually unlimited. In their observations to the Court, the Government accepted that, in principle, any person who sent or received any form of telecommunication outside the British Islands during the period in question could have had their communication intercepted under a section 3(2) warrant. Furthermore, under the 1985 Act, the authorities had wide discretion to decide which communications, out of the total volume of those physically captured, were listened to or read. Under section 6 of the 1985 Act, the Home Secretary was obliged to make such arrangements as he considered necessary to ensure a safeguard against abuse of power in the selection process for the examination, dissemination and storage of intercepted material. Although during the relevant period there had been internal regulations, manuals and instructions to provide for procedures to protect against abuse of power, and although the Commissioner appointed under the 1985 Act to oversee its workings had reported each year that the arrangements were satisfactory, the nature of those arrangements had not been contained in legislation or otherwise made available to the public.

The Court noted the UK Government's concern that the publication of information regarding those arrangements during the period in question might have damaged the efficiency of the intelligence-gathering system or given rise to a security risk. However, in the UK, extensive extracts from the Interception of Communications Code of Practice were now in the public domain, which suggested that it was possible for the State to make public certain details about the operation of a scheme of external surveillance without compromising national security. In conclusion, the Court considered that the domestic law at the relevant time had not indicated with sufficient clarity, so as to provide adequate protection against abuse of power, the scope or manner of exercise of the very wide discretion conferred on the State to intercept and examine external communications. In particular, it had not set out in a form accessible to the public any indication of the procedure to be followed for examining, sharing, storing and destroying intercepted material. The Court therefore held, unanimously, that the interference with the applicants' rights had not been in accordance with the law, in violation of article 8.[9]

To sum up, what I have tried to establish in this chapter is that the State's duty to protect its citizens is twofold. First, the State has a duty to protect the civil liberties and human rights of citizens. Second, it also has a duty to protect citizens in terms of their security. This balance is at best difficult to achieve and, at worst, perhaps impossible. However, achieving that balance fairly is surely the aspiration? The historical commitment to balancing these principles came about subsequent to two world wars at a time when – on the back of atrocities such as the Holocaust – there appeared to be political will to try to work to prevent such atrocities occurring again. These principles were primarily embodied in the principles of international law which were recognised in the Charter of the Nürnberg Tribunal. The commitment to safeguarding human rights and civil liberties has continued and has since been enshrined in the European Convention on Human Rights, and in the UK, embodied in domestic law in the form of the Human Rights Act 1998. Nevertheless, what I have also sought to demonstrate in this chapter is that in spite of these formal commitments, little appears to have changed. To demonstrate this I have used examples such as the treatment of suspects during internment in Northern Ireland; the abrogation of the right to a fair trial by the use of the Diplock courts – also in Northern Ireland; the sidestepping of the right to an independent inquiry into a murder in the case of Pat Finucane, and the retrospective enactment of legislation, namely the Inquiries Act 2005, to effectively gag the independence of the Judiciary in questioning the conduct of the Government. I have also referred in this chapter, to more recent examples pertaining particularly to the issue of the current so called 'war on terror.' For example the potential human rights violations in relation to the shooting of Jean Charles de Menezes on the London underground, the torture and killing of Baha Mousa in Iraq and in general terms the whole issue of the legality of the war in Iraq which is currently being analysed by the Chilcot Inquiry. The interesting question in relation to all of these rather disparate issues is that they appear to have one thing in common. That is the basis on which the Government has justified them – that is, national security and the prevention of terrorism.

Benjamin Franklin is alleged to have said that those who would give up essential liberty, to purchase a little temporary safety, deserve neither liberty nor safety. Writing in 2001, Garland could not have anticipated then the likelihood, nor the impact of the current 'war on terror'.

Nonetheless, what he wrote then seems strangely prophetic now. I have also written before (Moss 2009: 110) that:

> .... there has been a significant move towards a greater degree of social control, particularly during the last decade, which can be explained by reference to a number of factors. First, in spite of an overt commitment to the idea of 'open and democratic societies' attitudes to security and contemporary crime control in both Britain and the United States have undergone something of a transformation towards what Garland (1996) describes as an excessive concern with penality and social control. This can partly be explained by the response of numerous criminal justice agencies to rising crime rates and social changes from which a new 'crime control culture' has emerged. Second, this move has been underpinned by social policy developments which, contrary to what was predicted in the 1970's, have become more oppressive, rather than less so. This development has been encouraged by the intense interest in law and order that politicians in most countries have shown – probably because to pursue these interests is both ideological and pragmatic. Added to this, changes in ideologies about responsibility for crime have not only shaped attitudes, but have also changed the way in which many criminal justice and other agencies now respond to crime and its control. Finally, perceptions about increases in the crime risks to society – both from what we might term 'ordinary' crimes, to the threat posed by terrorism – have increased due both to media and political representations.

In the following chapter I will advance this argument further by illustrating the contemporary European safeguards for Human Rights and Civil Liberties with specific reference to the nature and purpose of the European Convention on Human Rights which took effect in 1953 with the objective of avoiding the atrocities and abuses of human rights that had taken place in World War I. It does not form part of UK law but has developed as a separate system of jurisprudence with its own institutions and procedures. There has been a clear expectation of compliance since this time and currently it seems that a theory of State obligation has developed whereby member states have to do more than just be seen to comply. The Human Rights Act 1998 gives 'greater effect' to Convention Rights in two main ways; first, by making it clear that as far as possible the courts in this country should interpret the law in a way that is compatible with Convention Rights and second, by allowing people the right to take court proceedings if they think that their

Convention Rights have been breached or are going to be. This chapter will also assess the relevance of the legal doctrine of the 'Margin of Appreciation' which reflects the ideal that maximum compliance from all parties about the general standards that the convention sets and the relevance of the legal 'Doctrine of Proportionality' which is a way of testing whether member states' actions are compatible with convention standards.

Notes

1. Jenkins, S. (2006) 'These Cartoon don't Defend Free Speech, they Threaten It.' *The Sunday Times* 5 February 2006 accessed 29 July 2010 at http://www.times-online.co.uk/tol/comment/columnists/guest_contributors/article727080.ece
2. All of these excerpts are from personal communications to the author.
3. Cory, P. (2005) Canadian Judge Slams Finucane Inquiry Legislation at http://www.patfinucanecentre.org/cory/pr050315.html accessed 31 August 2010.
4. http://www.ppu.org.uk/learn/infodocs/cos/st_co_wwtwo.html#conscription
5. 'Johnny' Sandhu was a Londonderry solicitor who pleaded guilty to inciting murder after police bugged his conversations with a suspected terrorist client inside a police station. The Shankill Butchers were members of the Ulster Volunteer Force (UVF) who carried out paramilitary activities in Belfast during the 1970s. They were most notorious for late-night abductions, torture and murder of Catholic civilians. Sean Kelly was convicted for his part in planting a bomb on the Shankill Road, Belfast, which was intended to kill senior members of the Ulster Defence Association (UDA) but which exploded prematurely, killing nine Protestant civilians. Christy Walsh was stopped in 1991 by soldiers in Belfast who alleged he had a jar containing Semtex explosive. Walsh was tried in a Diplock court in Belfast, found guilty and sentenced to 14 years' imprisonment. He was released in 1998 after serving seven years and continues to appeal his conviction.
6. On 5 August 1983 a number of IRA members were convicted largely on the evidence of a police informant, the so-called 'supergrass' Christopher Black. He was granted immunity from prosecution and is now believed to be abroad.
7. Pte Jason Smith's mother argued that troops should be entitled to the protection of human rights law on the battlefield and in conflict overseas.
8. http://www.independent.co.uk/news/education/higher/are-academics-being-put-at-risk-by-antiterrorist-measures-452977.html accessed 21 April 2011 [Please note that all the URLs listed hereafter have been accessed on 21 April 2011.]
9. For the full text of this judgement see http//www.echr.coe.int

3
The Context of the European Convention on Human Rights and the Human Rights Act 1998

This chapter illustrates contemporary European safeguards for Human Rights and Civil Liberties with specific reference to the nature and purpose of the European Convention on Human Rights (ECHR) which took effect in 1953 with the objective of avoiding the atrocities and abuses of human rights that had taken place in World Wars I and II. It does not form part of UK law but has developed as a separate system of jurisprudence with its own institutions and procedures. There has been a clear expectation of compliance with the ECHR since 1953 and currently, a theory of State obligation[1] has developed whereby member states have to do more than just be seen to comply. In the UK, the Human Rights Act 1998 gives 'greater effect' to Convention Rights in two main ways; first, by making it clear that as far as possible the courts in this country should interpret domestic law in a way that is compatible with Convention Rights and second, by allowing people the right to take court proceedings if they think that their Convention Rights have been, or are going to be, breached. This chapter will also assess the relevance of the legal doctrine of the 'Margin of Appreciation' which reflects the ideal that there should be maximum compliance from all parties about the general standards that the convention sets and the relevance of the legal 'Doctrine of Proportionality' which is a way of testing whether member states' actions are compatible with convention standards.

The origin of the 'human right'

In terms of the development of basic human rights, two philosophers in particular were influential – John Locke and Thomas Paine. John Locke, who would go into exile for his ideas, was writing at the time of significant constitutional change in the UK; changes which culminated in the Bill of Rights 1689. Locke (1689) expressed his views on Government in the *'Two Treatises of Government'*[2] in which he defended the suggestion that Government rests on popular consent and thus rebellion is acceptable when Government subverts the ends, i.e., the protection of life, liberty and property, for which it is established. Locke proposed that Governmental power should not be exercised arbitrarily in relation to society and that because power was vested in the Government by the people, it could never be increased on the basis that nobody can transfer, to another, more power than he possesses himself, and nobody has an absolute arbitrary power over any other, to destroy, or take away, the life or property of another. For Locke (ibid.) the power of legislators should be limited to

> the public good of society. It is a power that hath no other end but preservation, and therefore can never have a right to destroy, enslave, or designedly to impoverish the subjects... To this end it is that men give up all their natural power to the society they enter into, and the community put[s] the legislative power into such hands as they think fit, with this trust, that they shall be governed by declared laws, or else their peace, quiet, and property will still be at the same uncertainty as it was in the state of Nature.[3]

Locke's conclusion was that if a Government 'offended against natural law' it should be deposed by revolution. This philosophy lay behind the rebellions of both the American colonies in 1775, and the French in 1789. Thomas Paine's ideas were likewise influential in the revolutionary settlements in France and America – the French Declaration of the Rights of Man and the Citizen (1789) and the US Constitution (1787). Although Paine was born in Norfolk in 1737, he settled in Philadelphia, where he worked as a journalist, writing articles on a wide range of topics. In 1776, he published *Common Sense*,[4] which immediately established his reputation as a revolutionary propagandist. Paine became committed to the idea of American independence during his first year of residence there. He criticised monarchical Government, the British constitution, and was opposed to any reconciliation with Britain, urging the Americans to declare independence and establish a republican constitution. Paine's political ideology was founded on morals based on the natural equality of humans in the sight of God. He considered Government to be a necessary evil that had to be accepted by society as a means of protecting its natural rights. In keeping with the ideas of John Locke, he believed that the only legitimate Government was one established by all members of society, in which natural rights were preserved, where all individuals had an equal claim to political rights and where Governments' ultimate sovereignty rested with the people.

The notion of inalienable rights, based upon a perception of their 'naturalness', was thus enshrined in the political philosophy which accompanied the two revolutions of the late 18th century. From origins such as these, further developments have occurred in the drive to secure the protection of various human rights and fundamental freedoms, some of which have ultimately been enshrined within the ECHR and which I will discuss specifically later in this chapter. These developments have not, of course, been without setbacks. Although it is not the intention of this chapter to provide what would have to be a sizeable explanation of the historical development of human rights and civil liberties – even within the UK – it is worth mentioning that neither the Utilitarian movement nor the Victorian era were particularly conducive to the development of civil liberties. For example, Gibbard (1984: 1) mentions that:

> Jeremy Bentham, the founder of the utilitarian movement in nineteenth century England, accepted the incompatibility of utilitarianism and the rights of man, and rejected talk of the latter as 'anarchical fallacies'.[5]

The Victorian era was also notorious for its lack of consideration for basic human rights. During this period it was the norm to employ young children in factories and mines and as chimney sweeps. Similarly women had few rights as illustrated by the famous case of Elizabeth Garrett Anderson. Having met the American Elizabeth Blackwell – the first woman doctor – Garrett Anderson determined to become a doctor. This was unheard of in 19th century Britain and her attempts to study at a number of medical schools were denied. She enrolled as a nursing student at Middlesex Hospital and attended classes intended for male doctors, but was barred after complaints from other students. The Society of Apothecaries did not specifically forbid women from taking their examinations, so in 1865 she passed their exams and gained a certificate which enabled her to become a doctor. The society then changed its rules to prevent other women entering the profession this way. She finally went to the University of Paris, where she successfully earned her degree. In spite of this, the British Medical Register refused to recognise her qualification.

Following the Second World War the United Nations was formed, a successor to the League of Nations, and the Universal Declaration on Human Rights was adopted. The Declaration has been the focus for numerous other treaties worldwide, inspiring regional conventions such as the European Convention of Human Rights and Fundamental Freedoms 1950, the American Convention of Human Rights 1969 and the African Charter of 1987. The 20th century has seen significant developments in the political recognition of human rights, although many regimes throughout the world continue to conduct Government with a minimal respect for the rights of citizens. For example, June 2008 witnessed the problematic election process in Zimbabwe. On 22 June, Morgan Tsvangiri, who was opposing Robert Mugabe, withdrew from the election process as a result of the violence and torture being perpetrated against his supporters. In a statement at the time, he said that this was not a democratic election as a vote could cost his followers their lives. The right to a free election may be seen by many as a fundamental human right and yet as we can see this is by no means a right enjoyed universally.

The idea that basic human rights, derived from natural law, were superior to positive laws, enacted by man, became a driving principle in the development of constitutional theory during the late 17th and early 18th centuries. Implicit in these ideas was the assertion that a Government's right to rule was conditional upon a respect for, and acknowledgment of, the rights of individual subjects, who would be justified in over throwing a Government which violated their trust. This was famously posited by the constitutional writer Albert Venn Dicey (1915) who suggested a number of constitutional principles. First he stated that the rights of individuals are determined by legal rules and not the arbitrary behaviour of authorities. Indeed, there does appear to be a judicial aversion to arbitrariness which is demonstrated in case law such as the case of *Entick v Carrington (1765)* which established the need for warrants to search private premises, and the case of *Kelly v Faulkner (1973)* which established that British soldiers in Northern Ireland must have valid reasons for an arrest. Second, Dicey (ibid.) suggested that there can be no punishment unless a court decides there has been a breach of law. This is an idealistic and aspirational notion which the evidence suggests does not work in practise. For example (and I shall investigate this in more detail in Chapter 5), detention without trial operated during both World Wars and in Northern Ireland in 1971 and 1976. Currently detention without trial is still enforced, today facilitated by various pre-vention of terrorism laws which give statutory powers to detain. This has occurred most notoriously in the UK at Belmarsh Prison and in the US in relation to Guantánamo Bay, Cuba. It is also important to remember that the power to detain without trial also operates under the Mental Health Act 1983 which gives the further power (in certain circumstances) to detain indefinitely. Most recently the idea of 'pre-emptive incarceration' within an updated Mental Health Act, based on an assessment of risk was discussed but not implemented. Dicey (ibid.) also suggested that everyone, regardless of position in society, is sub-ject to the law. This is not true of the British constitution in reality. Dicey thought we should have a system like the French *droit administra-tif* which was a separate system for dealing with abuse by Government personnel, but the UK has never moved towards this model. Instead, within England and Wales and before the 1947 Crown Proceedings Act the Crown could not be sued in contract and was vicariously liable for the torts of its employees. MP's still of course possess privileges like legal immunity for things said in Parliament and diplomats also have some immunity under the Diplomatic Immunity Act 1964.

The relevance of the notion of Parliamentary Sovereignty

Highly relevant to any discussion of rights, liberties, the individual and the power of Government is the relevance – particularly within the UK – of aspects of the notion of Parliamentary Sovereignty. First, sovereignty is characterised by the competency of Parliament to legis-late on any matter whatsoever. In practise this means that Parliament can change constitutional principles no matter how long standing or important. For example, the Parliament Act 1911 removed the veto powers of the House of Lords; the Life Peerages Act 1958 provided for the appointment of life peers with full voting rights and the Abdication Act 1936 altered royal succession and allowed Edward VIII to abdicate in favour of his younger brother who became George VI. Parliament can also alter or extinguish rules of common law or equity. This ability to legislate on any matter whatsoever even applies to situations which fall outside normal UK jurisdiction. For example, the Continental Shelf Act 1964 asserted British jurisdiction over the sea bed well beyond the limits of the territorial sea. The War Crimes Act 1991 made it an offence – triable in an English court – for a foreign national to commit murder or other war crimes against foreign nationals in a foreign coun-try. More recently, Foreign Travel Orders, which allow for paedophiles to be banned from destinations where they could be a risk to children, form part of the Sexual Offences Act 2003. Offenders can thus be prosecuted in the UK for acts that amount to an offence in the country visited. It is even possible to contend that immoral or improper legislation is within Parliament's power. For example, the War Damage Act 1965 retrospectively deprived claimants of rights to compensation for destruction of their property by the State, reversing a previous decision of the House of Lords in the case of *Burmah Oil Co (Burma Trading) Ltd v Lord Advocate [1965] HL*. Indeed, many activities have been made lawful by Parliament that many consider immoral or improper; these include abortion, gay sex, the abolition of hanging, laws against discrimination, marriage between relatives, legalising gambling and liberalising alcohol laws. Significantly, the second aspect of sovereignty is relevant here; namely that no person or court can question the validity of what Parliament has passed. For example, in the case of *Cheney v Conn (1968)* a British taxpayer challenged the validity of the Finance Act 1964 because it provided for expenditure on nuclear weapons, contrary to international law (the Geneva Convention was incorporated into UK Law by the Geneva Convention Act 1957). However, the High Court held that a statute could not be challenged on the grounds that it was illegal, or made for an unlawful purpose, for if this was possible, the supremacy of Parliament would be denied. Further, the court commented that whilst there was a general presumption that Parliament would not wish to override the UK's international obligations it certainly had the power to do so; where an Act conflicts with a Convention, the Act prevails. Thus the taxpayer lost his case.

The third aspect of the notion of Parliamentary Sovereignty is that no Parliament can bind a successor by purporting to make a law that cannot be repealed; whatever one Parliament can do, another can undo. For example, in the case of *Godden v Hales (1686)* the defendant – an army officer – did not take the oaths required by the Test Act 1678 but claimed when prosecuted that he had a dispensation from the King. The court held that the power of dispensation was well established at common law, and that the defendant was not required to take the oaths; further that if an Act of Parliament had a clause in it that it should never be repealed; it was without question that the same power that made it may repeal it. More recently, in the case of *Blackburn v Attorney General (1971)* the Court of Appeal rejected the argument that joining the European Community would amount to an illegal surrender of sovereignty. Lord Salmon commented that Parliament could enact, amend and repeal any legislation it pleased. This point has similarly been made in relation to the Union with Ireland Act 1800 which united Great Britain and Ireland into a single kingdom. This legislation was clearly meant to be in force and have effect forever, nevertheless it was largely repealed in 1922 without any legal difficulty.

The debate about the sovereignty of Parliament has become more complex since joining the European Union (EU). Membership of the EU does not extend to all matters either foreign or domestic and generally speaking is limited to issues of trade, employment, agriculture, fisheries, consumer protection, competition, banking, health and safety and welfare benefits. It has limited concern with the criminal law (with the exception of the European Arrest Warrant and some rules on insider dealing for example) and also Contract law (except for consumer and employment law) Education, Health, and Family law. However, institutions of the EU *can* make laws affecting the UK, which the English courts have applied irrespective of the wishes of Parliament. For example, in the case of *Van Gend en Loos v Netherlands [1963]* the claimants objected to the imposition of certain customs duties, which they claimed were in breach of the Treaty. The court held that an individual (or a corporation) could rely on the provisions of the Treaties as against a national Government, and can enforce its rights there in a domestic court stating that 'the Community constitutes a new legal order of international law for the benefit of which the States have limited their sovereign right, albeit within limited fields.'

Parliament is also obliged to legislate (or let Ministers legislate by Order in Council) to implement obligations arising from EU membership. In the case of *Marshall v Southampton Health Authority (1986)* the claimant was forced to retire at the age of 62 from her employment within the National Health Service. This was deemed a breach of the Equal Treatment Directive 1976, but the Sex Discrimination Act 1975 excluded matters related to retirement from its provisions. The court held that the claimant was entitled to succeed, and could use the provisions of the Directive against her employers (who were an emanation of the State) because the UK had not properly implemented the directive. It follows from this that an Act of Parliament which is incompatible with any requirement of European law can and must be declared invalid and ineffective to the extent of that incompatibility. For example, in the case of *R v Secretary of State for Transport ex parte Factortame (No.2) [1991] HL* the UK Government enacted the Merchant Shipping Act 1988, which provided (inter alia) that to fish in British waters all fishing boats had to be majority British owned. The claimants – who were Spanish fishermen – claimed that this Act affected

UK fisheries policy (since the majority of vessels were joint British and Spanish owned) and was contrary to European Community (EC) Law. The claimants sought an order directing the Secretary of State not to enforce the Act pending a full trial of the issue. The Divisional Court referred the substantive question to the European Court of Justice (ECJ), but ordered by way of interim relief that the Regulations should not be applied against the claimants. The Court of Appeal (CA) and House of Lords (HL) held that no national court had the power to suspend the operation of an Act of Parliament, but the ECJ disagreed. It suggested that a national court judging a case before it which concerned EC law (and where EC law was considered to be the sole obstacle which precludes it from granting interim relief) must set aside that rule. They commented that:

> The full effectiveness of Community law would be impaired if a rule of national law could prevent a court seized of a dispute governed by Community law from granting interim relief in order to ensure the full effectiveness of the judicial decision to be given on the existence of rights claimed under Community law.

In response, the HL granted interim relief thus disapplying the 1988 Act and Lord Bridge expressed acceptance of the supremacy of Community law. Since Factortame therefore, UK courts will not apply an Act if it conflicts with Community law, and this effectively means that Community law overrides any national law that conflicts with it.

In the light of this, the question remains whether the UK could withdraw from the EU and thus retain the sovereignty of Parliament? The answer to this is that it could; in theory at least. Not only can Parliament legislate on any matter it thinks fit, but, as stated earlier, no Parliament can bind its successor. In other words, whilst the European Communities Act 1972 clearly implements all EU jurisprudence, a future Parliament could repeal the 1972 Act. Because of the same principle, the 1972 Act itself is not bound by its own provisions. The relevance of the notion of sovereignty to the idea of fundamental human rights and civil liberties is that basically what is being balanced here is the inalienable right of Parliament to legislate on any matter whatsoever – even in a way which may contravene civil liberties – and the rights of individuals to have civil liberties protected. Having provided some context for these issue and before moving on to discuss the nature and purpose of the European Convention itself, it is pertinent to describe the context of the European Institutions of Justice.

The European Institutions of Justice and the Convention on Human Rights

The Council of Europe was established in 1949, driven by the post-war ideal to rebuild Europe within a framework of political, social and economic unity. The European Convention on Human Rights was formulated by the Council and came into effect in 1953. The UK was a signatory to the Convention and was instrumental in drafting the document. The UK Government had reservations about the potential impact of the document on British constitutional law, and it did not form part of domestic law until 1998 with the passing of the Human Rights Act. The UK has never had a written (or, as Munro (2005) suggests, codified) constitution. A written Bill of Rights will normally be a feature of written constitutions. In the UK the view that prevailed was that liberties were respected, although not legally enshrined, and that Parliament would not legislate in a way that would deny basic liberties. Furthermore the influential author, Dicey (1915), argued that Judges through the development of common law principles, protected individual liberty. Rights in the UK were defined as 'residual', that is to say, individuals were free to do what they wanted as long as they did not break the law. This can be contrasted with the legal position where a written Bill of Rights forms part of the constitution and where rights might be described as 'positive'.

Politicians in the UK began to recognise the need for a written form of a Bill of Rights to be codified. Given that the Executive increasingly dominates Parliament the potential for Governments to ignore basic rights for political imperatives is very real. Furthermore confidence in the ability of the Judiciary to safeguard rights through the common law had become increasingly undermined. In 'Rights Brought Home: The Human Rights Bill' (Cmnd 3782) the Labour Government outlined the case for incorporation.[6] The European Convention on Human Rights was formulated by the Council of Europe and came into effect in 1953. The UK was a signatory to the Convention and had been instrumental in drafting the document, but it did not form part of domestic law until 1998. This was achieved by the Human Rights Act of that year. Until then rights in the UK were defined as 'residual' and the incorporation of the Convention has created positive rights rather than negative freedoms. Despite not forming part of domestic law the Convention was nevertheless influential in the development of policy on human rights in the UK. It is also important to recognise that the courts used Convention Rights as an aid to interpretation where there was an ambiguity in legislation, the presumption being that Parliament enacted laws that were in conformity with the Convention.

The European Court of Human Rights

The European Court of Human Rights sits on a permanent basis in Strasbourg. Each signatory State has a Judge, elected for six years, who enjoys security of tenure for that period. Once in office, a Judge cannot be dismissed unless the other Judges agree the dismissal by a two-thirds majority. Judges are expected to be independent of the political considerations of signatory States in applying the rights and guarantees set out in the Convention, decisions being based on legal considerations alone. The jurisdiction of the Court extends to all matters concerning the interpretation and application of the Convention, and when the court finds that a member state has violated one or more of the rights guaranteed the Court delivers a judgment, and the country concerned is under an obligation to comply with the judgment. The Court is not bound by precedent, and the Convention is regarded as a 'living instrument' – a statement of rights which develops to reflect changing values within European societies. Consequently, decisions of the Court on a given right have evolved over time. In terms of the application of the convention and the substantive rights that it affords, the European Convention on Human Rights is regarded as the most important achievement of the Council of Europe. Under Article 25 any person, non-Governmental organisation or group of individuals can apply to the Court. Complainants must first exhaust domestic remedies. The applicant submits the complaint to the Court's Registry, and attempts are made to achieve a 'friendly' settlement. In 1998 the Court was expanded creating a two-tier structure; a Chamber of seven Judges now presides. Exceptional cases may be referred to the Grand Chamber consisting of 17 Judges, outlined in Protocol 11.

The evolution of the European Union

Primarily the objective of the Community was to create an internal market with no restrictions on the movement of people, goods, capital and services. These objectives are defined in the Treaty of Rome. The means by which these objectives were to be achieved include the abolition of customs duties, the establishment of a common commercial policy and the free movement of goods. It was anticipated at an early stage that Community policy would extend beyond economic and commercial matters to include social and environmental policy and health protection. Political progress towards the achievement of Community objectives has, at times, been slow, certainly slower than the architects of the Treaties might have hoped. There is inevitably a tension between European objectives and the national interests of member states, and politicians of member states have to satisfy their own electorates of the benefits to their own countries of Community policy. In 1986 the Single European Act, a European Treaty, provided a timetable for achieving the objectives of the original Treaty. In addition to extending the competence of the Community institutions into areas such as the environment and regional development the Treaty revised the voting procedures in European Institutions which were largely driven by a requirement of unanimity amongst member states. As the Community enlarged it became increasingly difficult for this to be achieved. Accordingly, the Single European Act provided for a 'qualified majority voting system' which had the effect of reducing the power of individual Member States. The Single European Act was given effect in the UK by European Communities (Amendment) Act 1986.

The Treaty of European Union (the Maastricht Treaty) was signed by all member states in 1992. The UK negotiated an 'opt out' from some of the provisions, including the social chapter, although the Labour Government (elected in 1997) agreed that the UK should be bound by them. The Treaty expanded the aims and objectives of the Community, marked the creation of the European Union and signalled a move towards a more federal Europe. Barnett (2010) comments that in this respect it represents a compromise between the federalists who see an almost total political and economic union and those member states who wish to maintain a higher degree of national autonomy. The Treaty provided for the development of common policies in relation to foreign affairs, security and justice and home affairs. These became the three 'pillars' of the European Order. The Treaty also strengthened the powers of the European Parliament, created the concept of European citizenship and introduced provisions leading to economic and monetary union including the establishment of a common exchange rate and the use of a common currency. The Treaty of Amsterdam 1997 resulted from an intergovernmental conference and sought to address some of the issues which remained unresolved from the Maastricht Treaty. One of the concerns arose from the anticipated enlargement of the Union to 27 members, an enlargement that would inevitably require institutional changes. Difficulties between members existed over the Social Protocol, the European Monetary Union, border controls and a common defence policy. The third pillar of the Union – Justice and Home Affairs – was subsequently renamed 'Police and Judicial Cooperation in Criminal Matters' and was transferred to the jurisdiction of the European Community pillar, which resulted in the imposition of European laws through issue of regulations or directives by the Community institutions. Later, the Schengen Agreement, providing for the abolition of border controls, was formally incorporated into Community law, but special arrangements were reserved for Denmark, Ireland and the UK. The Treaty of Nice 2001 also introduced changes to the size and organisation of the Commission, revised the voting system in the Council and the powers of co-decision of the European Parliament in readiness for membership of the twelve additional countries. In June 2004 a draft constitution for the European Union was agreed.[7]

The Treaty on the Constitution for Europe had to be ratified by the then 25 members. Sixteen countries ratified the Treaty, but two countries – France and the Netherlands – rejected it in a referendum. This effectively derailed the process, and further progress came to a halt. The UK placed preparations for a referendum on hold. In June 2007, under the Presidency of Germany, European Union leaders agreed a Treaty which contained many of the reforms included in the failed constitution. The changes were to be effected through amendments to existing Treaties, thus avoiding the need for a referendum, although it was anticipated that the UK Parliament would be hostile to some of the proposals. In particular, the UK was opposed to the incorporation of a legally binding Charter of Fundamental Rights and the appointment of a High Representative for foreign affairs and security policy.

The Court of Justice

The Court of Justice consists of one Judge per Member State. The court receives written arguments, and the procedure is inquisitorial rather than accusatorial – more akin to the continental system. The court is assisted by Advocates General who prepare opinions for the court to consider prior to decisions. The court has the following jurisdiction;

(i) Proceedings brought by the Commission for breach of Community obligations.
(ii) Proceedings brought by a Community institution regarding the legality of any act or failure to act by the Council, Commissioner or Parliament.

(iii) A reference by the court of a member state on the interpretation of Community law

(iv) Actions by member states or European citizens for compensation in respect of the acts of community institutions

The most important of these are proceedings brought by the Commission or other member state under Article 226 against a member state for failure to comply with Treaty obligations and requests by national courts for preliminary rulings under Article 234. Proceedings under Article 234 arise when the courts of member states are uncertain on a point of interpretation of European law.

The jurisprudence of the European Court of Human Rights

The jurisdiction of the Court extends to all matters concerning the interpretation and application of the Convention. The Court is not bound by precedent and consequently, decisions of the Court on a given right have evolved over time. The Courts of signatory States are expected to take account of the decisions of the European Court in arriving at judgments within domestic jurisdictions. The UK incorporated the Convention Rights into UK law in 1998. Domestic courts can now rule on whether there has been a violation by a public body of a Convention right. UK courts must take account of the jurisprudence of the European Court of Human Rights in coming to a judgment. Before looking in more detail at some of the cases in which the European Court has developed Convention Rights it is appropriate to contextualise the origins of the European Convention on Human Rights.

The nature and purpose of the European Convention on Human Rights

The Convention does not form part of the law of the EC but has developed as a separate system of jurisprudence with its own institutions and procedures. Prior to 2000 the EC was an international treaty to which the UK was a contracting party. It imposed obligations on the UK Government but did not confer rights directly enforceable by individuals. This meant that if someone took a case to the ECHR prior to 2000, the UK courts did not have to recognise the judgements of the

EC.[8] However, there has been a clear expectation that the UK would not legislate directly contrary to what the convention said.

In 1998 the European Court of Human Rights was restructured so it could better deal with cases coming before it. Its Judges are thus elected by the Parliamentary Assembly from lists put forward by each member state. Initially the convention was seen as imposing negative obligations on member states – that is, that it identified a number of human rights with which member states should not interfere. Currently, it seems that a theory of State obligation has developed whereby member states have to do more than just be seen to comply.[9] The European Convention Rights were subsequently embodied in a UK version –the Human Rights Act 1998 (HRA). The incorporation of the European Convention on Human Rights into domestic law is a significant constitutional change in the UK. Previously rights were safeguarded either through the courts or by means of specific statutory enactments on rights-related matters. The Judiciary is now empowered to adjudicate on alleged violations of Convention Rights and, in so doing, to take account of the jurisprudence of the European Court of Human Rights.

It was established earlier in this chapter that under the doctrine of parliamentary sovereignty, legislation cannot be entrenched and the HRA thus seeks to retain the traditional supremacy of parliament. Under section 3 of the Act, primary legislation, passed or to be passed, is to be interpreted in accordance with Convention Rights 'as far as it is possible to do so'. The courts have adopted a purposive approach to interpretation with a view to achieving compatibility wherever possible. Where domestic legislation is not compatible with Convention Rights the higher courts must make a statement of incompatibility under section 4. Such a declaration does not invalidate the legislation in question. Under section 10 the appropriate Government Minister can making an amending order – a remedial order. Remedial orders are laid before Parliament for 60 days and approved by resolutions of each House under the 'fast track procedure'.

The following cases demonstrate how the European Court has developed Convention Rights. They are, of course, examples only; the body of case law is huge and for this reason I have given a selection of examples of the pertinent case law only, in order to give the reader a flavour of the development of some of these rights. The majority of the following examples involve the UK; some of the more recent cases are decisions of the House of Lords, and these cases give some indication of the way in which UK courts have begun to absorb the jurisprudence of the European Court of Human Rights.

In respect of Article 2, the right to life the Act provides that:

> Everyone's right to life shall be protected by law. No one shall be deprived of his life intentionally save in the execution of a sentence of a court following his conviction of a crime for which this penalty is provided by law.

This article provides that the Government and public authorities must protect the right to life. This may require, for example, that the police have to protect someone whose life is under immediate threat. It could also be used to argue that a patient should be able to get treatment that would save their life. Generally, there will be a breach of Article 2 if someone is killed by a State official (usually the police, but also the army or prison officers). The only circumstances where there will not be a breach are set out in the second part of the Article. However, where a death occurs in each of these three circumstances the police (or other State official responsible for the death) will have to show that they did not use any more force than was absolutely necessary. So, if someone is killed when the police are trying to arrest them, there will be breach of Article 2 if it is shown that the police used more than the minimum amount of force necessary to detain the person. The ECHR has made it clear that Article 2 also requires that there should be a proper investigation when the police or army kills someone or when someone dies in custody. There have been several cases in the British courts where the courts have had to consider what type of investigation is necessary to meet this requirement. There are some exemptions, for example, if death occurs while defending yourself against unlawful violence, or arresting someone, or putting down a riot. It has also been established that the State must positively promote the right to life and therefore cannot ignore life-threatening situations, such as someone in prison threatening to commit suicide. It may also apply where a hospital's negligent treatment causes death.

The application of Article 2 has been considered in a number of cases, some of which have received media attention. Notably, this includes the case of *Evans v UK (2006) 1FCR*, in which Natalie Evans, an ovarian cancer survivor, who had the embryos of her and her partner, Howard Johnston, frozen. After the breakdown of their relationship, Mr Johnston withdrew his consent to the implantation or continued storage of the embryos. Miss Evans complained that requiring the father's consent for the continued storage and implantation of the fertilised eggs was in breach of the rights of the embryos, under Article 2. However, the European Court of Human Rights held, unanimously, that there had been no violation of the right to life under Article 2, and the frozen embryos were duly destroyed. Article 2 was also considered in the high-profile case of *R(Pretty) v DPP 2001 3 WLR 1598* in which Mrs Pretty, who had motor neurone disease, sought an assurance that her husband would not be prosecuted should he assist in her suicide. Both UK courts and the European Court of Human Rights denied that the right to life encompassed a right to choose the timing and manner of one's death. The Judges also felt that any arguments premised on respect for patients' autonomy were outweighed by the State's interest in preserving life and protecting the vulnerable. More recently, a question which has been asked is, is there a case for alleging that a violation of Article 2 as a result of the tragic shooting of Jean Charles de Menezes?[10]

With respect to Article 3, freedom from torture, inhuman and degrading treatment or punishment, this will be dealt with in detail in the following chapter. However, the elimination of the practise of torture as a feature of interrogative procedure can be seen as fundamental to the development of international treaties on human rights.

Article 4 states that no one shall be held in slavery or servitude and that no one shall be required to perform forced or compulsory labour.

The essence of Article 5 – the right to liberty – is the obligation on the State to ensure that suspects are brought promptly before a court to answer a charge against them, and the right to a trial within a reasonable time. Law enforcement agencies must therefore be in a position to evidentially support charges laid following arrest within a short time scale. Legislation empowering the police to investigate terrorist acts and to detain suspects for interrogation for long periods requires derogation from the provisions of Article 5. This article will be dealt with in detail in Chapter 5.

Article 6 – the right to a fair trial – safeguards the right to a fair and public hearing within a reasonable time. Article 6 also ensures that accused persons are informed promptly of the charges, have adequate time to prepare a defence and obtain the attendance of witnesses. The presumption of innocence, a feature of Article 6, does not imply a right to silence. This article will also be discussed in detail in Chapter 6.

Article 7 provides that:

> No one shall be held guilty of any criminal offence on account of any act or omission which did not constitute a criminal offence

under national or international law at the time when it was committed. Nor shall a heavier penalty be imposed than the one that was
applicable at the time the criminal offence was committed.

Sometimes this refers to situations where a person is facing criminal sanctions on the basis of legislation which has retrospective
(backward looking) effect. This is considered to be contrary to the
Rule of Law and is an absolute right. But what does this mean exactly?
This article provides that no one can be tried and found guilty of a
criminal offence if what they did was not a criminal offence when
they did it. It also provides that an individual cannot be punished in
a way that was not the law when the offence was committed. Neither
can Parliament backdate a law that increases the length of time an
individual could be sent to prison for, or introduce a new punishment for an offence. A good example of this is the case of *Welch v UK
The Times 15 February 1995* in which Welch had been convicted of
drugs offences in 1988. The actual offence had taken place in 1986.
The Judge made a confiscation order against him (for £59,000) under
the Drugs Trafficking Offences Act 1986. However, this Act had not
actually been enacted until 1987; therefore, the Judge had made an
order under a piece of legislation that did not actually exist at the
time Welch committed the offence. The court held that Article 7 had
been breached because it was not possible to impose a penalty on the
defendant that was not in force at the time, even though it was by the
time he came to trial.

Article 8 – sometimes referred to as the right to privacy – provides
that:

Everyone has the right to his private and family life, his home and
his correspondence.

The Article is, in fact, more wide-ranging and encompasses the right
to respect for private and family life, home and correspondence. Article
8 may also be of importance where employers interfere with communications by staff, such as intercepting telephone calls or email or inter-
fering with Internet use. Also the disclosure of personal information
about an employee to third parties without that employee's consent
may breach Article 8, particularly if it is confidential medical information. Cases which demonstrate the application and interpretation
of Article 8 include the case of *R (on application of Robertson) v City of*

Wakefield Metropolitan Council [2001] EWCA 915 in which Article 8 was said to have been breached when information on an electoral register was sold to commercial businesses without telling the people whose names had been sold. Cases like this have also led to another common law becoming more important again. This is the common law rule of 'breach of confidence' which has not been used a great deal in recent times. However, since the media have become more aggressive particularly in respect of the private lives of those in the public eye, the Judiciary have now applied this rule more frequently. This has resulted in its development so that it can now be used by people seeking redress for what they consider to be abuses of private information. This can be in both written or picture forms. This development can be demonstrated by the case of *Douglas v Hello Magazine [2005] EWCA Civ 595* in which film star Michael Douglas and his wife Catherine Zeta-Jones said that *Hello* magazine had published pictures of their wedding without their permission.

In his judgment, Lord Phillips said:

> we conclude that in so far as private information is concerned, we are required to adopt... the course of action formerly described as breach of confidence.

The meaning of 'private life' under the terms of Article 8 can therefore extend beyond what we might consider to be normal, or personal matters, to cover issues such as a person's sexual identity, sexual orientation or moral identity. The broadness of this was commented on in the case of *Pretty v UK [2002] 35 EHRR 1* in which the court said:

> the concept of private life is broad... it covers the physical and psychological integrity of a person... an individual's physical or social identity. Elements such as... gender identification... sexual orientation and sexual life fall within the personal sphere protected by Article 8.

Issues of gender are more common today, for example, concerning people who have had gender reassignment therapy or surgery. Until recently, courts had refused to accept that the ECHR would give a person the right to have their sexual identity completely changed from one gender to another and so such people were not allowed to change legal documents such as birth certificates. This attitude changed recently and signifies that the convention is supposed to be a 'living instrument' – which means that it is capable of being interpreted in different ways in order to keep up with changes in society. A case which is important in demonstrating this is *Goodwin v United Kingdom [2002] 35 EHRR 18*. In this case, the applicant (G) was a UK citizen born in 1937 and was a post-operative male-to-female transsexual. G had dressed as a woman from early childhood and underwent aversion therapy in 1963 and 1964. In the mid-1960s, she was diagnosed as a transsexual. G had married a woman and had four children but claimed that she was a woman in a man's body. In January 1985, the applicant began treatment in earnest, attending appointments once every three months at the Gender Identity Clinic at the Charing Cross Hospital, London, which included regular consultations with a psychiatrist as well as, on occasion, a psychologist. She was prescribed hormone therapy and began attending grooming classes and voice training. Since this time, G lived fully as a woman. In October 1986, G underwent surgery to shorten her vocal chords. In August 1987, she was accepted on the waiting list for gender reassignment surgery. In 1990, she underwent gender reassignment surgery at a National Health Service hospital. Her treatment and surgery were provided for and paid for by the National Health Service. The applicant submitted that despite warnings from the Court as to the importance for keeping under review the need for legal reform, the Government had still not taken any constructive steps to address the suffering and distress experienced by the applicant and other post-operative transsexuals. She said that the lack of legal recognition of her changed gender had been the cause of numerous discriminatory and humiliating experiences in her everyday life. In particular, from 1990 to 1992, she was abused at work and did not receive proper protection against discrimination. She claimed that all the special procedures through which she had to go in respect of her NI contributions and State retirement pension constituted in themselves an unjustified distinction in treatment.

In 1996, the applicant started work with a new employer and was required to provide her National Insurance number. She claimed that the new employer traced her identity, and she began experiencing problems at work. Colleagues stopped speaking to her and she was told that everyone was talking about her behind her back. The UK court did not accept that there had been a breach of Article 8 and said that the case fell within their 'margin of appreciation'. That is, that it was an area where Europe should allow the UK to make its own decisions about morals. However, the European Court did not agree. They said;

(i) There were no significant factors of public interest to weigh against the interest of this individual applicant in obtaining legal recognition of her gender re-assignment;

(ii) The fair balance that is inherent in the Convention now tilts decisively in favour of the applicant.

(iii) There was indeed a failure to respect her right to private life in breach of Article 8 of the Convention.

The court also commented that there was a gap between social reality and the law in the UK; they considered it strange that a country should provide gender reassignment surgery but then not recognise that change in a person legally. There was clear evidence of this trend of recognising post-operative transsexuals and that there was no evidence that such recognition would damage the public interest. The outcome of the modern interpretation of Article 8 is that there is now full legal recognition given to post-operative transsexuals.

Article 9, sometimes referred to as freedom of thought, conscience and religion, provides that:

Everyone has the right to freedom of thought, conscience and religion; this right includes freedom to change his religion or belief, and freedom, either alone or in community with others and in public or private, to manifest his religion or belief, in worship, teaching, practice and observance.

This article guarantees that individuals can have freedom of thought and can hold any religious belief. No individual can be forced to follow a particular religion, and neither can they be prevented from changing religion. This extends to beliefs such as veganism and pacifism. This right is a 'qualified right' and it can be broken in some circumstances. The Government or public authority that breaks the right must show that their actions were carried out to protect the rights of others. They must also show that breaking the right was 'necessary and proportionate'. Perhaps the most famous recent case which demonstrates this is the case of *R (Shabina Begum) v Denbigh High School [2006]*. Shabina Begum took her school to court because they said she was not allowed to wear the Islamic jilbab. Initially the Court of Appeal delivered a well-publicised judgment declaring that 17-year-old Shabina Begum had been unlawfully excluded from Denbigh High School when she insisted on wearing the jilbab but in March 2006, in a remarkable u-turn, the House of Lords overturned the Court of Appeal's decision on all counts and said Shabina's Article 9 right to manifest a belief had not in fact been violated by the school.

Article 10 – the right to freedom of expression provides that:

> Everyone has the right to freedom of expression. This right shall include freedom to hold opinions and to receive and impart information and ideas without interference by public authority and regardless of frontiers. This article shall not prevent States from requiring the licensing of broadcasting, television or cinema enterprises.

The scope of freedom of expression is wide and pervades religious, political, artistic and moral issues. Article 10 underlines the view that Governments should create an environment where the enjoyment of ideas and beliefs is unrestricted unless such restriction is to ensure national security or public order. It also guarantees the right to pass information to other people, to receive information and to express opinions and ideas. Journalists and publishers of newspapers or magazines can use Article 10 to argue there should be no restrictions on what they write about or publish. Artists and writers can use it to defend themselves against censorship. Article 10 may also be used to argue for fewer restrictions on pornography and may cover expressing yourself through the way you look – how you dress or have your hair cut, for example – though this may also be covered by Article 8. The extent to which courts consider Article 10 as one of the most important of all the articles was highlighted by the case of *Rushbridger v AG [2003] UKHL 3* in which Lord Steyn commented that:

> freedom of political speech is a core value of our legal system. Without it the rule of law cannot be maintained. Whatever may have been the position before the HRA 1998....it is difficult to think of a rational argument justifying the criminalisation of a citizen who wished to argue for a different form of government.

A further case concerning Article 10 which demonstrates where the Article will *not* be allowed to succeed on the basis of protecting people is that of *Nilsen v Full Sutton Prison [2004] EWCA Civ 1540*. Dennis Nilsen was sentenced in 1983 to six life sentences for six murders. The murders were of homosexual partners whom he then cut up into pieces and stored in and around two properties he rented. The details of the murders and of what Mr. Nilsen did with and to the bodies are horrifying. He was eventually arrested because Dyno Rod came to unblock the drains to his property and found that they were blocked with human flesh. Nilsen wanted to publish all of these details in an autobiography. According to Paragraph 34(c) of Prison Standing Order 5, a prisoner's general correspondence may not contain material which is intended for publication, or which, if sent, would be likely to be published, if it is about an inmate's crime or past offences. The principal issue in this case was whether Paragraph 34 of the Prison Rules was lawful having regard to a prisoner's right to freedom of expression under Article 10 of the European Convention on Human Rights.

Nilsen began to write his autobiography in 1992. By 1996 his work amounted to 400 closely typed pages which he gave to the solicitor who was then acting for him at HMP Whitemoor.

His solicitor took it with him when he left the prison. Interestingly, a number of copies were made of it which are still outside the confines of the prison. Nilsen was transferred to HMP Full Sutton. His solicitor wished to return his typescript to him so he could do further work on it in order to prepare it for publication. However, the Secretary of State and the Prison Governor decided that it should be withheld from him, and Nilsen challenged this. He said the application of Paragraph 34 on the facts of this case was disproportionate and infringed his rights under Article 10. In a judgment delivered on 19 December 2003, the court held that there was no breach of Nilsen's rights under Article 10.

Article 11 – peaceful assembly and association provides that:

> Everyone has the right to freedom of peaceful assembly and to freedom of association with others, including the right to form and to join trade unions for the protection of his interests.

This article protects the right to protest peacefully by holding meetings and demonstrations. It also means that the police may have to act to protect people holding a meeting or demonstration from anyone trying to stop it. It also protects the right to form or join a political party or other group, and the right to belong to a trade union. However, the right to join a trade union does not include police officers, soldiers and some other groups who work for the Government.

At the moment, English law allows the police to restrict demonstrations or to ban them under Public Order Legislation. Article 11 may be used to challenge this. The obvious enjoyment of this right is in the context of peaceful marches or demonstrations to publicise a cause or collectively voice objections to political decisions and policies. The right can be limited; for example, restrictions can be imposed in the interests of public safety and public order. For an example of this we can note the case of *Pendragon v United Kingdom 19th October (1998) in which* Druids were banned from holding services at the summer solstice. This was held to be a proportionate response to the aim of preventing disorder; however, the court also took the view that the State has a responsibility to provide opportunities for legitimate demonstrations to take place even if that means policing demonstrations where groups with strongly held opposite views may also be present, thus raising the likelihood of disorder.

The extent of this responsibility can be demonstrated by the case of *R (on application of the countryside alliance) v AG [2006] EWCA Civ 817* which came about after the ban on fox-hunting by the Hunting Act 2004. Many people argued that to fox-hunt was a basic right to their freedom of expression and that if the Government legislated to say they could not do it, then this would be a breach of Article 10. The UK Court of Appeal held that the Hunting Act 2004 had prohibited assemblies which were specifically for the purpose of gathering to hunt foxes. It also stated that it was only a ban on assembling to hunt the fox, and not a blanket ban on assembling in exactly the same way for anything else. This might be to pursue a similar sport, or to drag hunt or just to ride without chasing the foxes.

Article 12 – the right to marry – provides that:

> Men and women of marriageable age have the right to marry and to found a family, according to the national laws governing the exercise of this right.

This Article has yet to generate a significant amount of UK case law. However, a number of things can be said of the Article currently. First, it does not give an absolute right to marry and procreate in all situations. Second, the courts give consideration to all the circumstances of a case, including any rational and legitimate policy consideration which might be relevant. This can be demonstrated in relation to the interpretation of the case of

Mellor v Sec of State for the Home Dept [2001] EWCA 472 in which a prisoner tried to argue under Article 12 that he should have the right as a prisoner to start a family, by means of artificial insemination. Because

prison policy did not allow this, the prisoner said that this was a contravention of his rights under the ECHR Article 12 and that it was irrational. The court, however, did not agree and stated that:

> the purpose of imprisonment...is to punish the criminal by depriv-
> ing him of certain rights and pleasures which he can only enjoy
> when at liberty. Those rights and pleasure include the enjoyment
> of family life, the exercise of conjugal rights and the right to found
> a family...a prisoner cannot procreate by the medium of artificial
> insemination without the positive assistance of the prison authori-
> ties. In the absence of exceptional circumstances, they commit no
> infringement of article 12 if they decline to provide that assistance.

More recently the right of transsexuals and same-sex couples to
have their relationship formally recognised has also been a focus for
cases under Article 12. Perhaps the most famous case in relation to this
issue is that of *Cossey v UK* (1992). Caroline Cossey (originally Barry
Cossey) was born in Norfolk and was raised as a boy. Cossey suffered
from Klinefelter's syndrome which means that instead of having XXY
chromosomes like most people with this condition, Cossey was XXXY.
At the age of seventeen, Cossey started hormone therapy and began
living as a woman. Soon after beginning transition, Cossey began a
career as a showgirl and, after breast augmentation surgery, was a top-
less dancer, working in nightclubs in London, Paris and Rome. After
initial shock, Cossey's parents were supportive. After years of hormonal
and psychological treatment, and legally changing her name, Cossey
had sex reassignment surgery on December 31, 1974 at Charing Cross
Hospital in London. In 1981 she was one of the Bond Girls in the film
'For Your Eyes Only'.

This case concerned Cossey's assertion that the refusal of the UK
Government to issue her with a birth certificate showing her sex as
female constituted an 'interference' with her right to respect for her
private life. In her view, the Government had not established that this
interference was justified under Article 8. She also took a case under
Article 12 because UK law at that time would not allow her to marry a
man. Miss Cossey accepted that Article 12 referred to marriage between
a man and a woman, and she did not dispute that she had not acquired
all the biological characteristics of a woman. She challenged, however,
the adoption in English law of exclusively biological criteria for determining a person's sex for the purposes of marriage. In her submission,
there was no good reason for not allowing her to marry a man. The

Court maintained a traditional view of what constituted marriage and concluded that there was no violation of Article 12 although subsequent to the case of *Bellinger v Bellinger*, EWCA Civ 1140 [2001] the Court commented that it was for Parliament, not for the Courts, to decide at what point it would be appropriate to recognise that a person who had been assigned to one sex at birth had changed gender for the purposes of marriage.

General principles applied by the courts

When the Convention was first drafted, it was understood that the contracting States would not enact legislation which would interfere with the rights guaranteed under the Convention. There was no positive obligation on the State to act to ensure that the activities of an individual do not affect the rights of another. In recent times, however, this has changed and has moved towards a positive obligation on the state to act to protect the individual's rights against interference from whatever source. This is based largely on the obligation contained in Article 1, which states that 'the High Contracting Parties shall ensure to everyone within their jurisdiction the rights and freedoms defined in section 1 of this Convention'.

In terms of its interpretation therefore, the Convention is seen as a 'living instrument' and as a result the court is able to interpret it in line with any modern shift in human rights thinking. It is not bound by precedent or the need for a rigid literal interpretation, and whilst using consistency to ensure reasonable certainty, may depart from previous decisions where necessary. Crucial to the interpretation of articles by member states is the doctrine of the 'margin of appreciation'. It is important to explain this further. When a signatory State puts into place facilities for securing the rights guaranteed under the Convention, it is allowed a 'margin of appreciation'. The concept recognises that the cultural traditions and national interests of each of the signatory states can result in differing legal expectations and that compliance with the Convention Articles should take account of this. The nature and scope of such measures must, however, be proportionate to the objective. Also of note are restrictions on the convention rights. The Convention contains absolute rights which may not be interfered with by the State. These include, for example, Article 3 (prohibition of torture) and Article 4 (slavery). There are no circumstances in which the State may interfere with these rights, even in a case of public emergency or for security reasons. Other rights, such as those contained in Article 2 (right to life) are subject to restrictions, but only in the limited circumstances set out in the articles. However, Article 15 gives the State an opportunity to derogate from the rights guaranteed in all but Articles 2, 3, 4(1) or 7 in a 'time of war or other public emergency threatening the life of the nation.... To the extent strictly required by the exigencies of the situation'. Any restriction must be based on clear legal authority and must be proportionate.

A further principle of interpretation is that of certainty which requires that any restriction on Convention Rights to be clear, precise and prescribed by law. Any restriction must be through an established law (in the UK this would be a statute or through the common law only), readily accessible to individuals, and sufficiently clear for individuals to understand. For example, in the case of *Steel and Others v United Kingdom (1999) 28 EHRR 603* it was argued that the common law offence of breach of the peace was not sufficiently certain and clearly defined. The applicants asserted that the powers of the police to deal with breach-of-the-peace situations constituted an interference with the right of assembly as guaranteed by Article 10 and that any interference with it should be 'prescribed by law' and sufficiently clear.

However, the court in this instance felt that although the offence had been vague in the past it had now been sufficiently defined in various cases to the point that the definition was clear. A similar argument arose in *Hashman and Harrup v United Kingdom (2000) 30 EHRR 241* involving demonstrations against fox-hunting, where it was argued that the common law power of a magistrate to bind defendants over to 'keep the peace and be of good behaviour' was also ill-defined. Here the European Court of Human Rights accepted the argument that the phrase 'to be of good behaviour' did not make it sufficiently clear to the defendant what they should do or not do. This was therefore not a sufficiently defined restriction to satisfy the requirements of Article 10(2) that any interference with the right of assembly should be 'prescribed by law'.

Also important in relation to the interpretation of the Convention is the doctrine of the 'margin of appreciation'. Essentially, the convention was not meant to set rigid and inflexible rules and therefore there has to be some element of discretion allowed to member states in relation to how they interpret and apply the convention in a national context. Clearly the thinking behind this was that it might lead to tensions between member states and between them and the European Court, and this could lead to a lack of consensus. Therefore, the idea is to achieve maximum compliance from all parties about the general standards that the convention sets. The margin of appreciation there-fore reflects this ideal and means that there should only be conflict if there is less than substantial compliance. The margin of appreciation permitted also depends on the nature of each right or situation. Each is judged on its own merits, and in some cases they will allow more flexibility than in others. The case of *Handyside v UK [1976]* for exam-ple established the principle that more flexibility will be allowed for member states to decide what they want in relation to issues such as public morality.

Alongside the margin of appreciation, the doctrine of proportional-ity also provides a way of testing whether member states' actions are compatible with convention standards. If a member state says that they acted in a legitimate way regarding the public interest the EC asks whether the action taken was proportionate to the aims pursued and whether the reasons given are relevant and sufficient. For example, in the case of *Bowman v UK [1998]*, the applicant distributed literature in the 1997 elections about the views of the main candidates on abortion. She was taken to court under section 75 of the Representation of the People Act 1983 because she spent more than the £5 that is allowed – under statute – to be spent on this. Bowman took a case to the European Court under Article 10 on the basis that it was her right to freedom of expression. The court held that some legitimate limit on expenditure was right to ensure fairness between candidates but that the £5 limit imposed by section 75 of the aforementioned Act imposed an unneces-sarily severe restriction on the dissemination of opinions. The court also commented that this appeared particularly odd to them since they were aware that in the UK, national publicity campaigns had no such restrictions on them.

Constitutional implications

The incorporation of the European Convention on Human Rights into domestic law was a significant constitutional change in the UK. Previously rights were safeguarded either through the courts or by means of specific statutory enactments on rights-related matters. The Judiciary is now empowered to adjudicate on alleged violations of Convention Rights and, in so doing, to take account of the juris-prudence of the European Court of Human Rights. In spite of this, under the doctrine of parliamentary sovereignty, legislation cannot be entrenched and therefore the Act seeks to retain the traditional supremacy of Parliament whilst at the same time, under section 3 of the Act, primary legislation, passed or to be passed, must be interpreted in accordance with Convention Rights 'as far as it is possible to do so'. The courts have adopted a purposive approach to interpretation with a view to achieving compatibility wherever possible, but where domestic legislation is not compatible with Convention Rights the higher courts must make a statement of incompatibility under section 4.

Thus Human Rights Act 1998 (HRA) gave legal effect in the UK to certain fundamental rights and freedoms which were originally contained in the European Convention on Human Rights (ECHR). Sixteen basic rights were taken from the European Convention on Human Rights. These rights not only affect matters of life and death like freedom from torture and killing but also affect rights in everyday life: what individuals can say and do, their beliefs, right to a fair trial and many other similar basic entitlements. In practise, the HRA is said to give 'greater effect' to Convention Rights in two main ways:

1. by making it clear that as far as possible the courts in this country should interpret the law in a way that is compatible with Convention Rights.
2. by placing an obligation on public authorities to act compatibly with Convention Rights.

The HRA also gives people the right to take court proceedings if they think that their Convention Rights have been breached or are going to be. Parliament makes laws but it is the courts that have to interpret them. The HRA makes it clear that when they are interpreting legislation the courts must do so in a way which does not lead to people's Convention Rights being breached. Moreover, the courts are now under a duty to develop the common law – the law which has been developed through decisions of the courts themselves – in a way that is compatible with Convention Rights. But what happens if the Courts cannot read the law compatibly? If the law is an Act of Parliament, the courts have no choice but to apply the law as it is, even though it breaches Convention Rights. However, the higher courts (the High Court, the Court of Appeal and the Supreme Court) have the power to make what is called a 'declaration of incompatibility'. This is a statement that the courts consider that a particular law breaches Convention Rights. It is meant to encourage Parliament to amend the law, but the courts cannot force the Government or Parliament to amend the law if they do not want to. It is against this background that I shall now concentrate in the following three chapters, specifically on Articles 3, 5 and 6.

Notes

1. This refers to the fundamental obligation of any State which is a party to the European Convention on Human Rights, to ensure that domestic law is compatible with the articles of the Convention and that alleged breaches of the articles of the Convention will be investigated effectively.
2. Locke's original essays were published anonymously in 1689 as *Two Treatises of Government. The first was entitled 'The False Principles and Foundation of Sir Robert Filmer and His Followers, are Detected and Overthrown' and the second was 'The True Original, Extent, and End of Civil-Government.'* For an up-to-date version see Laslett's (ed.) 1988 version or see http://www.constitution.org/jl/2ndtreat.htm
3. Ibid.
4. For the more recent version see Paine, T. (2010) *Common Sense*. Createspace.
5. Readers may also be interested to read Jerome Shestack's (1998) 'Philosophic Foundations of Human Rights', in *Human Rights Quarterly* 20, 201–234, John Hopkins University Press.
6. www.archive.official-documents.co.uk/document/hoffice/rights/contents.htm
7. http://news.bbc.co.uk/1/hi/world/europe/2950276.stm
8. For an example of this see the case *of Malone v MPC (1979)* in which no right to privacy was recognised by English law and none could be imported by way of Article 8 of the Convention.
9. For an example of this see *Plattform 'Artze fur das Leben' v Austria [1988]* which involved the right to protest and where the court said it was not sufficient just to allow marches and demonstrations, but that the State should take positive steps to make sure people could do this without interference from others.
10. See http://www.guardian.co.uk/menezes/story/0,,1884990,00.html

4
Article 3 and Torture

The aims of this chapter are to highlight the legal prohibition of torture and to illustrate judicial decisions in cases relating to its prohibition in order to assess how far the European Convention on Human Rights and the UK Human Rights Act 1998 are designed and deployed to prevent contemporary abuses of the ideals of the rule of law and essential civil liberties as enshrined by Article 3 of those statutes. The chapter discusses mechanisms for evading the law on torture and cruel and inhuman or degrading treatment or punishment and the circumstances in which this occurs and highlights such practices around the world. The relevance of human rights law will be assessed, and the effectiveness of legal challenges over the torture and ill-treatment of detainees held by the UK and US abroad will be highlighted as will the current complex moral and ethical dilemmas surrounding its use.

What is torture?

Article 3 of the European Convention on Human Rights prohibits torture and establishes that:

> No one shall be subjected to torture or to inhuman or degrading treatment or punishment.

One of the briefest of the Articles of the Convention, this definition is further elaborated on by the International Red Cross Society which defines torture as being the intentional infliction of severe suffering or pain and as having a specific purpose.[1] But *what is* torture and what is society's opinion of it? Has this shaped the current law on torture and indeed should it? The more I have thought about these questions, the more difficult this chapter has been to write. When I set out to write this book, I probably had what I thought were fairly firm, liberal views about many of the issues I am writing about. As time has passed, and the more I have studied these areas and the discourses surrounding torture in particular, the more difficult it has been to entirely reconcile myself to one overarching view which covers all situations. It seems logical to suggest that torturing people is morally and ethically wrong, but does this necessarily take account of all the different situations in which this might occur? Does it matter what those situations are; does it matter what the reasons are? Some would argue not and that it is always wrong. However, there are of course, competing discourses about this very sensitive subject. There are also debates surrounding issues of power and instrumentality which arguably should be part of the essential definition of torture. For example, if a terrorist organisation waterboards a soldier, that might well be considered as grievous bodily harm; but if the soldier waterboards a terrorist would that be defined as torture? What *is* clear is that torture has always been practised; it has historically and traditionally been a way of getting confessions, evidence and intelligence. The main difference between historical and modern torture is that historically torture was not hidden because it was not universally outlawed. In the modern world, torture is generally deemed to be unacceptable, and protection from it is found in a wide range of (albeit largely unenforceable) declarations, conventions and resolutions. Whilst this demonstrates that there is significantly more moral commitment to protecting people from torture, or inhuman or degrading treatment or punishment, today we also know that it still happens and that the nations that still demonstrably practise it are sometimes also those that have been most vocal in support of making sure it is not practised. Hypocrisy, the saying goes, is the tribute which vice pays to virtue. I start by looking at the differences between historic and modern torture in an effort to determine why and how views about it have changed and to ascertain whether this can provide any explanations as to why torture was historically acceptable but is contemporaneously not.

Historically torture was seen as an entirely legitimate means for criminal justice systems to extract confessions, to obtain the names of accomplices or other information about the crime in question, or to punish people. Torture was deemed a legitimate way of obtaining testimonies and confessions from suspects for use in legal inquiries and trials particularly during the Middle Ages. The barbarous custom of punishment by torture was also condemned on several occasions by the Church. As early as 866, we find from Pope Nicholas V's letter to the Bulgarians that their custom of torturing the accused was considered contrary to divine as well as to human law; Pope Nicholas being attributed as having said that confession should be voluntary, and not forced. Despite this, the historical practise of torturing victims continued. The Inquisition tortured for the good of the victim's soul, so that s/he should enjoy heaven.[2] Because medieval torture was a freely accepted form of punishment in the Middle Ages it was only legally abolished in England in 1640. According to Cobain (2008),[3]

> The last torture warrant in England was issued in 1641. Enraged by the mistreatment of religious dissenters and other enemies of King Charles I, parliament resolved to abolish the Star Chamber. The Habeas Corpus Act, passed that year, was to end forever what the lawmakers described as the 'great and manifold mischeifes and inconveniencies' of that tribunal, which had 'beene found to be an intollerable burthen to the subjects'.

However, in spite of this historic prohibition of torture it still occurs – perhaps more than we think and in more places than we might imagine. In modern times the UK has carried out torture in Kenya and Northern Ireland; France has used it in Vietnam and Algeria; Israel has used it in the occupied territories, and the US has used it in Vietnam, in Central America and in Afghanistan and Guantanamo. All of this has taken place after World War II, when it has been widely asserted that the western world has been experiencing a humanitarian revolution. Torture is therefore both historic and modern, but in spite of this and in spite of modern legal definitions, there is little academic agreement about what torture actually is. In relation to non-legal definitions, contemporary debates centre inevitably on whether torture can be justified in exceptional, one-off or emergency situations and also whether in countries where there may be an ongoing terrorist threat torture should actually be legal if carried out in relation to known terrorists in order to extract life-saving information. Clearly there are conflicting views about this proposition. Commentators such as Waddington[4] point to the moral permissibility of torture as demonstrated by the 'terrorist and the ticking bomb scenario.'

> It is merely tautological to say that all torture is bad, because 'torture' is a term of opprobrium. Because liberals shrink from the nasty realities of power, I don't think they've thought clearly enough about

this. If it is legitimate to coldly kill someone who poses an imminent threat to life (the hostage–taker problem), then why is it impermissible to torture that same person to prevent the execution of the same threat? It would be as wrong to kill someone for trivial or non-existent reasons, as it would be to inflict pain and suffering. The problem comes in assessing the level of risk and the likelihood of error. Is the gun that the hostage–taker is holding a real firearm? Is it loaded? Would the hostage–taker actually fire it? On any, or all, these counts the commander of the operation might get it wrong. The hostage–taker, who is threatening, not a person, but a city with a CBRN[5] device, may be a fantasist or deliberately tempting the authorities to act in a discreditable way, or an entirely innocent person mistaken for the terrorist. We can't eliminate risk and error, but neither is it specific to the ticking bomb problem, because the hostage–taker with a 'gun' to the head of the hostage presents just as much a risk.

This is a view which is supported by a number of academics such as Alhoff (2003) and Dershowitz (2003) who have argued for the legalisation of torture if restricted to extreme emergency situations and provided there were appropriate mechanisms for accountability in place. One example of the type of situation in which Dershowitz has suggested this could apply is torture warrants similar to those which have previously been used in Israel. He rejects the notion (as does Waddington) that it is *always* morally wrong to torture the terrorist and suggests that there are some circumstances in which it is morally permissible to torture someone. This argument therefore still allows an individual to suggest that the *routine* use of torture is not morally justified but if it could be proven that it was necessary to save life in a given situation then it would be permissible.

The difference with modern torture is that it is not necessarily just a form of interrogation or punishment. It *is* still used for those reasons, but arguably it also functions as a form of domination. This suggests that the existing legal definitions of torture are not sufficient and that broader definitions are really necessary. Academics are now suggesting that it should include the infliction of severe pain to gather information; the infliction of severe pain to punish; the infliction of potentially escalating mental or physical pain for the purpose of domination and the infliction of potentially escalating mental or physical pain for which responsibility is ascribed to the victim. It is interesting to note that the philosopher and historian Michel Foucault (1975) looked at some of the activities of European penal systems in the 18th century.

He was particularly interested in how people were punished and how this changed over time from public torture and executions to putting people in prison instead. Foucault said that these types of visual punishments were an attempt to dissuade people from criminality (a deterrent). People would have no excuse for committing crime because they would have seen what happened to others who did it. He also thought that these types of punishments served as theatrical re-enactments of the actual act of transgression. What he was most interested in though was the fact that he believed that whether people were tortured, executed or imprisoned by the state, this was all done for the same reason, and that was social control – so that the State had total authority over people. The same might still be true of the persistence of torture today in the modern world even though it is now hidden from sight. So perhaps one of the crucial issues which determines whether torture is moral in certain situations or not, is the purpose of that torture or, putting it a different way, what the motivation behind such behaviour is. The bottom line here seems to be that if your motivation for torturing someone is purely sadistic, then that it clearly immoral. If the motivation is the greater good and the preservation of life, then perhaps it is not immoral. However, this does not take account of other situations where the motivation for torture is not necessarily sadistic, but might be driven by commercial forces. Surely this would be similarly immoral and unethical?

One of the reasons why I raise this as an important issue is that torture is not necessarily confined to the types of state agencies we might initially think of as being potentially involved in this type of activity; for example, the police, the armed forces and paramilitaries, where we could resort to explanations of political legitimacy in the face of a terrorist threat, for example. Increasingly it is the case that multinational companies have allegedly been either supporting or actually perpetrating it in order to protect their interests in countries throughout the world. For example, in Burma, torture, rape and the use of slave labour have been reported in the construction of the Yetagun and Yadana natural-gas pipelines. Unocal (US) and Total (France) are the financial backers of this project, which is the country's largest foreign investment. It has been suggested that in order to achieve this, Unocal hired the Burmese military as security guards. Further examples are the systematic beatings, rapes and murders which have been used to intimidate the Ijaw people of Southern Nigeria who have resisted operations of oil companies such as Chevron, Shell, Agip and Exxon-Mobil. The Nigerian military even used a Chevron helicopter for one attack. Shell has also been linked to abuses in Ogoniland. In Aceh, Indonesia, the army has committed massacres in order to protect Mobil Oil and its partner PT Arun. The latter was responsible for building an interrogation centre that dealt with local uprisings. In Sudan there have been numerous reports of rape, slavery, murder and repression around the oil fields in the South. Talisman Energy, a Canadian oil company, has made investments which it is claimed help the Government to continue its genocidal war. The Chinese National Petroleum Corporation has also been accused of brokering arms deals with the Government for access to oil. In 1996 British Petroleum struck a deal to train a Colombian army battalion through a British mercenary firm. The soldiers were entrusted with monitoring the construction of a pipeline to the Caribbean coast. An unpublished report commissioned by the Colombian Government alleges that BP provided intelligence about local protestors to the soldiers who were involved in abductions, torture and murder.

It is also important not to forget that because information is more readily available in liberal democracies; it might appear that they are the worst offenders. For example, Amnesty International (2001) catalogues the atrocities carried out in Liberia, where they report that:

> Widespread and gross abuses against unarmed civilians, including women and children, continue unabated in Lofa County, the northern region of Liberia bordering Guinea and Sierra Leone. There has been armed conflict in the area since renewed incursions by armed opposition groups into Lofa County from Guinea in July 2000. Hundreds of civilians have been victims of killings, arbitrary detention, torture and rape and the number of civilians fleeing fighting – estimated to be tens of thousands – has now reached an unprecedented level.[6]

Saudi Arabia also has a well known but rarely discussed policy of corporal punishment, some of which – such as executions – are carried out in public under Sharia Islamic law. Only in fairly recent years has the United Nations Committee against Torture criticised Saudi Arabia over the amputations and floggings it carries out under this law and recommended (in 2002) that the Saudi authorities re-examine their penal code. Although Saudi delegates protested that Sharia law expressly forbade torture, the UN Committee did not accept this as being reflected in their domestic law. It appears to be the case therefore that torture continues to happen on a wide scale overseas, during military operations, and against people who have been labelled as either deviants or 'enemies'. In all of these situations the common factor is that it is usually hidden and as long as it is hidden, it can be denied. If it can't be denied, then officials call it something else and say it is not torture.

In the US, for example, there is documentation about what are called 'counter-terrorism techniques' which lists the conduct that the US Government has apparently been prepared to condone in particular (usually labelled terrorist) situations. There are also legal 'get out' clauses which allow states or officials to argue that torturing someone was justified. Two reasons are normally given in these situations. The first reason is 'necessity'. This defence was used in Israel in the case of *Public Committee against Torture in Israel v Israel (1999)* where the court held that interrogators who were being prosecuted for using coercion were entitled to raise the defence of necessity. This defence is also available in the US under their Model Penal Code. The second reason sometimes given for using torture techniques is 'exception or emergency'. This defence can be raised where a State says that treating people in a particular way was merited because at the time, an exceptional situation was taking place. Again this usually means a terrorism or national security situation. In Algeria, for example, there was denial by the French followed by an admission that rare incidents of torture had taken place, but these had been committed by the Foreign Legion, not by the ordinary French military. The language that was used to describe the procedures that had taken place was euphemistic and included phrases such as 'long established police practices', 'excesses' and 'methods'.

In the 1980's the Israeli armed forces had permission under the 1987 Landau Inquiry[7] to use 'moderate physical pressure'. The secret services interpreted this as allowing them to carry out violent shaking, food deprivation, sleep deprivation, forcing people into painful positions for long periods of time, putting urine- or vomit-soaked hoods over people's heads and subjection to loud music. These practices were not actually challenged until 1999 when the Israeli Supreme Court said such practices had no place in interrogation. In spite of this, in 2002 the World Organisation Against Torture reported that Palestinian children in Israeli prisons were being beaten, handcuffed and blindfolded, were denied access to medical treatment, food bedding and were released during the night in outlying areas. The problems with these situations are, who defines what is exceptional, and how far can states go in saying that things are exceptions? For example, the Weimar Republic said that it was dealing with exceptional circumstances in relation to the Jews. They used this justification over 250 times over a period of 13 years in an effort to defend the terrible things they were doing.

Clearly wars are often given as the reasons to justify behaving in what would otherwise be unacceptable ways. One might imagine that this only happens occasionally but you only have to think how many wars there have been since World War II and still are. For example, the Cold War between the US and Soviet Union which lasted from 1945 to 1989; numerous sub-wars in Korea, Vietnam, Africa, the Middle East and Central America; the Gulf War against Iraq which started in 1990 and all the military problems in the Middle East which have continued almost indefinitely and have culminated in the invasion of Afghanistan and the war in Iraq – called the 'war on terror'. So even since World War II there has never really been a time when there has not been a war some-where in the world and therefore a time when the defence of emergency could not be used to justify the use of torture. In terms therefore of the respective arguments about justifications, motivation and the purpose of torture, one argument might be that under 'normal' circumstances, torturing individuals would not be permissible, but in exceptional sit-uations it may be. Perhaps torture could thus be distinguished by its purpose or motivation. If torture could accordingly be more narrowly defined into categories of either permissible or non-permissible torture, would this result in a more preferable state of affairs than is currently the case, where all torture is denied, irrespective of motive? Langbein (1977: 31) suggests a notion of 'judicial' torture and comments:

> When we speak of 'judicial torture,' we are referring to the use of physical coercion by officers of the state in order to gather evidence for judicial proceedings.... Torture has to be kept separate from the various painful modes of punishment used as sanctions against per-sons already convicted and condemned. No punishment, no matter how gruesome, should be called torture.

Any definition of torture therefore relies to some extent on an accept-ance that the concept of purpose or motivation is central to that defi-nition. This seems to be the case with Amnesty International's (1973) definition of torture as 'the systematic and deliberate infliction of acute pain in any form by one person on another or on a third person, in order to accomplish the purpose of the former against the will of the latter.'

The law relating to torture

First let us contextualise the debate about torture by outlining the law that currently exists in relation to its prohibition. The intention is to establish first what the law provides in relation to torture, before moving on to discuss some of the more philosophical discourses surrounding this complex and sensitive issue. This is important because law should never, and perhaps can never, be isolated from the social situations in which it operates and therefore it is crucial to acknowledge the interaction between the law and the societies in which it operates in order to fully appreciate what it can and does achieve.

Article 3 of the European Convention on Human Rights and Human Rights Act 1998 describes the current legal prohibition against torture and specifically that 'no one shall be subjected to torture or to inhuman or degrading treatment or punishment'. Torture is also mentioned in several international conventions. For example, Article 1 of the Convention on Cruel, Inhuman or Degrading Treatment or Punishment, also known as the Convention against Torture, (1984) defines torture as:

> any act by which severe pain or suffering, whether physical or mental, is intentionally inflicted on a person, for such purposes as obtaining from him or a third person information or a confession, punishing him for an act he or a third person has committed, or intimidating or coercing him or a third person, or for any reason based on discrimination of any kind, when such pain or suffering is inflicted by or at the instigation of or with the consent or acquiescence of a public official or other person acting in an official capacity. It does not include pain or suffering arising from, inherent in, or incidental to lawful sanctions.

Torture is thereby banned absolutely. Article 2 states clearly that there cannot be any justification for it, and Article 16 mentions that state parties must undertake to prevent it. The International Covenant on Civil and Political Rights 1966 (ICCPR) also bans similar conduct, as do the Geneva Conventions 1949. The European Convention on Human Rights (Article 3) also prohibits torture and inhuman or degrading treatment or punishment, and the European Court of Human Rights has considered the definitions of the terms contained within the Article. Torture has a much higher threshold than inhuman or degrading treatment and amounts to 'deliberate inhuman treatment causing very serious and cruel suffering'.

Article 3 of the UK Human Rights Act 1998 imposes an absolute prohibition on torture with no exceptions and no possibility of derogation, even in times of war or public emergency. It is referred to as being 'deliberate, inhuman treatment causing very serious and cruel suffering'. But what exactly constitutes inhuman treatment? Case law suggests it includes:

(i) The threat of torture
(ii) Physical assault
(iii) Detention in oppressive conditions
(iv) Deportation
(v) Extradition to a place where someone may be at risk of serious ill treatment
(vi) Psychological interrogation techniques

So importantly, there appears to be a difference between what constitutes torture and what constitutes inhuman or degrading treatment or punishment; this is emphasised in various national and international laws such as the Convention against Torture and Other Cruel, Inhuman and Degrading Treatment or Punishment 1984. Currently there is a very tough test for what constitutes torture. This can be found in the case of *Cakici v Turkey [2001]* where the applicant's brother was beaten, one of his ribs was broken, his head was split open and he was given electric shock treatment – all in police custody. The court held that this *was* torture because it was 'deliberate, inhuman and caused serious and cruel suffering'. For a definition of what constitutes inhuman or degrading treatment or punishment we have to look at the case of *Ireland v UK [1978]*. This case concerned interrogation techniques used against IRA suspects arrested under the internment operations in 1971. Suspects had been hooded and forced to lean against the wall on their finger tips and tiptoes whilst being subject to white noise and continuous questioning. If they fell they were beaten. All were deprived of food, water and sleep. This was not held to be torture, and this represents how strict the test is for this offence. *Soering v United Kingdom* (1989), concerned a German national who was to stand trial in the US, accused of the murder of his girlfriend's parents. The applicants would possibly have been in breach of Article 3 if he had been returned to his own state because the death sentence is still imposed in certain US states. The UK Government could therefore have been guilty of a violation of Article 3 had it exposed a person such as Soering to the risk of execution, which is a breach of the Article. In *Z v UK [2002] 34 EHRR 310* a local authority was found to be in breach of Article 3 when it failed to protect children in its care from abuse and neglect. Therefore, the Article imposes a positive obligation on states to ensure that measures are taken actively to protect individuals from such breaches.

Article 3 has also been relied upon in a situation where the applicant would be returned to a receiving State with inadequate medical facilities and treatment. In *D v United Kingdom (1997)* the applicant had AIDS and was to be returned to an island in the West Indies where there would be inadequate treatment available, which would expose him to 'a real risk of dying under the most distressing circumstances'. However, the Court stated that the facts were exceptional. Applying the case in the domestic courts, it can be seen from *N v Secretary of State for the Home Department [2005]* that a very serious level of suffering would be required. A number of cases have concerned whether the UK is in breach of Article 3 if an individual is deported to a country which may then violate the terms of the Article. For example, in the case of *J v Secretary of State for the Home Department [2005]* , the Court stated that the principles which a court should consider when making a decision about the deportation of an individual to a country which may violate the Article should include;

- Assessing the severity of the treatment which the individual will receive. This must attain a certain level of seriousness.
- Demonstrating a causal link between the act and the removal.

It is worth noting that under Article 15, a contracting state may derogate from any of the Articles which interfere with the rights protected in the Convention 'in times of war or other public emergency threatening the nation' but this does not apply to Articles 2, 3, 4 or 7. This means that legally there can be no derogation from Article 3.

Similarly, what constitutes degrading punishment or treatment? Case law suggests that this would be the treatment of a person which grossly humiliates or debases them. For example, in the case of *Tyrer v UK (1978)*, a 15-year-old boy on the Isle of Man was given three strokes of the birch by a court after being found guilty of assault. This was held to be degrading treatment under Article 3. The court held that although it amounted to institutionalised violence, the treatment did not amount to torture. It took into consideration factors such as the boy's age and the fact that he had to undress to have the punishment inflicted by strangers. The conclusion reached was that this did amount to a breach of Article 3 in that it constituted a degrading punishment. As an outcome of this case, the practice of judicial birching on the Isle of Man was discontinued.

The interpretation of Article 3 has been extended to include the use of corporal punishment in schools, and even smacking as a means of parental discipline. For many years it had been the accepted practice of schools to employ such punishment. In the home, the common law defence of reasonable chastisement meant that smacking children was not against the law per se. However, many other European states such as Sweden historically do not hold the same opinion, and the climate towards this issue has gradually changed in many states. It was felt that it was wrong to seek to protect adults but not children from assaults within the home. The outcome of several cases concerning this matter provide instances of how domestic law has gradually moved to keep up with the findings of the European Court and with changing opinions on human rights, even before the coming into force of the Human Rights Act 1998. So what is the cumulative outcome of these cases, and how have they affected the law in the UK regarding the corporal punishment of children at home or at school? A number of cases can be used to highlight the current legal position. In *Y v UK* the caning of children was found to be a violation of Article 3, being sufficient to amount to 'degrading' punishment. In *Maxine and Karen Warwick v United Kingdom (1986)* the Commission's initial decision was also that such treatment amounted to a breach of Article 3, although this was not referred to the Court and was subsequently not agreed by a two-thirds majority of the Committee of Ministers. Such punishment is now banned from all schools in England, Wales and Scotland, both State and private, through the Schools Standards and Framework Act 1998. In *A v United Kingdom (1999)* the applicant was a boy who had been beaten by his stepfather with a garden cane. When prosecuted, the stepfather had relied on the common law defence of reasonable chastisement and was acquitted. However, the boy then successfully applied to the Commission alleging that the State had failed to protect him from breaches of Article 3. The UK was held to be in breach. Although as yet no statute has been imposed on parents to prevent the use of corporal punishment in the home, it is clear from such decisions that parents cannot simply rely on the defence of reasonable chastisement to excuse such excessive punishments as the ones imposed on the applicant in the previously mentioned case of *A v United Kingdom*. Article 3 has also formed the basis of various applications where an individual may face ill-treatment if returned to their home state. For example, in *Chahal v United Kingdom (1997)* the European Court of Human Rights ruled that to return a person to their country of nationality would violate Article 3 if they were likely to suffer torture at the hands of the State on their return.

Whilst it seems entirely humane for the UK not to deport such people, the most recent case in relation to this demonstrates the real difficulties of this situation. On 18 May 2010 it was reported that the most recent judgment from the UK's Special Immigration Court ruled that even though the alleged leader of an al-Qaeda plot to bomb targets in north-west England was thought to be an al-Qaeda operative, he could not be deported because he faced torture or death back home in Pakistan. Whilst security services believed the man – Abid Naseer – was planning attacks with other students, none were charged. Disclosure of the evidence would compromise the covert surveillance techniques which had yielded it. Clearly, whilst it is of the utmost importance that if people have committed a crime, then pertinent evidence ought to be available in order to put those individuals on trial, the difficulty of this situation is that the UK Government is now faced with a situation where, although there was a lack of disclosable evidence, this individual may still realistically pose a security risk within the UK. Exactly how the Government is to deal with this and ensure that further risk potentially posed by such individuals is avoided is a big ask. Casciani (2010a) comments that:[8]

> This judgement shines a public light on the difference between intelligence assessments and hard evidence – with the tribunal concluding that MI5 was on the right side of the line. Its conclusions will be regarded by security and police chiefs as a vindication of their assessment that there was a plot, even though detectives never found a bomb and the men were never charged with an offence. Abid Naseer will be added to the list of other suspects in similar situations – men who are unwanted by the UK but, simultaneously, cannot be deported because they could be tortured. The Home Secretary's answer for some suspects is to place them under a control order, a form of house arrest that restricts their movements.

Although the Court was satisfied that Naseer was an al-Qaeda operative who posed a serious threat to the security of the UK and that it was conducive to the public good that he should be deported, it also commented that because there is a long and well-documented history of disappearances, illegal detention and torture in Pakistan, it was impossible to return him.

There has also been debate about the admissibility of evidence procured by torture. In August 2004, for example, the UK Court of Appeal ruled that the ATCSA 2001 permitted the use of information procured through torture. However, the case of *A and others & FC and others v Secretary of State for the Home Department (2005)* subsequently overturned this ruling.

These cases demonstrate that the situations in which a person's rights under Article 3 may be protected are perhaps more diverse than might have at first been imagined. Social attitudes in many (albeit not all) countries have probably changed somewhat in more recent times. Generally speaking, this was not always the case historically and these are important points to which I address the next section of this chapter.

The hypocrisy of torture

In spite of the wide acceptance that there are both moral and ethical dilemmas surrounding the practice of torture, Green and Ward (2005) comment that there is huge hypocrisy around torture in relation to foreign policy and practice. Governments openly denounce torture but at one and the same time can be providing the means to do it (in terms of instruments of torture) and training in torture techniques to other countries. Amnesty International has documented that between 1998 and 2000 the US had the biggest number of manufacturers who produced 'instruments of torture' such as leg irons, shackles, and thumb cuffs. It is also the case that there are centres where people can be trained to be torturers. According to Amnesty (2001) the bulk of this training goes on in the US, China, France, Russia and the UK and is provided for the police, the military and security forces throughout the world:

> much of this training occurs in secret so that the public and legislatures of the countries involved rarely discover who is being trained, what skills are being transferred and who is doing the training. Both recipient and donor states often go to great lengths to conceal the transfer of expertise which is used to facilitate serious human rights violations.[9]

The most sinister of all the training centres is in the US Previously called the 'School of the Americas' (SOA) it is now known as the 'Western Hemisphere Institute for Security Cooperation'. It has undoubtedly trained torturers from Latin American dictatorships, senior members of Argentine and Chilean Juntas, and military officers from Panama and Guatemala. Its training manual first came to light in 1996 and in it, the use of torture, including beatings, blackmail, counter-insurgency and even executions were advocated. These manuals have been distributed for training purposes in Colombia, Ecuador, Guatemala, Peru and El Salvador.

The UK has not necessarily had a good track record in relation to its approach to this issue either. The [then] UK Foreign Secretary was reported in November 2004 as saying that:

> ...there are certainly circumstances where we may get intelligence from a liaison partner where we know, not least through our own Human Rights monitoring, that their practices are well below the line. It does not follow that if it is extracted under torture, it is automatically untrue.

In August of the same year the Court of Appeal had ruled that the Anti-Terrorism, Crime and Security Act 2001 permitted that information procured by means of torture *could* be admitted as evidence in UK courts, so long as its officials neither committed nor connived in the torture. Amnesty International condemned this ruling and arguably it also brought domestic law into conflict with the UK's international obligations flowing from the absolute prohibition of torture or other ill-treatment – specifically Article 15 of the Convention against Torture which states that; 'Each state party shall ensure that any statement which is established to have been made as a result of torture shall not be invoked as evidence in any proceedings, except against a person accused of torture as evidence that the statement was made'. In 2005 in the case *A and Others and FC and Others v Secretary of State for the Home Department* seven Law Lords unanimously confirmed that such evidence is inadmissible. They also ruled that there was a duty to investigate whether torture had taken place, and to exclude any evidence if the conclusion was that it was more likely than not that it had been obtained through torture.

In 2001, nine men were arrested under Part 4 of Anti-Terrorism, Crime and Security Act (ATCSA). Most were held in the High Security Unit (HSU) in Belmarsh between December 2001 and March 2002. The HSU is a prison within the prison. The cells are small with restricted natural light. Detainees are kept in their wing and can communicate only with detainees in the same wing, except during religious worship. Amnesty International refers to this restriction of movement and association as 'small-group isolation'. During their initial detention in the HSU, the ATCSA detainees were locked in their cells 22 hours a day and in the two hours out of their cell they were subjected to 'small-group isolation'. Many of these aspects of the HSU regime violate international human rights standards, specifically, for example, the lack of adequate association time and activities in communal areas; the lack of educational, sport, and other meaningful activities and facilities; and the lack of access to open air and the lack of natural daylight and exercise in a larger space. The European Committee for the Prevention of Torture and Inhuman or Degrading Treatment or Punishment (CPT) noted allegations that the detainees had been subjected to verbal abuse; expressed concern about the detainees' lack of access to legal counsel and remarked that the detention regime and conditions of the ATCSA detainees should take into account the fact that they had not been accused or convicted of any crime, and the indefinite nature of their detention. They commented that:

> Detention had caused mental disorders in the majority of persons detained under the ATCSA.... The trauma of detention had become even more detrimental to their health since it was combined with an absence of control resulting from the indefinite character of their detention... For some of them, their situation at the time of the [CPT] visit could be considered as amounting to inhuman and degrading treatment.

Another example is the case of *Chahal v United Kingdom (1997)*, referred to earlier in this chapter and in which the European Court of Human Rights ruled that to return a person to their country of nationality would violate Article 3 if they were likely to suffer torture at the hands of the State on their return. Returning briefly to *Chahal*, the applicant had been politically active in various affairs which were considered by the Home Secretary to be undesirable on the grounds of national security and the fight against terrorist activity. The Court of Human Rights held that the UK had violated Article 3 by deciding to deport Mr Chahal, as he would be exposed to the risk of torture in India, where he had previously been subjected to such treatment. This case illustrates the fact that even if the state feels that an individual's presence is detrimental to national security, the State is still not at liberty to deport that individual to a place where they may be subjected to breaches of Article 3. Since then, the UK Government has been interested in a Dutch case concerning a man called Mohammed Ramzy, a 22-year-old Algerian challenging deportation. His asylum application was rejected and he was challenging a decision to deport him from the Netherlands. He argued that he would face a real risk of torture or other ill-treatment if sent back to Algeria. The Dutch Government said it was not seeking to reverse the *Chahal* precedent; it was arguing that Mohammed Ramzy's return to Algeria would *not* expose him to a real risk of torture. The UK Government – and three others – decided to intervene in this case. Amnesty International is very concerned that this intervention is attempting, in the context of this case, to persuade the European Court of Human Rights to abandon its jurisprudence in *Chahal v the United Kingdom* in favour of a position that the risk to the individual should be balanced against the national security interests of the state.

There is also clear evidence of European Union countries trading in the tools of torture.[10] For example, in May 2010 Amnesty International published a report demonstrating that European companies are trading in the equipment that is commonly used in torture such as wall restraints, thumb cuffs and electric shock devices. This is in spite of the introduction of the European Council Regulation No 1236/2005 of 27 June 2005 which was passed to ban the trade in goods which can be used for capital punishment, torture or other cruel, inhuman or degrading treatment or punishment. Specifically it states that:[11]

> Under this regulation, any export or import of goods that have no practical use other than for the purpose of capital punishment, torture and other cruel, inhuman or degrading treatment or punishment is prohibited. Moreover, authorisation is required for the export of goods that could be used for purposes of torture or other cruel, inhuman or degrading treatment or punishment, irrespective of the origin of such equipment.

In spite of this, many manufacturers continue to trade in instruments of torture, and many European countries continue to buy imported goods of this nature. One example is a Florida-based company called Stinger Systems[12] which both manufactures and exports a wide range of this equipment worldwide, although they do not normally disclose to whom. Those involved in the import and export of torture tools usually rely on the defence that they sell to law enforcement and military personnel only. This seems to them to be perfectly admissible – as though the use of torture equipment by such agencies has been condoned somehow or is in fact legal if used by such agencies. An article in Time Magazine (Cendrowicz 2010) recently reported that:

> An official at one company known to produce such items, the Belgian firm Sirien, denied any wrongdoing in an interview with TIME. Sirien makes products like electric-shock stun shields and S-200 projectile stun guns – devices that export manager Erwin Lafosse insists save lives. 'If you want to ban electroshock pistols, then policemen

will have to use firearms to defend themselves,' he says. 'The problem with Amnesty International is that they only see the bad side to everything. Yes, these can be used to torture someone, but so can all sorts of ordinary devices like knives, forks and spoons.'[13]

Aside from the availability of torture equipment, techniques of torture are also well known. Much has been made of the ill-treatment of prisoners at well-known detention facilities such as Guantánamo Bay and Abu Ghraib. However, Leigh (2004) reports that these examples are not merely isolated cases of ill-treatment by maverick guards but part of a much more entrenched and well-accepted process of interrogation commonly practiced by British troops known as 'R2I' or resistance to interrogation. These methods include sexual insults and degradation and in many cases they involve stripping prisoners naked. It is asserted that both British and US Special Forces (such as the SAS) have to learn about degradation techniques in order to be able to resist them personally, should they be captured. However, Leigh (ibid.) includes the following comment from a British former officer who said that:[14]

> The crucial difference from Iraq is that frontline soldiers who are made to experience R2I techniques themselves develop empathy. They realise the suffering they are causing. But people who haven't undergone this don't realise what they are doing to people. It's a shambles in Iraq.

Leigh (ibid.) also comments that such is the normality of the use of such techniques, that even the US commander in charge of military jails in Iraq, Major General Geoffrey Miller, has confirmed that there are at least 50 coercive techniques which can be used against enemy detainees to extract as much intelligence as possible, as rapidly as possible.

Modern torture

Modern torture is therefore both hidden and denied. However, the evidence that it occurs is fairly unequivocal, and for this reason it is pertinent to highlight some examples of evidence that have come to light regarding the practise of interrogation and torture techniques. First is the case of Abed Hamed Mowhoush, one of Saddam Hussein's generals who turned himself over to US forces in Iraq in 2003, a short time before Saddam Hussein himself was captured. Clearly at this time there would have been huge pressure on the US Army to detain and interrogate captured prisoners in order to produce useful information. According to Shamsi and Pearlstein (2006) a Chief Warrant Officer called Lewis Welshofer stated that a memo he had received in late August 2003 indicated that there were no specific rules of engagement for interrogations in Iraq and that captured detainees were to be considered unprivileged combatants, which meant that detainees were not to be afforded the protections of the Geneva Conventions. Mowhoush was interrogated by a number of people, including Welshofer. The interrogations began with direct questions but quickly changed. Mowhoush was slapped, had his hands bound, and was beaten with sledgehammer handles which a subsequent autopsy revealed broke five of his ribs. It was at this point that Welshofer then began to employ 'SERE' (Survival, Evasion, Resistance, Escape) interrogation tactics which he had learned at military training school. These tactics are apparently based on North Korean and Vietnamese methods and include prolonged isolation, sleep deprivation, and painful body positions which are designed to induce overwhelming stress, despair, anxiety, hallucinations and delusions. After being subject to these techniques for several months and during which time he was threatened with the execution of his sons who were also in US detention at that time, Welshofer eventually put Mowhoush head-first into a sleeping bag, wrapped it with electrical cord and sat on Mowhoush's chest to block his nose and mouth. Shamsi and Pearlstein (ibid.) report that it was at this point that Mowhoush died (according to the autopsy report) of asphyxia due to smothering and chest compression. The day after his death, the US military issued a press release stating that Mowhoush had died of natural causes. It is interesting to note that, in spite of the brutality of Mowhoush's death, Welshofer was not convicted of murder, but only of negligent homicide and negligent dereliction of duty. He could have been sentenced to more than three years in prison, but received only a written reprimand, a $6,000 fine, and 60 days of movement restriction. Other officers implicated in Mowhoush's death received even lesser punishments and no charges were ever brought against CIA personnel or Special Forces Command.

There have, of course, not only been allegations of ill-treatment and torture by US forces in relation to the conflict in Iraq, but also allegations that British soldiers have committed serious human rights violations in Iraq. The UK Government has repeatedly asserted, including in subsequent court proceedings, that neither the ECHR nor the HRA applies to the conduct of UK personnel in Iraq, in spite of the fact that the parliamentary Foreign Affairs Committee acknowledged that there have been abuses, concluding in its March 2005 report that some British personnel have committed grave violations of human rights of persons held in detention facilities in Iraq. One such case is that of Baha Mousa, who was among eight Iraqi citizens arrested and reportedly beaten in a hotel by members of the British military. Baha Mousa was 26 years old and worked as a receptionist at a hotel in Basra City. In the early morning of 14th September 2003 a unit from 1 Queen's Lancashire Regiment raided the hotel. The troops were particularly concerned to ascertain the whereabouts of one of the partners who ran the hotel. They rounded up a number of the men they found there, including Baha Mousa, whose father, Daoud Mousa, had been a police officer for 24 years and was by then a colonel in the Basra police. He had called at the hotel that morning to pick up his son at the end of his shift, and he told the lieutenant in charge of the unit that he had seen three of his soldiers pocketing money from the safe. During this visit he also saw his son lying on the floor of the hotel lobby with six other hotel employees with their hands behind their heads. The lieutenant assured him that this was a routine investigation and would be over in a couple of hours. Colonel Mousa never saw his son alive again. Four days later he was invited by a military police unit to identify his son's dead body. It was covered in blood and bruises, the nose was badly broken, there was blood coming from the nose and mouth, and there were severe patches of bruising all over the body. Witnesses said there was a sustained campaign of ill-treatment of the men who were taken into custody, one of whom was very badly injured, and they suggested that Baha Mousa was picked out for particularly savage treatment because of the complaints his father had made.

The UK Government initially decided not to hold an independent inquiry into the deaths. The Ministry of Defence claimed that neither the ECHR nor the Human Rights Act was applicable to the conduct of its military in Iraq at the time of the deaths, because Iraq was outside Europe and was not a party to the ECHR. So is it actually the case that human rights law does not protect prisoners of UK troops abroad? A ruling by the House of Lords in a landmark case has recently established that the jurisdiction of the Human Rights Act *does* apply overseas, including in relation to detention centres over which British troops have control. Of interest also is the fact that this ruling paves the way to an independent public inquiry into the Mousa killing and other alleged abuses of Iraqi civilians. However, the UK High Court will have to decide whether to demand such an inquiry. The UK Government may have to conduct an independent inquiry since the European Convention on Human Rights obliges Governments to carry out independent, timely, open and effective investigations when someone dies allegedly at the hands of agents of the State. Is it likely, however, that this will actually happen? It is possible that the Government could argue that the military police investigation and the court martial fulfilled the state's obligations to conduct an independent investigation. This will not necessarily be an easy argument to make as the ECHR requires states to carry out an adequate and effective investigation where an individual protected by the convention has been killed as a result of the use of force.

The final example, and possibly the most well known of all these cases, is that relating to the Binyam Mohamed litigation. Mohamed, from Notting Hill in west London, had been detained without trial since he was picked up at Karachi airport three years earlier after trying to leave Pakistan with a false passport. During subsequent court proceedings it became evident that he had been tortured by Pakistani agents and had been questioned by a bearded British man. He was flown to Morocco and for the next eighteen months was beaten, bombarded with white noise and scalded with burning liquid. His limbs were stretched, and scalpels were used to slice inch-long incisions in his body. After being released and returned to the UK, he alleged that he had been tortured in order to confess to his involvement in terrorist plots against the US He sought the release of documents from the US authorities relating to his detention and about which the UK Government claimed public interest immunity in order to prevent the documents being released – which basically means that their argument was that the release of the documents would not be in the public interest. The UK High Court deemed he was entitled to the documents because his case concerned allegations which involved the UK Government as a third party but agreed not to publish seven particular paragraphs which the UK Government claimed would breach the diplomatic rule that intelligence provided by one Government to another should not be disclosed without the consent of the Government which provided it. This is called 'the control principle'. More recently, however, the UK Court of Appeal decided on 10 February 2010 that the seven paragraphs should be published. Currently there is to be a High Court challenge over the UK Government's torture guidance in relation to this case. The human rights group Reprieve alleges that British ministers failed to ensure UK intelligence staff were not complicit in the torture of detainees abroad, and according to Norton-Taylor (2010):[15]

The organisation said it has 'compelling evidence' that British intelligence agencies have been engaged in the practice of 'systemically providing information and questions and of conducting interviews with detainees in the custody of a foreign state in the knowledge, or constructive knowledge, that the individuals were being subjected to torture.

Reprieve is currently involved with litigation in the High Court in relation to a judicial review based on evidence from the Binyam Mohamed case and others. It contends that this is necessary because the Government has refused to answer questions about its current guidance on torture which was established initially in 2002. This guidance is said to have given MI5 and MI6 officers advice that legally they would not have to intervene even in situations where they knew that prisoners were being treated in a way which would breach the terms of the Geneva Conventions because strictly speaking it could be argued that such prisoners were not in the control of British agents. The Government has since reported that this guidance was changed in 2004, but it has not allowed this to be published. The question is, why? Clearly the most likely explanation for this is because it would be politically embarrassing for the Government to freely admit that it has been complicit in torture first, because it is legally prohibited and second, because the Government purports to abide by those legal prohibitions even though the evidence suggests otherwise. If the Government supports the use of torture in exceptional circumstances, then why does it not admit to this and end the speculation about it? Is it because it would not be politically advantageous; because they don't wish it to overtly bring them into conflict with European law; because they want to avoid an embarrassing media campaign against their tactics fuelled by influential pressure groups; or it just easier to systematically deny it than to embark on a complex explanation about the justifications for it? These and other questions merit further analysis.

The persistence of torture

This chapter has established that Article 3 of the UK Human Rights Act 1998 imposes an absolute prohibition on torture with no exceptions and no possibility of derogation, even in times of war or public emergency. Torture is also mentioned in several international Conventions, for example, the Convention on Cruel, Inhuman or Degrading Treatment or Punishment (also known as the Convention against Torture 1984), the International Covenant on Civil and Political Rights 1966 (ICCPR) and the Geneva Conventions 1949. Whilst under Article 15 a contracting state may derogate from any of the Articles which interfere with the rights protected in the convention 'in times of war or other public emergency threatening the nation', this does not apply to Articles 2, 3, 4 or 7 and this means that legally there can be no derogation from Article 3. Clearly, therefore, there are numerous legal prohibitions on torture but what does the interpretation of this law by the Judiciary tell us?

It has already been established earlier in this chapter that there is a very tough test for torture. The few cases which demonstrate the type of conduct which can amount to torture include *Cakici v Turkey [2001]* where broken ribs, head injury and electric shock treatment *were* deemed to amount to torture because it was 'deliberate, inhuman and caused serious and cruel suffering'. Similarly in *Soering v United Kingdom (1989)* exposing a person to the risk of execution in another jurisdiction would also amount to a violation of Article 3. In *D v United Kingdom (1997)* returning a person to a country where there would be inadequate medical treatment available, which would expose that person to 'a real risk of dying under the most distressing circumstances', was also held to be a violation of Article 3. It is important to note, however, the circumstances in which certain conduct has *not* been held to amount to torture. For example, in *Ireland v UK [1978]* interrogation techniques used against IRA suspects including hooding, white noise, continuous questioning and food, water and sleep deprivation was not held to be torture. In *Tyrer v UK (1978)* , the birching of a 15-year-old boy did not amount to torture and In *Y v UK (1992)* the caning of children was only found to amount to 'degrading' punishment.

So the law exists, the prohibition is there, but is it enforceable? The evidence presented in this chapter suggests that it is not. But why is this, and what makes it largely unenforceable? There are two reasons for this. First, case law demonstrates that the test for it is very strict; second, in spite of legal prohibitions, the cases of Mowhoush, Baha Mousa and Binyam Mohammed and the evidence of the widespread trade and training in torture all demonstrate that torture continues whether legally prohibited or not. This means that Article 3 is largely unenforceable and does not provide adequate protection against torture and inhuman or degrading treatment or punishment. The legal prohibitions are largely ignored by Governments who appear to condone a covert acceptance that torture remains an acceptable means for the military to obtain information in difficult situations. The lenient way in which military personnel who have perpetrated this behaviour upon others have been dealt with underpins this attitude as does Governmental sidestepping of the issue. It appears that the world over, attitudes have not really moved on and that the legal prohibition of this behaviour merely pays lip service to what ought to be happening ethically or morally but this does not reflect what is actually happening the world over, nor does it reflect states' real attitudes to this important issue.

According to Amnesty International, one-third of the world's nations have practised torture since 1980. There are six acknowledged US terrorist detention facilities; three in Iraq, two in Afghanistan and one at Guantánamo Bay. At least 45 detainees have died in US custody due to suspected or confirmed criminal homicides, and at least 8 of these were tortured to death. At least 98 detainees have died while in US custody in Iraq or Afghanistan. There have been nearly 600 criminal investigations into allegations of detainee abuse; each investigation tends to include more than one US soldier, more than one instance of abuse and more than one victim. Allegations against 250 Soldiers have been addressed in courts-martial, non-judicial punishments and other administrative punishments but no CIA personnel have ever been charged with wrongdoing in connection with alleged involvement in any of these deaths. Reportedly between 100 and 150 individuals have been rendered from US custody to a foreign country known to torture prisoners, including Egypt, Syria, Saudi Arabia, Jordan and Pakistan. There are believed to be at least 11 'secret' detention locations that have been used since September 2001. There are, or have been, CIA facilities in Afghanistan, Guantánamo, Poland, Romania and Jordan; detention facilities in Alizai, Kohat and Peshawar in Pakistan; a facility on the US naval base on the island of Diego Garcia, and detentions of prisoners on US ships, particularly the *USS Peleliu* and *USS Bataan*. Over 15,000 people have been held in Iraq, Afghanistan and Guantánamo Bay. A world poll was taken in 2008 asking people in nineteen countries how they felt about torture. Five countries did not want a total abolition of torture. According to Human Rights Watch the use of torture has been documented in China, Egypt, Indonesia, Iran, Iraq, Israel, Malaysia, Morocco, Nepal, North Korea, Pakistan, Russia, Syria, Turkey, Uganda and Uzbekistan.

Are we close to the truth about torture, or is our reliance on the effectiveness of the clearly unenforceable and largely ignored legal prohibitions misplaced? This chapter has demonstrated that torture still continues and that, more than this, it is regarded by both the UK and US Governments as a legitimate means of obtaining evidence – usually from terror suspects. Given the examples of the cases of Baha Mousa and Binyam Mohammed, it is unrealistic to imagine that both [then] Prime Minister Tony Blair and other senior figures in Government would not have been aware of the existence of Britain's secret interrogation policy. This would have included David Blunkett and Jack Straw who were at that time responsible for MI5 and MI6. This policy was doubtless influenced by the UK's 'special relationship' with the US and both countries' commitment to obtaining and sharing intelligence about the threat from al-Qaeda. It is all the more odd to imagine that this issue was sidestepped politically given the fact that, aside from the Geneva Conventions, the UK Government had already banned a number of torture techniques that had been employed by the British Army in Northern Ireland in 1972. Perhaps one explanation is precisely because of the UK Government's relationship with the US and the influence of their changed attitude to terrorism post-9/11 when, according to Tony Blair, the rules of the game had changed. This attitude fails, however, to take account of Article 4 of the 1984 UN Convention against Torture, to which the UK is a party, and which criminalises 'any act by any person which constitutes complicity or participation in torture'. Clearly, given that senior ministers at the time must have known that prisoners were being mistreated, this means that the UK Government was thus culpable and complicit in breaching the UN Convention as well as Article 3 of the ECHR and the HRA 1998.

It has long been argued that any information gained from torture is not necessarily the truth and, as such, the reliance placed on this intelligence should realistically be questioned. A 2002 US military memo prepared by the agency that helped train interrogators in torture methods such as waterboarding warned about the prospect of gaining 'unreliable information' as a result. Koppelman (2009) reports that the document suggests that:

> The requirement to obtain information from an uncooperative source as quickly as possible – in time to prevent, for example, an impending terrorist attack that could result in loss of life – has been forwarded as a compelling argument for the use of torture. Conceptually, proponents envision the application of torture as a means to expedite the exploitation process. In essence, physical and/or psychological duress are viewed as an alternative to the more time consuming conventional interrogation process. The error inherent in this line of thinking is the assumption that, through torture, the interrogator can extract reliable and accurate intelligence. History and a consideration of human behavior would appear to refute this assumption. (The application of physical and or psychological duress will likely result in physical compliance. Additionally, prisoners may

answer and/or comply as a result of threats of torture. However, the reliability and accuracy information must be questioned.)[16]

Similarly Bell (2008) hypothesises on the 'torture myth' which she postulates is the idea that torture is an effective interrogation practice although it is widely acknowledged that its use gives rise to a wide range of practical problems which diminish any claimed effectiveness. Contrary to the myth, Bell suggests that torture does not always produce accurate information, and any benefit it offers is marginal because traditional techniques of interrogation may be as good, or better at producing valuable intelligence.

In spite of this, torture persists and this in turn signals that Governments and the agencies working for them either believe, or want to believe, that it is valuable. As a result, torture remains hidden and is systematically denied, and thus the moral and ethical dilemmas which ought to surround this issue can be sidestepped by governments who condone it. In attempts to deny and conceal it, politicians instead seek to focus people's attention on the global threat of terror and in so doing negate human rights and human rights obligations in favour of the need for security. Principal in relation to this has been David Miliband, the former Foreign Secretary, who has been trying to block the public release of a summary of 42 US documents relating specifically to the treatment of Binyam Mohamed. Two Judges have already said that these documents contain powerful evidence of torture. Aside from the perpetration of torture being an offence under Article 3, it is worth noting that it is also an offence in international law to conceal evidence of torture. However, it is fairly clear that the UK Government has been concealing such illegal acts from judicial authorities and from oversight organisations to protect itself from liability, criticism and embarrassment. The question remains, therefore, how does this persist given the numerous prohibitions which exist?

A contributing factor to this situation in the UK was the enactment, in 1994, of the Intelligence Services Act. This Act was passed with little resistance in either the House of Commons or the House of Lords and ensures that British intelligence and security officers can commit serious criminal offences overseas and escape prosecution in the UK, thus enjoying complete immunity as long as either the Foreign, Home or Defence Secretary of the day has signed a warrant authorising that crime. The implications of this piece of legislation are significant since potentially it facilitates the intelligence agencies having a green light to engage, in the course of their profession, in virtually any sort of otherwise illegal behaviour ranging from bribery to the famous 007 licence to kill (also known as 'class seven authorisations', if readers think that this is the stuff of fiction). One can only speculate as to why such an Act would meet with little resistance unless it is because there is some entrenched acceptance by the majority of people that security personnel actually require this type of protection in order to carry out their functions effectively. If this is the case, it merely fuels notions of denial and covert approval and of course underpins the ineffectiveness of other civil liberty protecting legislations such as those embodied in Article 3 of the ECHR and HRA 1998.

Further evidence of the type of tacit approval for such behaviour which exists has also been provided by the Binyam Mohamed case where, at the High Court hearing, an anonymous MI5 officer who interrogated Mohamed in Pakistan told the Court that he had been led to believe that what he was doing was lawful. Two things are of note here. First, this certainly gives credence to the argument that the security services had indeed been given a green light to implement these practices since it is logical to assume that they would not have done so if they had not been assured of both political support at the highest level, and subsequent legal cover, should it become necessary. Second, it must be likely that the evidence of these practices is what former Foreign Secretary David Miliband wanted to prevent being disclosed from the US documents mentioned earlier in this chapter. As a result of this, the High Court ruled that this MI5 officer was probably involved in what they termed 'criminal wrongdoing' when he questioned Binyam Mohamed in Pakistan, and this in turn led to the former Home Secretary, Jacqui Smith, asking the Attorney General to investigate the case. A short time later Scotland Yard were asked to look at the case. The problem with this is that if officers such as this had been given the authority to question Mohamed under a 'class seven authorisation', whatever they then did could not be pursued legally because under the Intelligence Services Act 1994, they would have complete immunity from prosecution because these acts took place abroad. What seems of far more importance to Government ministers and to security officials is not whether they have either authorised or committed acts of torture, but whether they can evade getting caught in the process. It is with this as the backcloth that the evasive answers and statements from ministers about torture should be viewed. Nor should we be under any illusions about how high up the chain of command this complicity goes.

Similarly, in the US the Government has repeatedly tried to portray any evidence of abuse as isolated incidents, and perpetrated by officers who must have been acting without orders. However, more realistically, subsequent to the September 11 attacks on the US, it appears that the push against the so-called 'war on terror' has produced numerous situations whereby the US, like the UK, has endeavoured to circumvent international law. The present author (2009) describes the process by which the first detainees to arrive at Guantánamo in 2002 were labelled not as prisoners of war (POWs), but as 'unlawful combatants' – a term which immediately deprives them of any status or rights which are normally attributed to POWs. This made it possible for the US Government to argue that, because they were unlawful combatants, they thus did not have any rights under the Geneva Convention. There have subsequently been a number of legal challenges by such detainees; however, the US Government has always claimed that US courts would have no jurisdiction over these detainees even if they were being tortured or summarily executed. In the American case of *Gherebi v. Bush (2003)* it was reported by the court that the US Government had claimed that it could

> do with [them] as it will, when it pleases, without any compliance with any rule of law of any kind, without permitting [them] to consult counsel, and without acknowledging any judicial forum in which its actions may be challenged. Indeed, at oral argument, the government advised us that its position would be the same even if the claims were that it was engaging in acts of torture or that it was summarily executing the detainees. To our knowledge, prior to the current detention of prisoners at Guantánamo, the US government has never before asserted such a grave and startling proposition. ... a position so extreme that it raises the gravest concerns under both American and international law.

Added to this, almost nothing is known about investigations or prosecutions of US military personnel for alleged violations of international humanitarian law in Afghanistan. It is as though the US does not even find it necessary to deny or defend its actions. There has been no release of information or official responses about investigations that are supposed to have taken place into deaths at detention camps in Afghanistan. Two reports have been published about these allegations. The first was the Report of the International Committee of the Red Cross (ICRC) on the treatment by the Coalition Forces of Prisoners of War and other Protected Persons by the Geneva Conventions in Iraq during arrest, internment and interrogation (2004) – also known as the

ICRC Report, and second a report by Major General Antonio Taguba on alleged abuses at US military prisons in Abu Ghraib and Camp Bucca, 'Article 15–6 Investigation of the 800th Military Police Brigade' – also known as the Taguba Report. In the latter it was reported that 'numerous incidents of sadistic, blatant, and wanton criminal abuses' were inflicted on detainees, including;

- Punching, slapping and kicking detainees; jumping on their naked feet;
- Videotaping and photographing naked male and female detainees;
- Forcibly arranging detainees in various sexually explicit positions for photographing;
- Forcing groups of male detainees to masturbate themselves while being photographed and videotaped;
- Arranging naked detainees in a pile and then jumping on them;
- Positioning a naked detainee on a box, with a sandbag on his head, and attaching wires to his fingers, toes and penis to simulate electric torture;
- Writing 'I am a Rapist' *[sic]* on the leg of a detainee alleged to have forcibly raped a 15-year-old fellow detainee, and then photographing him naked;
- Placing a dog chain or strap around a naked detainee's neck and having a female soldier pose with him for a picture;
- A male military police guard having sex with a female detainee;
- Breaking chemical lights and pouring the phosphoric liquid on detainees;
- Threatening detainees with a loaded 9-mm pistol;
- Pouring cold water on naked detainees;
- Beating detainees with a broom handle and a chair;
- Threatening male detainees with rape;
- Allowing a military police guard to stitch the wound of a detainee who was injured after being slammed against the wall in his cell;
- Sodomizing a detainee with a chemical light and perhaps a broom stick;
- Using military working dogs (without muzzles) to frighten and intimidate detainees with threats of attack, and in at least one case biting and severely injuring a detainee;
- Forcing detainees to remove their clothing and keeping them naked for several days at a time;
- Forcing naked male detainees to wear women's underwear;
- Taking pictures of dead Iraqi detainees.[17]

Interestingly this was a much longer list than that which appeared in the report of the International Committee of the Red Cross (ICRC). The bottom line appears to be that in both jurisdictions, and in spite of international law or the pronouncements of startled judiciaries, both the UK and US Governments have been, and remain, determined to covertly proceed with their secret condonation of these policies, thus rendering international law completely ineffective. Writing in the *Guardian*, recently Cobain (2009)[18] commented that:

> The *Guardian* has repeatedly asked Blair about any role he played in approving the policy, whether he knew that it led to people being tortured, whether he personally authorised interrogations that took place in Guantánamo and Afghanistan as well as Pakistan, and whether he made any effort to change the policy. Blair's spokesman responded by saying: 'It is completely untrue that Mr Blair has ever authorised the use of torture. He is opposed to it in all circumstances. Neither has he ever been complicit in the use of torture.' When the Guardian pointed out to Blair that it had not suggested that he had authorised the use of torture – as opposed to asking him whether he had authorised a policy that led to people being tortured – and that his spokesman had not answered the questions that were asked, his spokesman replied: 'Tony Blair does not condone torture, has never authorised it nor colluded in it. He continues to think our security services have done and continue to do a crucial and very good job.' So Blair knew of the policy, but refuses to say whether he authorised it.

The extent of this complicity can also be demonstrated by the case of Moazzem Begg, who was kidnapped from Pakistan in 2002 by the Americans and taken to an interrogation camp in Afghanistan where torture was practised. Whilst there, he witnessed the murders of two other detainees. He was moved to Guantánamo Bay before being returned to the UK in 2005. Throughout this time, nothing was known about the fact that a British agent had actually been present at his kidnapping. The Foreign and Commonwealth Office told his father that they had no information about Begg and also said that the Americans would tell them nothing. Peirce (2008: 7) comments:

> We inhabit the most secretive of democracies, which has developed the most comprehensive of structures for hiding its misdeeds, shielding them always from view behind the curtain of 'national security'.

From here on in we should be aware of the game of hide and seek in which the government hopes to ensure that we should never find out its true culpability.

It would no doubt be satisfying to opponents of torture to imagine that the growing evidence of Britain's involvement in torture result might result in public pressure on the Government to stop the denials and to give real credence to a more realistic commitment to either a total or more narrowly defined prohibition on torture. The real problem though is that many people are either ignorant of, or not particularly troubled that their fellow citizens are being tortured because they have been conditioned to suspect that those victims might be terrorists. This approach facilitates the possibilities for torture to continue and highlights the continuing difficulty of achieving an ethical balance between the need for security on the one hand and essential civil liberties as enshrined in legislation, such as Article 3, on the other. Is it realistic therefore to expect such a balance to be achievable or is this merely an idealistic notion which could never be attained? If that is the case then we come back to the question of why successive Governments perpetuate the notion of denial in relation to torture. Would it be better to argue some moral or legal justification for it – however narrowly that is defined?

Justifications for torture

In a recent article, Frick (2008) cites [then] US Vice President Cheney as having admitted to personally approving the torture of a number of high-profile detainees. Specifically Mr Cheney defended the morality of torture, suggesting that it would actually have been immoral for the US *not* to torture certain individuals:

> In my mind, the foremost obligation we had from a moral or an ethical standpoint was to the oath of office we took when we were sworn in, on January 20 of 2001, to protect and defend against all enemies foreign and domestic. And that's what we've done.[19]

Although there are many people who would find this view unpalatable, one thing at least can be said about it – it is honest. Honesty is a factor totally lacking from current debates about torture and perhaps this, more than anything else, is what distinguishes it from historical torture. Historically states and Governments carried out the practice of torture and admitted to it. Now, states and Governments the world over do the same thing but pretend they do not and claim that there are no circumstances when it should be done. In stark contrast to this, Dick Cheney insisted that the torture policies he helped craft were directly responsible for helping to avoid any further terrorist attacks after 9/11. So would it be better if there were less hypocrisy and if torture were legalised? It is sometimes easy to maintain an ethical stance on something until you have been affected by it yourself. If your wife/husband/ mother/father had been in one of the twin towers and that atrocity could have been prevented by some form of interrogation, would you say it were permissible then? If your son/daughter had been kidnapped by a paedophile, would you say it were acceptable to pull someone's fingernails out to get them released unharmed? These are difficult, and some would say unrealistic questions – but are they?

There are thus a number of major philosophical views relating to this issue. Sussman (2005) offers an up-to-date and detailed account of what is wrong with torture. A qualified version of this perspective has been given by Davis (2005) who argues that in practice, if not theory, there is no justification for torture. A third version combines elements of both of these two groups, namely, that torture can in some extreme emergencies be morally justified, but that torture ought never to be legalised or institutionalised. This position has also been argued for by Tibor Machan (1990). Alternatively it has been argued by writers such Luban (2005) and Waldron (2010) that the inherent injustice involved in legalising such practices would result in irreparable damage to liberal institutions. Dershowitz (ibid.) rejects the notion (as does Waddington) that it is *always* morally wrong to torture the terrorist and argues that there are some circumstances in which it is morally permissible to torture someone. This argument therefore still allows an individual to suggest that the *routine* use of torture is not morally justified but if it could be proven that it was necessary to save life in a given situation then it would be permissible. It follows therefore that advocates of this view might suggest that because torture is arguably not impermissible in all situations, that it should be legalised. Citing Article 3 as ineffectual would no doubt bolster this view as would the contention that torture is already prevalent within many military and police organisations who in turn have to respond to numerous emergency situations in which torture is not immoral and thus, for which some institutional arrangement – such as its legalisation in such situations – should be in place to facilitate it. Added to this there is also the psychological angle to consider. Waddington (2010)[20] comments:

> In a famous experiment conducted forty years ago, the psychologist Professor Stanley Milgram of Yale University was able to convince ordinary people to inflict significant physical pain upon what those people believed was an unsuspecting fellow experimental subject, but who was in fact an actor. All that was required was to locate the experiment in a prestigious location (the University) and surround it with the trappings of 'science': an experimenter in a white coat and impressive looking machinery. The quietly spoken imperative, 'the experiment demands that you continue', was sufficient to induce ordinary people to administer progressively severe electric shocks to another person whose cries of pain and protest that were broadcast via a loudspeaker.

Against this, it is interesting to highlight the work of Philip Zimbardo, who designed the Stanford Prison Experiment (S.P.E). Hailed as one of the most significant and controversial psychological experiments ever conducted, it focused on the psychology of imprisonment, dividing a group of undergraduate students into 'guards' and 'prisoners'. Marriot (2007) reports:

> Zimbardo witnessed levels of cruelty he'd never have predicted or imagined. Within no time, liberal undergraduates became sadists, tormenting prisoners, even forcing them, in an uncanny premonition of George W Bush's Iraq 33 years later, to simulate sodomy with one another. After six days, Zimbardo called a halt to the experiment. Although the 'guards' knew the 'prisoners had done nothing criminally wrong to deserve their lowly status', he writes in his new book, 'some ... were transformed into perpetrators of evil'. The experiment taught him that 'most of us can undergo significant character transformations when we are caught up in the crucible of social forces.[21]

In a recent interview Zimbardo was asked about his reactions to the evidence of torture at Abu Ghraib. His response was:

> I was shocked. But not surprised. I immediately flashed on similar pictures from the S.P.E. What particularly bothered me was that the Pentagon blamed the whole thing on a 'few bad apples.' I knew from our experiment, if you put good apples into a bad situation, you'll get bad apples. Milgram quantified the small steps that people take when

they do evil. He showed that an authority can command people to do things they believe they'd never do. I wanted to take that further. Milgram's study only looked at one aspect of behavior, obedience to authority, in short 50-minute takes. The S.P.E., because it was slated to go for two weeks, was almost like a forerunner of reality television. You could see behavior unfolding hour by hour, day by day.[22]

The fact that Article 3 does not work to completely prohibit torture is an interesting fact in itself. Because the law has to apply itself to numerous and sometimes generalisable situations, it cannot therefore be too specific. Most statutes are drafted specifically with this in mind, the point being of course that it is the Judiciary who will subsequently interpret the law in the way in which they think Parliament intended. Thus, when one considers applying the law to complex situations where issues of morality are of prime importance, it is perhaps not surprising that the two do not easily go hand in hand and sometimes cannot be reconciled at all. Consider for a moment an example which is often given to demonstrate this; the soldier who deserts to return to his terminally ill wife would no doubt be morally justified in doing so, but the law relating to desertion in times of war will allow him no exception to this rule, and some would say that this is completely justified albeit morally harsh. So the argument for a change in the law is not simple for a number of reasons. We know, for example, that organisations other than the organs of State perpetuate torture for a variety of reasons. Legalisation would arguably give them *carte blanche* to go further without having the limitation of legal prohibition. It has also been suggested that this in turn could lead to a culture of torture developing with the innocent having no recourse to justice.

Some writers have argued that torture is endemic – whether we like it or not – to many social institutions, particularly correctional, military and police organisations both in democratic and non-democratic nations. It follows that to change the way in which vast organisations have operated for ages would be difficult, if not impossible, and for which there would be very little, if any, political will in any case. The job would be one of combating cultures of torture which pervade the very essence of vast institutions. Whilst arguably it would be fairly easy to legalise torture (because there are those who would argue that many institutions do it anyway) it would clearly de-sensitise people to the moral and ethical considerations surrounding it. It would also allow the lawful exercise of enormous power, perhaps ultimately leading to the development of torture cultures in military and police agencies. Plus, once legalised it would be very difficult to go back and change things if it proved unsuitable or unworkable. This can be demonstrated by the situation in Israel, mentioned earlier in this chapter. Before 1999, certain forms of torture were in fact legal but subsequently outlawed. One might presume that this meant that torture no longer occurred at all, but this is a naive view; it continued because it was a deeply entrenched practice.

The effectiveness of the current legislation as it appears in Article 3 in both the European Convention on Human Rights and the Human Rights Act1998 is clearly poor. Hypocrisy surrounds the issue; democracies the world over claim they do not condone it but the evidence suggests that it occurs with some frequency. Governments arguably torture too many people too often and on too many occasions make mistakes about who they are torturing. Arguably whilst total prohibition is not realistic because it does not work, perhaps it is the only (imperfect) option because the dangers of legalising torture and thus undermining the fundamental principles of any democratic society would be far less preferable. Added to this, the elimination of torture cultures and sub-institutions can only realistically be achieved if torture remains unlawful, however unsatisfactory the current legislation appears to be. Logically there is a clear distinction between torture and other legally permissible punishments like imprisonment and a distinction also between torture and related concepts like cruelty or sadism because of the instrumental nature of torture. However unpalatable we may find it, torture may be effective (if morally objectionable) for certain purposes, such as counter-insurgency. Waddington's view (ibid.) is:

> The prohibition on torture focuses on the means rather than the ends of coercive action. It is like saying that shooting someone is acceptable but causing an explosion is not. It is generally accepted that in extreme circumstances it may be justified to kill, why then do we not admit that in equally extreme circumstances it may be permissible to extract information that will save life?

In order to come to a view about this complex issue, it has been necessary to acknowledge the distinction between torture and more nebulous concepts like state repression, sadism and cruelty, and to judge the action on its own terms. Whatever the case, it is clear that the law as it stands, although fairly ambiguous and clearly ineffective in preventing torture, is probably better than nothing or the alternatives discussed here. One final point is worthy of note. I have commented elsewhere (Moss 2009: 254) that:

> Criminologists around the world seem to me to be strangely silent in relation to many of the issues I have raised here and many others besides. Perhaps they no longer see these issues as being part of their domain, and would rather leave it to other organisations such as Liberty and Amnesty International. But although the work of these agencies is a valuable contribution, this surely does not negate the need for academics to involve themselves in an informed debate about such matters and once more to be in a position to raise awareness at all levels about the importance of other aspects of society besides security – namely human rights, privacy, freedom of expression and other essential liberties about which we appear to be increasingly complacent.

The issue of torture is seemingly no exception to this, but what interests me most is that although torture has clearly been a concern for many human rights advocates for some time, it had not really been on the academic radar until after the events of 9/11 in the US and 7/7 in the UK Only since this time and since the announcement of the 'war on terror' has the topic of torture really taken off. Previously not an issue of major concern within the academic world, it has now been catapulted into the consciousness of many current political commentators and philosophers. Although there is clearly a debate there as to why this is the case (which this book does not seek to address) it should nonetheless be seen as a welcome development, since whatever one's view, the meaning attached to torture and the transparency of the debate about it is of deep significance, and it is crucial that this debate continues.

Notes

1. http://www.icrc.org/web/eng/siteeng0.nsf/html/69MJXC
2. Readers may be interested to read about the Inquisitions treatment of Galileo in relation to his seminal work the 'Dialogue' in which he raised the question of whether the Sun or the Earth was at the centre of the Universe. The Inquisition convicted Galileo of heresy, banned the 'Dialogue', imprisoned Galileo (although this was at the Archbishop of Siena's palace) and demanded that he recite seven penitential psalms once a week for three years. For more on this see Sobel, D. (1999) *Galileo's Daughter*. London: Fourth Estate Ltd.
3. Cobain, I. (2008) 'The Truth about Torture: Britain's Catalogue of Shame'. The Guardian.co.uk 8 July 2008 http://www.guardian.co.uk/politics/2009/jul/08/mi5-mi6-acccused-of-torture/print accessed 15 May 2010
4. In a personal communication to the author, 18 May 2010.

5. Chemical, biological, radiological or nuclear.
6. See Amnesty International's report, *Guinea, Liberia and Sierra Leone. A human rights crisis for refugees and the internally displaced*, 25 June 2001 (AI Index AFR 05/005/2001).
7. An inquiry set up by the Israeli Government subsequent to a scandal concerning the deaths of two Palestinian prisoners in Israeli custody. The Inquiry, headed by former Supreme Court Justice Moshe Landau, found that security service interrogators had routinely used force during the interrogation of prisoners and then committed perjury at subsequent trials. In its conclusion it laid down guidelines for the use of what it referred to as 'moderate physical pressure'..
8. http://news.bbc.co.uk/go/pr/fr/-/1/hi/uk/8688501.stm
9. See http://www.amnesty.org.uk/books_details.asp?BookID=25
10. http://www.statewatch.org/news/2010/apr/02eu-torture-trade.htm
11. http://europa.eu/legislation_summaries/external_trade/r12535_en.htm
12. http://www.stingersystems.com/
13. http://www.time.com/time/world/article/0,8599,1976495,00.html
14. http://www.guardian.co.uk/uk/2004/may/08/iraq.iraq
15. http://www.guardian.co.uk/uk/2010/feb/23/government-legal-challenge-torture-detainees
16. http://www.salon.com/news/politics/war_room/2009/04/24/jpra_memo
17. Reproduced from the Taguba Investigative report, on alleged abuses at US military prisons in Abu Ghraib and Camp Bucca, Iraq by Maj. Gen. Antonio M. Taguba: 'Article 15–6 Investigation of the 800th Military Police Brigade.'
18. http://www.guardian.co.uk/politics/2009/jul/08/mi5-mi6-acccused-of-torture/print
19. http://thinkprogress.org/2008/12/18/cheney-morality-of-torture/
20. In a personal communication to the author, 18th May 2010.
21. http://www.guardian.co.uk/books/2007/apr/29/politics1
22. http://www.harpers.org/archive/2007/04/horton-zimbardo-torture

5
Article 5 and Detention without Trial

> Indefinite detention without charge or trial is anathema in any country which observes the Rule of Law.[1]

This chapter deals specifically with the effectiveness of contemporary legislative safeguards in the forms of the European Convention on Human Rights and the UK Human Rights Act 1998 by specifically undertaking an analysis of judicial decisions in relation to cases brought under Article 5 in order to determine how UK law is being interpreted in relation to this article and whether or not it is compatible with, or is deviating from, these basic libertarian principles. Contemporary and controversial cases such as those involving Khalid el-Masri and Maher Arar will be used to highlight this assessment as will case law such as the *Secretary of State for the Home Department v JJ and others [2006]* where the respondents successfully challenged the compatibility with Article 5 ECHR, of control orders issued against them. It is necessary to highlight that detention without trial under Article 5, torture under Article 3 and extraordinary rendition and Article 6 cannot easily be discussed separately as in many situations these issues all appear to go hand in hand. There will, therefore, be occasions throughout these chapters where the issues of torture and extraordinary rendition will be mentioned albeit the main focus within this chapter is on the subject of detention without trial. For this reason, I have tried to avoid repetition of materials used in the previous chapter and in the penultimate chapter which follows this.

According to Article 5;

> Everyone has the right to liberty and security of person. No one shall be deprived of his liberty save in the following cases and in

accordance with a procedure prescribed by law. The article states various circumstances in which a person's liberty may be denied, which are:

(a) the lawful detention of a person after conviction by a competent court;
(b) the lawful arrest or detention of a person for non-compliance with a court order or any legal obligation
(c) the lawful and necessary arrest or detention of a person in order to bring him before a competent legal authority
(d) the detention of a minor for educational supervision or his lawful detention for the purpose of bringing him before the competent legal authority;
(e) the lawful detention of persons for the prevention of the spreading of infectious diseases, of persons of unsound mind, alcoholics or drug addicts, or vagrants;
(f) the lawful arrest or detention of those attempting an unauthorised entry into the country or prior to deportation or extradition.

The article also provides that everyone who is arrested shall be informed promptly, in a language which he/she understands, of the reasons for the arrest and the relevant charge.

Everyone arrested or detained in accordance with those provisions must, according to the article, be brought promptly before a Judge or other officer authorised by law to exercise judicial power and is entitled to trial within a reasonable time or to release pending trial. Everyone who is deprived of his liberty by arrest or detention shall be entitled to take proceedings by which the lawfulness of his detention shall be decided speedily by a court, and his release ordered if the detention is not lawful. Anyone who has been the victim of arrest or detention in contravention of the provisions of the article has an enforceable right to compensation. Before going into further detail about the article, what it provides and the specific circumstances when it has been brought into question, it is pertinent to contextualise the current UK and global position regarding liberty of the person.

On 12th June 2008 the [then] British Prime Minister, Gordon Brown, won the vote on the 42-day detention for terror suspects by just nine votes, having to rely on the support of the Democratic Unionist Party. The UK Government said the growing complexity and international nature of terror plots meant the police would need more time to question suspects before charging them. This split the Labour Party and was subsequently defeated in the House of Lords. Peirce (2008) comments:

> It would have been difficult to match Bush's executive onslaught on constitutional rights in the US, by means of the Patriot Act; the designation of 'enemy combatants' and their detention by presidential order; the abolition of habeas corpus; the subjection of detainees to torture in Afghanistan and Guantánamo or their unofficial outsourcing via rendition flights to countries specialising in even more grotesque interrogative practices, many of them those same regimes which had pressured the UK to take action against their own dissidents. Claiming that a parallel emergency faced Britain, Blair bulldozed through Parliament a new brand of internment. This allowed for the indefinite detention without trial of foreign nationals, the 'evidence' to be heard in secret with the detainee's lawyer not permitted to see the evidence against him and an auxiliary lawyer appointed by the attorney general who, having seen it, was not allowed to see the detainee. The most useful device of the executive is its ability to claim that secrecy is necessary for national security.

The debate about the proposed Counter-Terrorism Bill which would have introduced this measure in June 2008 was predictably tense. I make no apology for including some lengthy quotations from Hansard[2] (11 Jun 2008: Column 373 – 385) as the comments are both interesting and enlightening and demonstrate the strength of feeling about this issue within Parliament.

Mr. Mark Hendrick:

Let me be perfectly honest and say that, despite my regard for civil liberties, if proper, urgent and telling evidence had been produced of the need to bring in the proposed law, I would seriously have had to reconsider the position, take off my civil libertarian hat or wig and start thinking carefully. However, nothing of that sort has been produced, including during the whole period of the Public Bill Committee. I have heard nothing to persuade me even the slightest way towards the Government's view. We know that the Law Society has made its view clear, as has the Joint Committee on Human Rights [and] I have seen nothing of a persuasive nature. When the Home Secretary was interviewed on Radio 4 a few months ago, she admitted that she had no idea at all how many days were required. I intervened on the right hon. Lady earlier, but I am none the wiser. If, as we are told, the alleged plots are becoming more and more complex to unravel, why is the magic figure now half that of the previously recommended 90 days? Can anyone explain that?

Mr. Redwood:

The Hon. Gentleman is making a powerful case. Does he agree that, under this procedure, arresting someone who was a terrorist could be a disaster for the anti-terrorism campaign, because there might be no evidence or knowledge of what that terrorist had been up to? They might not know the network and all the other members of it would be alerted by that single arrest. Evidence would then get destroyed, which would make things very difficult.

Mr. Llwyd:

Indeed it does. I shall deal briefly with the safeguard – the parliamentary scrutiny. It is a complete fig leaf and a waste of time, for two main reasons. If we are given merely an outline of the case and the need for an extension on the view of the Secretary of State, Parliament will nod it through and vote yes. What if the matter goes to appeal and a court says no? Where will we be at that point? That is one of the problems involved with dressing Parliament up in a quasi-judicial function – a constitutional experiment that is doomed to failure.

On the other hand, if we are given all the details, as we arguably should be if we are to supervise the thing properly and scrutinise it, that will make a fair trial impossible. In the rush to try to get Back Benchers on board, the Government have made a complete mess of this part of the Bill. It is not even logical, let alone workable. It is nothing other than a fig leaf and, in the words of the Joint Committee on Human Rights. This is still all part of Mr Llwyds speech and should therefore be cited in the same way as the rest of this section and verbatim as written since it is a direct quotation from Hansard.

a virtually meaningless safeguard against wrongful exercise of the power.

Sir Menzies Campbell:

I will vote against the Government because any time any Government seek to diminish the freedoms that are the cornerstone of our system, it is our duty collectively and individually to hold that Government to account and to subject them to the most rigorous scrutiny. That duty transcends all our other responsibilities; it is our primary duty....

The concessions leave far too much to the discretion of the Home Secretary, they are...complicated to the point of incomprehensibility and ambiguity, and they blur the distinction between the responsibility of Parliament and the administration of justice. If we make a judgment that it is necessary to introduce the reserve power, and if that judgment is based on the circumstances surrounding an individual case, we inevitably become engaged in the administration of justice...I have searched my memory, and searched elsewhere, but I can think of no other instance when the House of the Commons has been called on to pass legislation based on individual circumstances after criminal proceedings have been commenced against an individual. If that is not a novel constitutional doctrine, I do not know what is.

MP David Davies actually resigned over the issue subsequent to the vote. His view, expressed at the Commons debate prior to the vote on 12th June 2008 (11 Jun 2008: Column 383),[3] was expressed thus;

In the Home Affairs Committee and in the Public Bill Committee, I approached the subject with a very open mind. I have not been shy about expressing my view in the House that we need more people locked up in prisons; I have even argued with my Front-Bench colleagues on the subject. We need prisoners to serve longer sentences, and we need a lot more prisons to be built to house them all. I add one important caveat: people should not be locked up in prisons or police cells unless they have been charged and convicted of an offence. That is absolutely fundamental to the liberties of people in this country.

When the Home Affairs Committee took evidence, and in the Public Bill Committee, it became obvious that the Government have not properly thought out their case. They were setting all sorts of constitutional precedents that some people have not considered.... We have seen the selective way in which the Government have used the evidence that was put before them, and their selective quoting of the Home Affairs Committee report on the 42-day limit. There was not unanimous support for an extension beyond 42 days.... we said that if there was to be an extension beyond 42 days, there would, of course, have to be safeguards. We went along with that, rather unwillingly, so that there could be some form of consensus, and so that we did not have to divide the whole Committee on the issue. We said that although it would have to be amended, the Civil

Contingencies Act 2004 could be used in some form instead of the so-called safeguards that the Government came up with, to which I shall turn in a minute.

I was not in Parliament when the decision was taken to invade Iraq. I suspect that I would probably have gone along with the consensus, had I been there, because I have always thought that those bright people in all parties in Parliament must know more than me, even though my gut instinct told me that the invasion was wrong. I even trusted Tony Blair when he said, 'Trust in me.' I have learned the hard way that we should never trust Ministers or assume that people in positions of power are any better than us.

I did not appreciate the way in which the evidence that the Home Affairs Committee heard was twisted and turned by Ministers. On one of the first times that the Director of Public Prosecutions gave evidence to the Committee, he made it absolutely clear that he was against an extension beyond 42 days, yet his words were twisted and turned. We met the director general of MI5, and I met a senior member of one of the security services. They spoke to us in confidence, but now that a statement on pre-charge detention has been published on MI5's website, it is fair to say that we knew months ago that MI5 was not calling for the measure, yet we had to listen while Ministers gave a different impression. We have heard lots of quotes from Sir Ian Blair, and that is reasonable enough, but we did not hear about all the other senior police officers, such as Sir Paul Condon, who did not believe that any extension was justified. Throughout the process, the Government have quoted selectively.

The fact is that the issue comes down to something very simple: if the police have enough evidence to arrest somebody, they must have something tangible to go on. I can say that as a serving police officer. A police officer cannot simply go around arresting people without any evidence that they have done something wrong, and rightly so. Of course, it might take a little while to get together enough evidence for a charge. I am sure that in the past there was a temptation to get as much evidence as one possibly could, so that the strongest possible charge could be bought, but in some ways, the case for doing that has been removed, because we are to implement post-charge questioning – a measure that all my colleagues and I fully supported. That part of the Government's case no longer arises. As Sir Ken Macdonald said to us, if within 28 days enough evidence cannot be found to bring some charge against someone, any prosecution is likely to be very unsafe.

Many colleagues have spoken about the Civil Contingencies Act and the fact that we would have the longest detention in the western world. I shall not add to that, as I want to allow others an opportunity to speak.

One would have to be sentenced to more than three months in prison to serve 42 days, because of early release, release on tagging and all the other Government initiatives to turf genuine criminals out of prison. Somebody who has been held for 42 days or longer without charge would have done the equivalent of a prison sentence of more than three months. What is the latest proposal that the Government have come up with today to try to make those people feel better? 'Okay, we arrested you at 5 o'clock in the morning, quite possibly at gunpoint, took you off, kept you there for 42 days, didn't even tell you why we had you in there, but here's some money. Don't worry about it. You were innocent, but have some money' – as if that will make anything better.

The Government have relied on emotion to try to get their case across today. They have not relied on facts. I am glad to be able to distinguish myself from rebels on the Government Benches by saying that if they wanted to do something about terrorism, they have had plenty of opportunity. They could, as my hon. Friend the Member for Shipley (Philip Davies) said, have done away with the Human Rights Act, which has given so much succour to terrorists. It has allowed people who we know have been involved in terrorism to come into this country. The Government have then found that they are prevented from deporting them, prevented from putting them in prison until they go back, and prevented even from keeping them in their own homes while tagged – all because of the Human Rights Act.

The Government tried to blame the judiciary, yet they brought in the Human Rights Act, which allowed the judiciary to do that. They could get rid of the Human Rights Act in a matter of weeks, if they wanted to. They could insist that people who come to this country learn our language and start to integrate, instead of allowing them to set up their own communities and maintain practices that are unacceptable in this country, such as forced marriage, polygamy and female genital mutilation, to which a blind eye is being turned by the Government. They should insist on integration, getting people to learn our language and getting them to fit in with our culture and traditions, rather than passing legislation that will do away with the liberties that British subjects and citizens have enjoyed for hundreds of years.

Just as King John had to be brought to book by the barons and the lords when they brought in the Magna Carta in 1215, if we lose the vote tonight, I hope that, once again, the Lords will come to our rescue – the rescue of the liberties of British people.

Clear strength of feeling was thus expressed by MP's in the Commons debate, but was it justified? How do plans to increase the length of time terror suspects can be held without being charged compare with other countries, for example? In France, suspects can be held without access to a lawyer for 72 hours and in pre-trial detention for up to four years. In Germany, suspects must be seen by a Judge within 48 hours but can be held without trial during the period of investigation. This must be reviewed by a Judge at least every six months. In Greece, suspects may be held without charge for up to 12 months, or 18 months in extraordinary cases, which requires a warrant to be issued by the public prosecutor whilst in Italy suspects may be held for 24 hours without seeing a lawyer. In Norway, suspects can be held for a maximum of 48 hours, but a Judge can increase this period to cover the period of an investigation if it passes a test of 'proportionality'. In Spain, terror suspects can be held for 72 hours without their lawyer or relatives being informed, and this can be increased to a maximum of 13 days. Finally in the US, under the 2001 Patriot Act, the Attorney General can detain foreign suspects but must start deportation proceedings within seven days. Suspects can be held for periods of six months but cases must be reviewed within a further six months. Currently in England and Wales[4] the level of restriction under normal circumstances is such that if an individual is arrested for a criminal offence, the maximum length of time that this person can be detained without charge is 96 hours. Where that detention is carried out on the basis of terrorism, however, the period of detention can be longer. Originally under section 41 of the Terrorism Act 2000 the initial period of time that an individual could be detained was 7 days. This was subsequently extended to 14 days by the Criminal Justice Act 2003. After the July 2005 London bombings an argument was put forward to raise the length of time to 90 days but after a defeat in the House of Commons a period of 28 days was finally agreed. In relation to suspects' rights in detention, during the first forty eight hours the position of the terrorism detainee is comparable to that of a suspected criminal detained under the provisions of the Police and Criminal Evidence Act 1984 (PACE). This difference comes at the end of the 48 hour period. At that point, the decision about continued detention passes to a Judge. Under PACE 1984, the power to extend detention rested with the Home Secretary and appeared to be entirely at his or her discretion. The lack of any judicial review of this extended period has brought the UK Government into conflict with the European Court of Human Rights. This can be demonstrated by the case of *Brogan v United Kingdom* [1989] in which four applicants had been detained, on the authorisation of the Home Secretary, for periods of between four days and six hours, to six days and 16.5 hours. The European Court of Human Rights recognised the particular problems presented by terrorist offences. It also acknowledged that these difficulties might have the effect of prolonging the period during which a person suspected of terrorist offences may, without violating Article 5, be kept in custody before being brought before a Judge. Stone et al. (2006: 396) ask:

> What is the rationale for extended detention in terrorist cases? It cannot be simply that such cases are more complex: serious fraud cases, for example, may be equally involved and contain international elements. Due to the international nature of modern terrorism, there exists the need to employ interpreters, the need to decrypt large numbers of computer hard drives and to analyse the product as well as disclose prior to interview, the need to make safe premises where extremely hazardous material may be found, the need to obtain and analyse communications data from service providers, the need to allow time for religious observance by detainees, and the fact that suspects often use one firm of solicitors which causes delay in the process.

In spite of sentiments such as this and the defeat of 42-day detention in the Counter-Terrorism Bill on 12th June 2008, the Government have subsequently restated their intentions in a Statement made by the Parliamentary under-Secretary of State for the Home Office, Lord West of Spithead on 24th March (Column 567 – 569: 2009.) Hansard[5] reports this as follows:

> Mr Speaker, I have today published the revised version of the Government's strategy for countering international terrorism. Protecting the safety of everyone in Britain is the primary duty, and abiding obligation, of government. Recent events in Northern Ireland were a chilling reminder that the threat of terrorism has not left our shores. They demonstrate the need to continue to adapt our approach so that we can deal with this threat wherever it emerges. As we set out in our CONTEST strategy today, the greatest security threat we

face comes from al-Qaeda and related groups and individuals. Our aim will always be to reduce the risk to the United Kingdom and our interests overseas from international terrorism, so that people can go about their lives freely and with confidence. We know that the threat is severe. We know that an attack is highly likely and could happen without warning at any time. And we know that this new form of terrorism is different in scale and nature from the terrorist threats we have had to deal with in recent decades. This new form of terrorism is rooted in conflicts overseas and the fragility of some states. It is grounded in an extremist ideology that uses violence to further its ends. It exploits the opportunities created by modern technologies and seeks to radicalise young people into violent extremism.

The threat now comes from the al-Qaeda leadership and its immediate associates located mainly on the Pakistan/Afghanistan border, as well as from its affiliates and from others, including rogue individuals, who espouse similar views. As honourable Members across the House will know, not least my right honourable friends my predecessors, on whose important work this strategy builds, these groups have planned a succession of attacks against the United Kingdom, with the aim of causing mass casualties. Thanks to the hard work and dedication of thousands of people, we have had considerable success in stopping terrorists in their tracks and bringing those responsible to justice. I pay tribute to their work. We have disrupted over a dozen attempted terrorist plots in the UK, and since 2001 almost 200 people have been convicted of terrorist-related offences. But the threat remains and is always evolving. This strategy takes that into account, draws on what we have learnt about how to counter it, and reflects the increased resources we have rightly made available to keep Britain safe. In recent years, the number of police dedicated to counterterrorism work has grown from 1,700 to 3,000. The Security Service has doubled in size. We have trained tens of thousands of people throughout the country in how to prepare for and protect against a terrorist attack, and we are working with communities to prevent the spread of violent extremism. We currently spend £2.5 billion on countering terrorism. By 2011 this will rise to £3.5 billion, the majority of it on the main focus of work–pursuing terrorists wherever they are and stopping their attacks.

The CONTEST strategy remains centred on four key areas: 'Pursue', 'Prevent', 'Protect' and 'Prepare'. We have updated each of these. 'Pursue' will make use of new resources and new legislation available to the intelligence agencies and police to investigate and disrupt terrorist networks here and overseas, and to prosecute those responsible. 'Prevent' will reach more people than ever before, as we step up our efforts to stop people becoming terrorists or supporting violent extremism. This reflects our better understanding of the causes of radicalisation and includes new programmes and new partnerships with communities here and overseas. 'Protect' aims to strengthen our defences against an attack, through a strong border, improved resilience in our critical national infrastructure and greater protection for the crowded places where we all live, work, shop and play. 'Prepare' will limit the impact of any attacks that do occur, with tens of thousands of emergency services workers, security guards, store managers and others trained and equipped to deal with an incident. Every region of the country now has plans to deal with an attack, and so to improve our ability to recover and ensure a return to normal as soon as possible. There is also dedicated cross-government work on the specific threat posed by terrorist use of chemical, biological, radiological or nuclear weapons and explosives.

The vital work to counter terrorism cannot be done by central government, the police and agencies working alone. That is why this revised strategy is based on work right across central, devolved and local government, together with our international partners and with local communities. In addressing both the immediate threats and their longer-term causes, and how we will deliver action at a local, national and international level, our aim has been to publish as full and as open an account of our work as possible. The strategy also draws close links with other government policies that are essential to its delivery, including conflict reduction, our international aid programme, counter-proliferation, our work in Afghanistan and Pakistan, and our support to communities here, building cohesion, empowerment and equality in this country.

The challenge that all of us in this House face is to strike the right balance between measures to protect security and the right to life with the impact on the other rights we hold dear. CONTEST is based on clear and unambiguous principles. And my approach to protecting Britain's security in the face of the terrorist threat will always be underpinned by our core shared values, including the protection of human rights, the rule of law, and democratic and accountable government. The Government have sought that balance at all times. But we remain uncompromising on a number of issues. We oppose the use of torture in all its forms. We have always condemned the practice of extraordinary rendition and will continue to do so. This strategy is comprehensive and wide-ranging. In publishing it, my primary aim is to reassure the British people that we are doing all in our power to protect this country through our relentless pursuit of terrorists and our determination to prevent violent extremism. We continue to depend on the determination, engagement, and vigilance of all in Britain to keep us safe. I commend this Statement to the House.

Unsurprisingly, concern has been expressed at the Government's 'Pursue', 'Prevent', 'Protect' and 'Prepare' strategy. A recurring theme in the development of State powers in any democratic society is the balance between the ideals of liberal legalism, with their emphasis on protecting the citizen from the coercive potential of the State, and the need to have a police force with sufficient powers to enforce the law effectively and efficiently. Thus there may be circumstances when certain restrictions upon individual freedom are sometimes necessary and are implemented for the safety and well-being of the majority of people. In a previous publication (Moss 2009) I gave an example of this in the case of air steward Gaetan Dugas[6] where I discussed what the driving forces might be for the deprivation of liberty. In this case, it could have been justified on the grounds of a known and quantifiable health risk. I demonstrated also that a somewhat different approach was taken in the US in relation to a man who may have exposed passengers on board two trans-Atlantic flights to a dangerous form of tuberculosis. The infected man travelled from Atlanta to Paris and then from Prague to Montreal in May 2007 and was subsequently quarantined by the US Centre for Disease Control and Prevention. CDC officials said the man was potentially infectious during this period, and recommended that crew members and passengers onboard the same flights seek medical attention. It was the first such federal quarantine order to be issued in over 44 years; according to the CDC the last such order was issued in 1963, to quarantine a patient with smallpox.

Importantly, what do these examples tell us about who decides what is reasonable for whom and in what circumstances, in relation to security, risk and individual liberty? First, it appears that in certain circumstances there may be principles which drive the kind of restrictions that might legitimately be imposed. One of these driving forces might be quarantine. In the second example concerning the spread of tuberculosis, this risk was the driver for the deprivation of liberty on the grounds of a known and quantifiable health risk. However, in relation to the first example, in which the potential spread of HIV was similarly a known and quantifiable risk, this did not result in deprivation of the individuals' liberty. What could the explanation for this difference be? I have commented previously (Moss 2009) that potentially, where issues of finance, politics or prestige are involved, risk factors might become subordinate. Could the same be said in relation to issues of national security? More specifically, when a threat to the nation is perceived and the organs of Government feel the need to be seen to be doing something in the face of a moral panic created by postulations about the war on terror, then arguably this might pave the way for a greater level of restriction based precisely on the importance of political expediency. Perhaps this is also how the idea of detention without trial has become acceptable. It is pertinent at this point, therefore, to focus on exactly what is meant by detention without trial.

What is detention without trial?

Detention without trial means that people are deprived of their freedom even though they have not been tried or found guilty of any offence in a court of law. For this reason, within this chapter the ideology of habeas corpus is crucial to any debate about prolonged detention without trial. *Habeas corpus* is Latin for 'You may have the body'. Originally a writ requiring that any detained individual must be brought before a court of law so that the legality of their detention may be examined, it is unfortunately rarely used in modern times although it could be used by anyone who believes they are being unlawfully detained. Habeas corpus does not determine guilt or innocence, but whether an individual is legally detained, and if not, they must be set free. The origins of the right to habeas corpus dates back to Anglo Saxon times but the Habeas Corpus Act was passed by Parliament in 1679 and thus guaranteed this right in law. As I mentioned in Chapter 1 it establishes that;

> ...no man of what estate or condition that he be, shall be put out of land or tenement, nor taken, nor imprisoned, nor disinherited, nor put to death, without being brought in answer by due process of law.

Although it would be fair to assume, on the basis of this, that everyone has a right to habeas corpus, and it is inconceivable that a time would come when that would not be the case, there have been, and continue to be, many examples of when the right appears to have been suspended for various reasons. Examples I have discussed before include internment in Ireland in 1971 but the most recent example is the pro-longed detention of 'terror suspects' post-9/11 and 7/7 facilitated in the UK by the Anti-Terrorism, Crime and Security Act 2001.

Detention without trial is usually justified on the basis of a need (or heightened need) for national security when it is alleged that the person in question poses a threat to the State.

However, it is possible for detention without trial to occur in other circumstances. For example, in the UK a person may be sectioned under the Mental Health Act 1983 if s/he is deemed (by two independent medical practitioners) to be either a danger to him/herself or to others. For the purposes of this chapter, however, I want to highlight the very particular circumstances where individuals are detained by virtue of the fact that they are thought to be actively involved in terrorist activities and are known as either 'special interest detainees' or 'illegal combatants.' It is, of course, important to remember that the right to liberty is not absolute. Most societies limit this right in certain circumstances where it is deemed by law to be necessary for the proper functioning of society. As a result, imprisonment is the most widely used criminal sanction, but this is normally only used where such detention is based on a pre-existing domestic legal norm establishing both the reason and the procedures for that detention, including the transparency of the period of detention and the likely time of release. Under the normal circumstances of detention therefore, the law allows individuals to foresee what sort of conduct will lead to detention and that it will not be arbitrary, and to have some awareness of the likely period of detention associated with particular criminal sanctions and an expected time for release. Detention without trial is, of course, a very different matter, because it undermines fundamental notions of personal liberty and makes assumptions about a person's potential risk to society.

Governments like those in the UK and US therefore justify detaining individuals without trial on the basis of the need for national security. This has most recently occurred in relation to the current concern over the so-called 'war on terror' subsequent to the attacks of 9/11 in the US and the 7/7 bombings in London. It has also resulted in the assertion by Governments that the safety and well-being of the majority outweigh an individual's right to personal liberty. The opposing view is that citizens *do* have a right to security but the greater the perception of a crisis is, then the easier it is to justify this. More important, if we accept that detention without trial is being exercised, then it is all the more important to determine whether this approach is being abused, or used for the wrong reasons. In chapter two I made reference to Locke's theory of fundamental civil liberties and human rights and Rousseau's notion of the social contract, both of which make reference to the paradigm of the contract between individuals and the state which allows for the ceding of power to the State in return for the state overseeing the application of the law and acting as guarantor of the fundamental rights of each of its citizens. I also mentioned that Rawls (1971) takes this theory further by arguing that in order to enjoy a society that will provide each of us with the 'good life', it is necessary to accept existence within a society that not only protects fundamental human rights but does so irrespective of a person's standing, class or any other individual difference. Further to this, Rawls (ibid.) has suggested that for this to work for the majority of people they will accept this situation based upon general considerations, not necessarily having regard to their own personal situation. He argues that such personal knowledge merely tempts people to select principles of justice that are advantageous to them – thus 'rigging the rules of the game.' The process of reasoning without personal bias is referred to by Rawls refers to as 'The Veil of Ignorance'. It is relevant to highlight this further within the context of this chapter as another possible explanation as to why the majority of people appear to accept the unfairness of detention without trial without much comment. Generally speaking, the problem of detention without trial is one which does not affect the majority of people either here or in the US Rawls suggests that in the majority of social situations a general consensus about what is accepted as fair is usually agreed by the majority of people and thus so are the rules, or laws that are subsequently passed to underline this. He refers to this as a form of procedural justice operating at the highest level. Unlike Locke (1690) whose social contract exists between free, equal individuals who have some knowledge about themselves and one another and thus choose to accede to a fair justice system for all, Rawls contends that this version can only result in unfairness because within any society people will take advantage of their skills, social situation, wealth or gender (to give just a few examples) in order to bias the system to try to gain a more advantageous result. Rawls claims that the only way that this can be neutralised is by redefining the initial situation in order that individuals no longer have access to the type of knowledge which can distort their judgement and thus result in unfair or biased principles. He comments (1971: 12) that:

> Among the essential features of this situation is that no one knows his place in society, his class position or social status, nor does anyone know his fortune in the distribution of natural assets and

abilities, his intelligence, strength and the like. I shall even assume that the parties do not know their conceptions of the good or their special psychological propensities. The principles of justice are chosen behind a veil of ignorance.

With respect to Rawls, I do not agree with the paradigm of the veil of ignorance in relation to the exercise of justice. Ignorance is not bliss, and it is precisely because of the lack of transparency about issues such as detention without trial (and, of course, torture and extraordinary rendition) that many people are not aware of the realities of the current situation with regard to these issues. This suits Governments since keeping people in ignorance serves a purpose. The less people know, the less they are able to criticise and the easier it is to govern. In my opinion this does not result in a fairer system of justice but one where although laws exist (which may lull populations into a false sense of security), the Government can covertly choose whether to apply that law, to ignore it or to sidestep it, depending on what appears necessary at the time. If they are exposed subsequently as not following the law, they can then justify their actions on the basis of defence, national security, or, most recently of course, the war on terror.

It is pertinent to highlight that Dworkin (1986) argues that often, the moral principles that societies are wedded to, are wrong – even to the extent that some crimes can appear acceptable if your principles are skewed enough. Dworkin suggests that in order to discover and apply these principles, courts interpret legislation in order to achieve an interpretation that best explains and justifies past legal practice. Therefore, in order to make sense, subsequent interpretation flows from the notion of law as integrity. Thus, Dworkin's argument is that the law is 'interpretive' and where legal rights are controversial, the best interpretation involves the what he calls (1986: 119) the 'right answer' thesis.

Suppose the legislature has passed a statute stipulating that 'sacrilegious contracts shall henceforth be invalid.' The community is divided as to whether a contract signed on Sunday is, for that reason alone, sacrilegious. It is known that very few of the legislators had that question in mind when they voted, and that they are now equally divided on the question of whether it should be so interpreted. Tom and Tim have signed a contract on Sunday, and Tom now sues Tim to enforce the terms of the contract, whose validity Tim contests. Shall we say that the judge must look for the right answer to the question of whether Tom's contract is valid, even though the community is deeply divided about what the right answer is? Or is it more realistic to say that there simply is no right answer to the question?

Dworkin (ibid.) admits that this is not to say that everyone will have the same answer (a consensus of what is 'right') nor that any answer would necessarily be justified in exactly in the same way for every person. His suggestion is that there will be a necessary answer for each individual if he applies himself correctly to the legal question. So in relation specifically to the question of detention without trial, what safeguards *do* exist in relation to the abuse of such a power?

The law relating to detention without trial

The International Covenant on Civil and Political Rights 1966 (ICCPR) currently protects an individual's right to liberty and security of the person, under Article 9.

Article 9 gives several procedural rights of protection from arbitrary detention:

- The detainee must be informed of the reasons for his/her arrest
- The detainee must be given appropriate and relevant legal information in relation to the specifics of any acts or threats that s/he was supposed to be involved in.
- It is not be sufficient to justify the detention purely on the basis of a vague or more general accusation about the risk such an individual posed.

The position that International Humanitarian Law takes on this issue is also important. In relation to this, situations of armed conflict give rise to another set of rules for the protection of the individual. These are the rules of international humanitarian law which limit the conduct of states in times of war. The major codified bases of humanitarian law relevant to this are the Geneva Conventions of 1949. Under these Conventions, persons are either 'combatants' (meaning that they actively participate in hostilities) or they are 'non-combatants' (meaning those who do not actively participate). These two theoretical groups of individuals have the right to be treated as Prisoners of War (POW's) which means they can be detained for as long as active hostilities are taking place. However, because they have POW status, they are supposed to have special protection. The purpose of their detention therefore is not punishment but simply to prevent them from actively taking part in a war situation. The special status of a POW also means that they are supposed to be released and repatriated as soon as a war situation is at an end. The Geneva Conventions are relevant, but it is important to remember that they were drafted after the cessation of two conventional world wars which were rather different from the wars that are waged today. For example, in World Wars I and II, the termination of active hostilities could more easily be determined than it is today. In the case of the 'war on terror' how do you tell when the war is over? This means identified terrorist 'combatants' may be detained indefinitely in case they 'take up arms again' and re-engage in terrorist action. In such a situation, the so-called 'war on terror' has no end and the terrorist detainee has no realistic prospect of release.

According to the international law of human rights, for detention to be considered non-arbitrary and legal, a number of conditions have to be satisfied as follows;

1. Detention must be objective in each individual case.
2. In human rights law, such grounds must be stated in some prior legal basis and, in addition, comply with standards of basic justice, that is they must be reasonable, appropriate and proportional.
3. Humanitarian law authorises the detention of combatants by reason of their status as POW's as well as the detention of civilians for imperative security reasons of absolute necessity.
4. Detainees must be told why they have been arrested and detained.
5. Decisions to detain must be reviewed by a neutral third authority, who must be impartial and competent and rely on fair procedure.
6. Although a specific time limit cannot be found in human rights law and jurisprudence, the permissible period of administrative detention without trial must be measured in hours or days as opposed to weeks, following which judicial review must commence.
7. Indefinite detention without judicial review is prohibited.

There is also case law relating to this area which sheds important light on other issues. For example, the case of *Brogan v United Kingdom (1988)* established that Article 5 requires that the review of the need for continued detention take place promptly. The applicant in Brogan was detained for four days in accordance with section 12 of the Prevention of Terrorism Act 1984 and it was held by the Court that this breached the promptness requirement of Article 5. It is also possible, according to the terms of Article 15, that a contracting state may derogate from certain articles in times of war or when there is a public emergency threatening the life of the nation. This means that the state can in certain circumstances depart from the terms of the Convention if it can justify the need to do so by demonstrating that such a state of emergency exists but this must be significant and severe. The precedent for this, but which is still relevant today, was set in the *Greek Case (1969)* in which it was stated that the public emergency must be;

- actual or imminent
- affecting the whole nation
- threatening the continuance of the organised life of the community
- a crisis or danger which is exceptional, where the normal measures permitted by the Convention for the maintenance of public safety, health and order are plainly inadequate.

Most recently, of course, the Article 15 derogation order was considered in the light of the threat posed by terrorism subsequent to the attacks on New York and Washington on September 11th 2001. It was a as a direct result of this that the UK considered there to be a threat to the nation from individuals suspected of involvement in international terrorism. In particular, the Government's focus has since been on foreign nationals present in the UK who are suspected of being concerned in the commission, preparation or instigation of acts of international terrorism, of being members of organisations or groups which are so concerned or of having links with members of such organisations or groups, and who are a threat to the national security of the UK. As a result, a public emergency, within the meaning of Article 15(1) of the Convention, was declared to be in existence in the UK.

The US has always been rather vocal in support of human rights, but it also has quite a severe international policy on terrorism. It has enjoyed a position of importance as a driving force for strengthening the human rights ideal and took the lead in drafting the Universal Declaration of Human Rights, building the international human rights system and lending its voice and influence on behalf of human rights in many parts of the world. It has been at the forefront of numerous human rights battles and has contributed significantly to building a global consensus regarding the importance of human rights as a restraint on legitimate Governmental conduct. However, the US administration has adopted a rather narrow interpretation of aspects of the Geneva Convention, which effectively allows detainees to be kept in long-term arbitrary detention despite international prohibitions. The Third Geneva Convention provides that captured combatants are to be treated as prisoners of war until a 'competent tribunal' determines otherwise. The US has refused to bring any of the detainees before a tribunal and continued to claim that none of them qualified as a prisoner of war. Similarly, the UK used indefinite detention as a means of counter-terrorism in Northern Ireland between 1971 and 1975. As stated earlier, they called it 'internment.' The UK has not employed the 'enemy combatant' approach but has used immigration laws to justify the detention of terrorist suspects. Since 9/11 and following the terrorist bombings of the public transport system in London in July 2005, former Prime Minister Tony Blair stated, 'the rules of the game had changed' and outlined ideas for amending the law in the UK to tackle this threat to society. Simultaneously, concerns were expressed by civil liberties organisations that the Government might respond to these attacks in a way that amounted to a significant attack on individual human rights while at the same time proving to be counterproductive in the fight against terrorism. In terms of what UK law currently exists in relation to detention without trial, it was the Anti-Terrorism, Crime and Security Act 2001 (hereafter referred to as ATCSA) which first mentioned detention without trial for foreigners suspected of being involved in terrorism. The Prevention of Terrorism Act 2005 subsequently made it possible for the UK Government to expand the emergency provisions to which foreigners are subjected within the context of war on terror to cover the whole population. This change is important because it calls into question the notion of habeas corpus, the ancient common law rule which has historically been an important instrument for the safeguarding of individual freedom against arbitrary state action. The newly enacted law arguably attacked the formal notion of the separation of powers (the accepted British principle that Parliament, the supreme law-making body, and the Judiciary – the supposedly non-political body which interprets the law passed by Parliament – should operate entirely independently). It does this by giving to the Secretary of State for Home Affairs, judicial prerogatives to detain suspects without trial on the basis not of what they have done, but according to what the Home Secretary thinks they could have done or might do in the future. Article 21 allows for indefinite incarceration based on a certificate issued by the Secretary of State for Home Affairs because it effectively suspends the law for all persons not having either British citizenship or legal residence and those who do not have the right of protection as refugees. Therefore, the suspension of habeas corpus is less extensive than in the US, where all foreigners are affected. In order to pass this law, the UK Government instituted an exception to the European Convention on

Human Rights. This exception is based on the notion of a state of emergency and is thus an exception to Article 5, paragraph 1 of this convention, which guarantees personal liberties. According to Article 15 of the Convention, exceptional measures must be limited strictly to the minimum necessary as required by the situation. The Act does not allow for appeals to be made to the Special Immigration Appeals Commission. It is at this point pertinent to highlight where the legality of detention under the ATCSA has been challenged through the courts.

For example in the case of *A and Z and others v Secretary of State for the Home Department (2005)* , some of the applicants had been detained in a high-security prison for three years, with no prospect of release or trial. Due to the importance of the case, nine Judges in the House of Lords heard the case instead of the usual five, and the House held that the detentions were unlawful. By late 2004, the British Law Lords ruled that, because only foreigners suspected of being capable of, or implicated with, terrorist acts, could be detained without trial, that such anti-terrorist law was discriminatory, disproportionate and unlawful under Article 14 of the European Convention on Human Rights. It was subsequently proposed that rather than abolishing this measure, the power of detention without trial should be extended to all British citizens as well as foreign nationals. This caused an outcry concerning human rights and the principle of the burden of proof (an accused person is innocent until proven guilty), central to English constitutional tradition established since the Magna Carta in 1215. On December 22, 2004, the Secretary-General of the Council of Europe demanded the immediate abrogation of the 2001 Terrorism Act, stating that:

> Anti-terrorist legislation in the United Kingdom must be changed immediately. We will not win the war on terrorism if we undermine the foundation of our democratic societies.[7]

Subsequently, this legislation was repealed and replaced by the Prevention of Terrorism Act which was passed on March 11, 2005. This authorised the Home Secretary to initiate control orders over a person, potentially leading to house arrest, in cases where s/he has reason to suspect that an individual is or was implicated in an action linked with terrorism. The implementation of house arrest is the first time that this measure has been used in the UK.

Up to sixteen different restrictions can be placed on an individual who is subjected to such a control order, examples being the use of electronic tagging, surveillance, permission to search their premises and a curfew order. Such orders are made by the High Court following an application by the Home Secretary and imposed where an individual is suspected of having been involved in terrorist-related activity. Breach of a control order, without reasonable excuse, is a criminal offence punishable by up to five years imprisonment. Interestingly, justification for the decision to place a person under supervision is not founded upon objective facts, but in the suspicion that falls on that person or in the intention that is attributed to that person.

If we remind ourselves that according to Article 5, everyone has the right to liberty and security of person and that no one shall be deprived of his/her liberty unless they are lawfully arrested and detained after being convicted by a competent court, it is relevant to consider the fact that cases taken under Article 5 have reached the courts several times in the context of many different issues including prison sentences, parole opportunities and tariffs. It is in looking at the decisions of the Judiciary within these cases that it is possible to establish what sort of legal safeguard against unlawful detention without trial is afforded by Article 5 and whether this is, in fact, effective.

In *R (on the application of Smith) v Secretary of State for the Home Department [2005]* it was held that an independent tribunal, and not a minister, should determine the length of time that a prisoner serves when sentenced to be detained at Her Majesty's pleasure. Perhaps the most well-known case in relation to Article 5 however is that of *Republic of Ireland v UK (1978)* in which the UK Government, faced with serious acts of terrorism perpetrated by members of the Irish Republican Army (IRA) and Loyalist groups in Northern Ireland, introduced special powers of arrest and detention without trial, which were widely used, chiefly against the IRA. Under Article 15(1) it is possible for the UK Government to apply for what is called a 'notice of derogation' from Article 5. This essentially means that should the Secretary-General of the Council of Europe accept the UK Government's argument that in view of the 'public emergency threatening the life of the nation' they should be allowed to sidestep the prohibition on detention without trial. The Government of the Republic of Ireland brought an application before the Commission alleging, amongst other things;

(i) that the extrajudicial detention infringed Article 5 (right to liberty) and was not saved by Article 15;
(ii) that various interrogation practices – in particular the so-called 'five techniques', which included wall-standing, hooding and deprivation of sleep and food – and other practices to which

suspects were subjected amounted to torture and inhuman or degrading treatment contrary to Article 3; and

(iii) that the use of the special powers primarily against IRA members constituted discrimination in violation of Article 14.

Specifically in relation to the issue of detention without trial, the court also considered the subject of extrajudicial deprivation of liberty and in particular the question of whether it was possible to derogate from the right to liberty under Article 15 if it could be argued that this was as a result of a public emergency threatening life of nation. In relation to this issue the court found that;

(a) The relevant legislation on extrajudicial deprivation of liberty did not involve derogations from paragraphs 1 to 4 of Article 5.

(b) The existence of a public emergency threatening the life of the nation within the meaning of Article 15 was perfectly clear from the facts.

(c) A State had a wide margin of appreciation, but not an unlimited power, to determine whether the life of the nation was threatened by a public emergency and, if so, how far it might go in attempting to overcome it, the Court being empowered to rule on whether the State had gone beyond the 'extent strictly required by the exigencies' of the crisis in derogating from the Convention.

(d) Neither the Convention nor the general principles applicable to international tribunals required observance of the strict rules of evidence.

(e) The British Government was reasonably entitled, in the circumstances, to have recourse to measures outside the scope of the ordinary law in the shape of extrajudicial deprivation of liberty, even where the person was arrested solely in order to obtain information about others, bearing in mind that the maximum period of detention in such a case was 48 hours.

(f) It was not for the Court to substitute, for the British Government's assessment, any other assessment of what might have been the most prudent or expedient policy to combat terrorism. The Court had to take account of the conditions and circumstances prevailing when the measures were taken and not assess their efficacy retrospectively. Accordingly, the fact that the policy of extrajudicial detention had subsequently been abandoned did not justify the conclusion that its previous use had not been 'strictly required'.

(g) A State struggling against a public emergency threatening the life of the nation would be rendered defenceless if it were required to accomplish all safeguards at once and the interpretation of Article 15 must leave a place for progressive adaptations.

(h) As the requirements of the Article were met, the derogations from Article 5 were not in breach of the Convention.

(i) The use of extrajudicial detention chiefly against the IRA and not against Loyalists could not in the circumstances be said to violate Article 14, which prohibits discrimination in the enjoyment of the rights and problems guaranteed by the Convention.

Notwithstanding decisions such as that in *Ireland v UK (1978)*, more recent judgments by UK courts have taken a different stance. This can best be demonstrated by the case of *Secretary of State for the Home Department v JJ and others [2006]* in which an 18-hour curfew had been imposed on an individual living in a one-bedroom flat who was also tagged and monitored. The police had the power to search the flat at any time and the individual in question was only able to socialise inside or outside the flat if he obtained prior Home Office permission. In coming to a decision about whether this treatment constituted an unlawful deprivation of liberty, the House of Lords considered a number of other cases including *Engel v The Netherlands* (1976) and *Guzzardi v Italy* (1980). These cases had established, amongst other things, that;

(i) Deprivation of liberty could take a number of forms and would not necessarily be limited to traditional ideas of deprivation such as being detained in custody.

(ii) Each individual's situation should be judged on its own merits and in relation to this, the court should take into consideration the affect that situation had on each individual in terms of the type of detention, its length and how the detention was implemented.

(iii) Deprivation of liberty should be judged not on a single feature of an individual's situation taken on its own, but in the context of a combination of measures which might have that result.

Taking into consideration the precedents laid down in these cases, as well as the facts of the individual case in question, the House of Lords decision was that the type of non-derogating control order made by the Home Secretary in *JJ and others [2006] did* amount to a deprivation of liberty, contrary to Article 5 of the European Convention on Human Rights, and was therefore unlawful. The court also commented that although a common sense approach would probably suggest that deprivation of liberty normally meant being locked in a prison cell, the court in each case would have to consider the nature of the confinement, its duration and intensity and the overall effect on the life of the person involved. In this particular case the 18-hour curfew, together with the exclusion of social visitors, meant that the individuals were, to all intents and purposes, being kept in solitary confinement and although their lives were no more regulated than a traditional prisoners life, the penalties for breaching the conditions of their detainment were potentially much more severe than for an ordinary prisoner. It is interesting to note that although this was the majority view expressed by the House of Lords, Lord Hoffman in his dissenting judgment commented that:

> ... the liberty of the subject and the right to habeas corpus were too precious to be sacrificed for any reason other than to safeguard the survival of the state. But one could only maintain that position if one confined the concept of deprivation of liberty to actual imprisonment, or something little different from it. To describe a person in the position of one of the present respondents as being for practical purposes in prison would be an extravagant metaphor; true his freedom was greatly restricted compared with an ordinary person; but that was not the comparison the law required. The question was whether he could be compared with someone in prison and, in his Lordship's opinion, he could not.

Contemporary examples of detention without trial

Contemporary examples of detention without trial have been slightly more in the public consciousness since the events of 9/11 and 7/7. At the forefront of this has been the treatment of detainees at Guantánamo Bay which remains the subject of much debate and contention in spite of US President Barack Obama's recent promise to close it down. This detainment camp, which serves as a joint military prison and interrogation centre, has occupied part of the US Navy base at Guantánamo Bay, Cuba, since 2002. The detention area has three camps; Camp Delta, Camp Iguana and Camp X-Ray. It has been argued that the war on terror had rendered the Convention virtually 'obsolete' because Guantánamo Bay has been a 'legal black hole' effectively beyond the reach of any jurisdiction. Certainly one of its most salient features is that Guantánamo and its prisoners have been effectively beyond both American and international law. Amnesty International released their *Memorandum to the US Government on the Rights of People in US Custody in Afghanistan and Guantánamo Bay* in 2002, which criticised the failure of the US Government to comply with standards of international law in the detention and treatment of detainees both in Afghanistan and Guantánamo Bay. It summarised the specific concerns of both the humanitarian and legal communities and stated that the US Government had:

- Transferred and held people in conditions that may amount to cruel, inhuman, or degrading treatment, and that violate other minimum standards relating to detention;
- Refused to inform people in its custody of all their rights;
- Refused to grant people in its custody to legal counsel, including during questioning by US and other authorities;
- Refused to grant people in its custody access to the courts to challenge the lawfulness of their detention;
- Undermined the presumption of innocence through a pattern of public commentary on the presumed guilt of the people in its custody in Guantánamo Bay;
- Failed to facilitate prompt communications with or grant access to family members;
- Undermined due process and extradition protections in cases of people taken into custody outside of Afghanistan and transferred to Guantánamo;
- Threatened to select foreign nationals for trial before military commissions;
- Raised the prospect of indefinite detention without charge or trial, or continued detention after acquittal, or repatriation that may threaten the principle of non-refoulement ('non-return' – laws which protect refugees from being returned to places there their lives or freedoms could be threatened.)

The first detainees arrived in January 2002 but in spite of the fact that they had been captured in Afghanistan – with whom the US had said it was at war – they were detained not as prisoners of war, but as 'unlawful combatants'. The effect of this labelling has effectively been to deny them any rights under the Geneva Conventions. Added to this, they have never been charged with terrorist crimes, will most probably never be charged and have merited no right to a fair trial – being effectively deemed guilty until proven innocent. The isolation of this site at the south eastern tip of Cuba means those detained there have been denied access to due process. Many prisoners past and present have given consistent and repeated testimony of serious abuse and ill treatment. There is also significant evidence both from US officials and in Government documents, of widespread abuse at the camp. The British detainees known as the Tipton Three alleged they were repeatedly beaten, shackled in painful positions for long periods and subjected to strobe lighting, loud music and extremes of hot and cold. Other detainees have reported beatings, sexual assaults and death threats. At least one man was 'waterboarded'. The US administration and the US military have sought to justify this detention by saying that it is a special programme of measures and does not amount to torture. Whilst it is true that based on European decisions about what amounts to torture, there is a very stringent test, the Red Cross have already reported that detention at Guantánamo has caused psychological suffering that has driven inmates mad, with scores of suicide attempts and three inmates killing themselves in 2006. It is pertinent to discuss in more illustrative detail some of the most high-profile examples of the process of detention without trial.

The first of the two examples within this chapter is that of Khalid el-Masri, a German national of Lebanese birth who claimed that he was kidnapped whilst on holiday in Macedonia in 2003 by the CIA – a US intelligence organisation – which transported him to Afghanistan and held him there for five months – during which he was tortured – before releasing him on the grounds of mistaken identity. Masri subsequently brought a case in 2005 for damages against the former Director of the CIA, three airlines and twenty other individuals who have not been publicly named (presumably because they are intelligence agents). An interesting issue which impacts upon this case substantially is the fact that during the Bush administration, the US Government invoked a judicial doctrine known as 'State secrets privilege'.[8] This effectively protects the Government from having its actions reviewed by the courts in all matters concerning national security. In this sense it is very similar to precedents that have been set in British courts[9] concerning what is known in UK constitutional law as the exercise of the prerogative. It also establishes that discovery of documents cannot take place if it is felt to compromise national security. El-Masri's lawyers[10] argued that cases should not be dismissed on the basis of inability to produce evidence due to the 'state secrets privilege' rule and subsequently took the case to Inter-American Commission on Human Rights[11] asking it to recommend that the kidnapping and torture of El-Masri was a violation of the US Declaration of the Rights of Man. This is an important development since although the US has always considered itself at the forefront of human rights, there have been no trials in relation to any individual who has alleged that they have been tortured by the US and, more recently, Barack Obama's Government – in spite of declaring initially that they would close down Guantánamo Bay and other similar detention facilities – has stated that it will continue to render and detain those suspected of terrorism. Diplomatic assurances have been given that suspects will not be mistreated but it remains to be seen what the difference between this policy and that of the Bush administration will be.

The implications of the El-Masri case are potentially far-reaching. Although 'State secrets privilege' is clearly supposed to be based on specific evidence and can be invoked both during requests for the discovery of documents and also at trial, both the Bush and Obama administrations have suggested that this immunity can be used in relation to a whole trial and not just specific evidence. Arguably the role of the US Judiciary ought to be to ensure that the effect of this type of doctrine should not be spread more widely on an ad hoc basis, as and when a particular Government decides it is efficacious or, in effect, to give them an immunity against allegations of illegal activity. This is in line with the basic notion of the separation of powers. The case of *Mohamed v Jeppeson Dataplan Inc* (2009)[12] established that a claim by the Government for a case to be dismissed in its entirety on the basis of 'states secret privilege' would not be accepted by the Judiciary on the basis of the doctrine of separation of powers and also a precedent set in the case of *Totten v United States* (1875)[13] which established that:

> complete dismissal requires a secret agreement or contract between the plaintiff and the government such that the very fact of the lawsuit would reveal a government secret–a reading that limits Totten to its facts. Here, there was no such secret agreement or contract between the plaintiffs and the government. Instead, the agreement was between the defendant and the government (as intervenor, not a party). The court thus treated the contract not as the very object of the suit (which might trigger the Totten privilege) but rather merely as a piece of evidence in the suit. This, according to the court, is not enough to trigger the Totten privilege; at most, it would trigger the Reynolds privilege.

However, as Davis (2007) reports:

> The US Court of Appeal for the Fourth Circuit in a unanimous decision dismissed the action of Khaled el-Masri asserting claims related to his extraordinary rendition. The basis of the dismissal is the state

secrets doctrine. This decision presents us with the lawlessness of the internal law situation we have. The Executive cannot be criminally prosecuted domestically...for its acts because it controls the federal prosecutors. If the Executive charges someone in court, then as a defense the person can seek to have evidence of horrible treatment brought in but will be confronted with the state secrets doctrine. If the Executive charges the person in a military commission the evidence issues again will come up against the state secrets doctrine. If the person injured brings a civil suit as did el-Masri, the Fourth Circuit has told us that the state secrets doctrine will be allowed to trump and dismissal will occur.[14]

The implications of this decision are important because it represents an enlargement of the doctrine of 'states secret privilege' with the ensuing effect of allowing far greater presidential powers to control any situations which the Government claims hinge on defence or national security. Essentially, therefore, this represents a worrying challenge to the rule of law and suggests that a much more transparent and in depth debate regarding 'state secrets privilege' should be undertaken given its current (apparent) limitless breadth and its corresponding potential to undermine the basic notions of habeas corpus.

The most well-known case concerning detention without trial is perhaps that of Maher Arar, a Canadian citizen who was born in Syria in 1970. Well educated, Arar had a master's degree in computer engineering and worked in Ottawa as a telecommunications engineer. After a holiday in Tunisia in September 2002, US officials detained Arar, claiming he had links to al-Qaeda. After holding him in solitary confinement for several weeks, during which he was denied access to a lawyer, he was then deported to Syria – even thought he had a Canadian passport – and was held there for a year during which he was tortured. A Canadian Commission of Inquiry subsequently found that he *had* been tortured and that he had no links to terrorism and awarded him a settlement of $10.5 million. It categorically stated that there was no evidence that Arar had committed any offence or that his activities constituted a threat to the security of Canada. In spite of this, however, the US Government has never apologised nor even accepted that Arar has no links with terrorism. The Arar Commission of Inquiry, headed by Sir Dennis O'Connor also made number of detailed recommendations about national security, including a review of the Royal Canadian Mounted Police's (RCMP) national security activities and other federal departments and agencies; a recommendation for increased information sharing; the creation of the Independent Complaints and National Security Review Agency for the RCMP (ICRA) with jurisdiction to review all of the RCMP's activities, including those related to national security; the extension of independent review, including complaint investigation and self-initiated review, to the national security activities of the Canada Border Services Agency (CBSA); the creation of INSRCC (Integrated National Security Review Coordinating Committee) – a review coordinating committee – to provide a unified intake mechanism for complaints regarding national security activities of federal entities, to help ensure that the statutory gateways are functioning as intended, and to report to the federal Government on accountability issues relating to Canada's national security practices, including their effects on human rights and freedoms.

There have been some doubts expressed about Arar's version of events and his subsequent £10.5 million payout – most particularly in Canada. Steel (2007) reports that if Arar was detained unlawfully, he would deserve compensation but suggests that the US or Syria should have paid this, not Canada. He also raises the issue of the RCMP's suspicion of Arar as far back as 2001, resulting from what he describes as 'frenetic' cross-border travel as well as the fact that Arar himself confessed to having been to Afghanistan and Pakistan in 1993 but then contradicted this by saying that he had never been to Afghanistan and never had any desire to go there. Steel (ibid.) comments that like the torture claims, these statements have never been followed up and that in his opinion the O'Connor Commission (2006) does not address these issues. Levant (2009) is also unconvinced by Arar's allegations and suggests that although the payout he received is unjustified, he is more concerned about the demoralising effect that his case had had on the Canadian police and security services and the possible encouragement that it may give to accused terrorists to wage what he calls 'legal and political war against Canada'. He continues that it is:

.... ironic that our western legal system, with its checks and balances designed to protect our liberal freedoms, has become the favourite instrument of illiberal attackers of the West. The Western Standard itself has been a victim of that abuse: In 2006, after we published a story about the Danish cartoons of Mohammed, a radical Calgary Imam used Alberta's human rights law to attack us. One year and thousands of dollars in legal fees later, we're still fending off that contortion of our justice system, while the Saudi-trained Imam's case is funded by Canadian taxpayers. His concept of 'human rights' is alien to our Canadian values, but that doesn't stop him from using a legal shield as a sword against his enemies. Unlike the federal government, we won't cave in to political pressure. Regrettably, the most important facts about Arar likely will remain confidential for security reasons. How frustrating it must be to be an RCMP officer or diplomat, knowing [about] the secret dossier on Arar, but unable to disclose it, either for reasons of security or a political gag order. We don't know those details either–but we know there is enough on the public record to conclude that there is more to Maher Arar than the media darling the mainstream press have manufactured.

Maher Arar's rendition also represents an example of an approach to the 'war on terror' which has been called the 'preventive paradigm'.[15] What are we to understand by this term which essentially explains the violation of both the US Constitution and the rights embodied in it? The paradigm is based on two arguments which the US Government used to justify their position in relation to the case. First, anyone who is rendered would be an 'alien' who would thus be subject to preventive techniques such as detention without trial or torture because their status afforded them no constitutional rights. Second, the Judiciary should not be able to question the Government's actions in such matters which are unreviewable – presumably because they concern matters of national security. Arar counterclaimed that because it was US officials who rendered him to Syria to be tortured and detained without trial, this represented a departure from due process and a violation of the universal prohibition on torture established in the case of *Rochin v California (1952)*. Second, that this was a violation of his Fifth Amendment right. In response, the US Government stated that Fifth Amendment protection did not extend to Arar because he was a non US unadmitted alien who lacked physical presence in the US and therefore was not protected either by the Fifth Amendment or from being tortured according to a precedent established in the case of *Harbury v Deutch (2000)*.[16] Clearly no country would claim that it has a legal right to torture people, or would normally even admit to being complicit in such torture, therefore the more pertinent question is not whether it happened but whether its use is ever practicable or whether it is anomalous to uphold its total prohibition. However, as international law totally prohibits Government officials from being involved in torture, it is *not* impractical or anomalous to uphold this. Perhaps, therefore, courts should in future focus their attentions not on the practicalities of implementing particular rights, but on the question of whether a particular constitutional provision applies abroad and whether the rights involved are those which belong to the citizens of all free Governments or are implicit in the concept of ordered liberty.

There are naturally conflicting views regarding specific cases such as those described here; however the question remains, whether detaining any individual without allowing the basic right to a fair trial within a reasonable amount of time is a credible way of dealing with even the most politically sensitive of situations. These issues remain important as this approach continues despite a historical commitment to the underlying notion of habeas corpus, current legal prohibitions and various political promises. For example, in May 2010 the US Court of Appeals for the District of Columbia Circuit held that three men held at Bagram Air Base for several years had no right to a hearing which could review their continued detention based on the evidence against them because the location of Bagram was within the sovereign territory of another Government, and as such, there were obstacles to allowing hearings for such detainees in what has been described as an 'active theatre of war'. What remains troubling about this type of precedent is that it suggests that a Government can detain individuals without necessarily having to present evidence in court to prove what they are alleged to have done. Second, it gives credence to, and provides a precedent for, the exercise of unlimited executive power as well as the possibility of the executive effectively evading any sort of judicial review of their actions, thus making it unaccountable. This can be compared with a recent case in the UK where courts released two Algerians who had been detained in Belmarsh because the US had failed to produce any evidence to substantiate their claim that the suspects trained individuals involved in the 9/11 attacks in the US Peirce (2010) has commented that:

> The case raised fundamental questions about the role of crown prosecutors and about evidence against people interned in Britain on terrorist charges. Mr Haddad is an entirely innocent man who has lost everything, he has no place to go, no money and no accommodation.[17]

Whatever the view about high-profile cases such as those of El-Masri and Arar, the fact that detention centres such as Guantánamo Bay remain open underlines that detention without trial in whatever form continues to exist. One question therefore remains.

Is detention without trial a credible means of dealing with suspected terrorists?

Detention without trial is arguably a way of circumventing, if not entirely abandoning, the criminal justice system as a means of dealing with suspected terrorists. Suspected terrorists have thus been labelled enemy or unlawful combatants and have been detained without trial in Guantánamo Bay Prison Camp and other such detention facilities as well as being denied access to legal representation. This represents an abandonment of due process under the rule of law which clearly states that all people should have an opportunity to prove their innocence before a court of law and has been referred to conveniently as the 'preventive paradigm'. Arguably, even when a person's safety is threatened by terrorist activities, it remains of critical importance that these safeguards are able to protect the individual from unlawful actions by the Government. At present, detainees have a right to appeal to a special tribunal, presided over by Judges of the High Court. The Special Immigration Appeals Commission (SIAC) deals with appeals from people the Home Secretary wants to deport on grounds of national security). Under the 2001 Anti-Terrorism, Crime and Security Act, a detained suspect can request a hearing, which takes place behind closed doors. The detainees are not told the charges against them. Former Lord Chief Justice Woolf has said this is no good and that 'secret courts are an affront to our liberty'[18] stating that proceedings ought to be held in public whenever possible and when there is no threat to national security. The person detained should be charged and tried whenever this is a realistic possibility. If this is not possible, detention should be limited to the period absolutely necessary and in any event should be subject to a limit laid down by Parliament. Such an example is provided by Northern Ireland. The 'Diplock courts' were established in 1972 in order to address the problem of paramilitary violence through means other than detention. These courts attempted to overcome the widespread jury intimidation associated with the 'Troubles' by trying suspects in front of a Judge alone. The Diplock courts contributed to the provision of justice in the most difficult of times. They were 'open' to public scrutiny and thus accountable. Detention without trial is certainly an infringement – and a dangerous one – of civil liberties. However, terrorism is equally a dangerous abuse of civil liberties. Does a 42-day detention erode fundamental British freedoms or is it necessary to protect the community from the threat of terrorism? It appears to be a case of trading off one hazard against the other. This is a complex issue at best and one in which it could be argued that even the courts are constrained. In the case of *Secretary of State for the Home Department v AF and another (2009)* the House of Lords ruled that the closed part of a hearing regarding a control order was contrary to Article 6. This means that unless an individual is provided with 'sufficient information' a control order can no longer be made. More recently the SAIC stopped the deportation of two men arrested following a counter-terrorism operation in spite of the fact that they accepted that both men posed a significant threat to national security. Thus the interpretation of the Human Rights Act 1998 has resulted in the UK not being able to deport an individual, or to subject a person to a control order, even if they are a suspected terrorist. The question is whether this is a step too far in using the protection of Human Rights legislation for suspects and perhaps supports the case for a bespoke piece of legislation to replace the HRA, based on UK specific needs rather than European ideals. I shall return to this issue in the final chapter.

The Terrorism Act 2000, The Anti-Terrorism, Crime and Security Act 2001 and the Prevention of Terrorism Act 2005 in the UK and the USA Patriot Act of 2001 all represent important extensions of State power which have been passed by Parliament in the usual way. Much of this legislation has provided the police with greater powers specifically in the areas of stop and search and detention and have also introduced new offences such as 'supporting terrorism'. In addition, the Government campaign to extend pre-charge detention for those suspected of terrorist offences to 28 days limit was secured in the Terrorism Act 2006 (Moran, 2005). The debate to extend this further to 42 days trundles inexorably on. Added to this, control orders can now be applied to individuals on the basis of intelligence presented to special tribunals as opposed to the standard judicial process. This means that if a person is identified as being involved in terrorist-related activity s/he may become the subject of a control order which has the potential to impose a wide range of restrictions such as wearing an electronic tag, refraining from contact with specified individuals or movement outside a demarcated area and being subjected to curfews and house arrest, to name but a few. The essence of Article 5 is to ensure that nobody is deprived of liberty in an arbitrary manner; any deprivation of liberty must be lawful and justifiable, and the emphasis is on bringing the detained person before a competent court within as short a time as possible. Article 5 therefore requires that the review of the need for continued detention takes place promptly. In recent times, the tension between respecting the human rights of all individuals to be free from arbitrary arrest and detention, whilst needing to protect the wider community from possible threats from terrorism, has been at the forefront of much political controversy. One of the most high-profile advocates of the need for extended detention has been Sir Ian Blair, former Metropolitan Police Commissioner who has commented that:

> We do not have a case that has required us to go beyond 28 days. Our position remains that the number of the conspiracies, the number of conspirators within those conspiracies and the magnitude of the ambition in terms of destruction and loss of life is mounting, has continued to mount, is increasing year by year and a pragmatic inference can be drawn that at some stage 28 is not going to be sufficient. The worst time to debate whether an extension should be granted would be in the aftermath of an atrocity.[19]

Whilst it is sensible to suggest that no such decisions should be made on a knee-jerk basis after some tragic event, Sir Ian's position is that extension is inevitable in the face of the terrorist threat that he clearly feels is real. The opinion of the formerly high-profile police officer, who must have been privy to a great deal of information that the general public will never share is difficult to rebut. However, whether or not the threat of terrorism is as pressing as Sir Ian suggests, and whether or not there is an unprecedented amount of information to collect and sift through, is it not still possible to collect enough evidence to charge a person within 28 days after which the police could continue to collect information and subsequently charge an individual with other crimes should they come to light? It has also been argued that the British constitution, with its inherent traditions of liberty and freedom, is strong enough to withstand this type of restriction, characterised as it is by Judicial and Parliamentary safeguards. However, it has already been noted within this chapter that both judicial and Parliamentary safeguards are all but ineffectual when matters of defence or national security are at stake. At such times, the true sovereignty of the British Parliament as the ultimate law-making authority, which cannot be questioned in any court, is much more significant. The former Labour Government made no secret of the fact that it wanted to extend detention to 58 days. It is as yet unclear what the present Coalition Government will do. A previous Conservative suggestion that the 58-day extension suggested by Labour could actually be achieved by the back door in the form of the Civil Contingencies Act which, if invoked, could extend 28-day detention by another 30 is of concern. The mere fact that this might be possible is interesting in itself since I have previously commented (Moss 2009: 4) on the:

> ... deluge of criminal justice and associated legislation – not mention Government Directives – which have filtered down on the unsuspecting public over the last ten to fifteen years. Arguably much of this has been prompted by what could be described as 'knee jerk' reactions to social problems.

It is almost as if the previous Government has made a stockpile of legislation, something which could potentially be used for every eventuality. Whilst it is true that the national security of any state depends in large part on having a sound legal basis from which to defend a democracy, it also means that the term 'security' and all that it implies can become a formidable and influential symbol of power for those in authority who, in turn, may stifle debate about crucial issues in order to support their policies. Whilst the terrorists need to believe that the State is determined to overpower them, the mechanisms which facilitate this also mean that Governments can justify almost any policy by saying that it is necessary for national security. Peirce aptly comments (2003: 2) that:

> The more extravagant the declarations about the needs, claims or rights of a state couched in the same language of national security ought always to be treated with extreme suspicion.

It is just this type of justification that has led to exceptions being granted for states to deviate from the essential principles laid down in the European Convention on Human Rights and the Human Rights Act 1998 and specifically, in relation to detention without trial, has enabled the UK Government to claim that in exceptional circumstances, such as the post-9/11 'war on terror' it should be allowed to withdraw from the obligation of not detaining individuals without trial, and this in spite of the fact that no other European member state has done the same thing. Steyn (2003) has commented that:[20]

> It is a recurring theme in history that in times of war, armed conflict, or perceived national danger, even liberal democracies adopt measures infringing human rights in ways that are wholly disproportionate to the crisis.

I have stated previously (Moss ibid.) that in the current climate political leaders appear to believe that all social problems can be resolved through the statute book. Whilst no one would diminish 9/11 or any other terrorist act, a badly conceived of and executed response does not help solve the problem. Arguably, such responses are a simplistic way of demonstrating that Governments are 'being seen to be doing something'. That does not make for good law or provide a solution to the problem. Crucially the fact remains that the Government will continue to deviate from its libertarian obligations on the basis of national security as long as there is little or no real informed debate about the issues. As such, Rawls' 'veil of ignorance' provides the perfect backdrop against which these departures from due process and the rule of law – established centuries ago – can take place. Human nature dictates that if individuals can get away with something, they invariably continue in the same course of action. The UK Government has thus far not really been questioned about the technicalities of detention without trial and the basis upon which this has been a justified departure from Article 5. As long as this persists, Article 5 will remain ineffectual. In conclusion, Peirce (ibid.: 16) comments that:

> What is now completely clear to us is that internment for the UK just as detention in Guantanamo Bay for the US is in the nature of an experiment and that a significant part of the experiment is the degree of protest and successful protest including by the Courts that those procedures will arouse. To a significant extent, for the present moment, that experiment has been a success for the governments concerned. There has been very little protest, even less in relation to internment, than there has in relation to Guantanamo Bay. No wonder the United Kingdom cannot effectively protest about the fate of British detainees in Guantanamo. Of course it cannot. It is complicit, far more than we originally thought, in the process.

The following chapter deals with my final example which highlights some of the contemporary deviations from Article 6 – the right to a fair trial – as illustrated by cases of extraordinary rendition.

Notes

1. Lord Nicholls in the case of *A v Secretary of State for the Home Department* (2005)3 All ER 169.
2. Counter-Terrorism Bill. House of Commons Hansard Debates for 11 Jun 2008 (pt 0015). Can be accessed at http://www.publications.parliament.uk/cgi-bin/newhtml_hl?DB=semukparl&STEMMER=en&WORDS=hendrick%20mark&ALL=&ANY=&PHRASE=&CATEGORIES=&SIMPLE=&SPEAKER=Hendrick%20Mark&COLOUR=red&STYLE=s&ANCHOR=80611–0015.htm_spnew2&URL=/pa/cm200708/cmhansrd/cm080611/debtext/80611–0015.htm#80611–0015.htm_spnew2

3. http://www.publications.parliament.uk/pa/cm200708/cmhansrd/cm080611/debtext/80611–0016.htm

4. It is important to note that Scotland's detention limits are very different from those in England and Wales. Any reference to detention times in the UK therefore only applies to England and Wales and not to Scotland.

5. http://www.publications.parliament.uk/pa/ld200809/ldhansrd/text/90324–0003.htm#09032428000425

6. Moss (2009: 73) comments that 'Researchers at the Centre for Disease Control in Atlanta, USA postulated in the early 1980's that the spread of Aids was most likely to have occurred because of the movements of a single individual around the world which introduced the disease to North America. In order to test this they traced sexual contacts and in 1982 found a man they called patient zero who, through his sexual liaisons could be linked to nine of the first 19 cases in Los Angeles, 22 cases in New York City and nine more in eight other cities – in all, some 40 of the first 248 cases in the US Shilts (2000) identified this man as Gaetan Dugas, a steward for Air Canada, who travelled extensively and picked up men wherever he went. Dugas developed Kaposi's sarcoma, a form of skin cancer common in Aids victims, in June 1980, before the epidemic had been perceived by physicians. Told later he was endangering anyone he slept with, Dugas carried on with an estimated 250 partners a year until his death in March 1984. Shilts (2000) argues that the Aids epidemic spread wildly because the federal government put finances ahead of the nation's welfare and health authorities placed political expediency before the public health. Added to this he claims that some scientists were more concerned with international prestige than saving lives. He suggests that all of these institutions failed the public and from the point of view of this book, it seems strange that in the face of such a health risk, no attempt was made to prevent this man from being at liberty when the risk to the lives of others was known and quantifiable.'

7. *Statewatch News Online*, 22 December, 2004.

8. This doctrine was first established in the case of *United States v. Reynolds* (1953) 345 US 1 where the survivors of three civilians who died in the crash of a military aircraft asked for the official accident report prior to the trial. The US Government refused to reveal the documents because it claimed that the report contained secret information about the plane's mission and equipment. The Supreme Court found for the Government and held that evidence should not be disclosed when there was a reasonable danger that it would expose military matters which, in the interest of national security, should not be divulged.

9. This concept was most famously established in the case of *CCSU v Minister for the Civil Service* (1984).

10. In the case of *El-Masri v United States* No. 06–1613.

11. The IACHR is an autonomous body created by the Organisation of American States to promote and protect human rights in the Americas.

12. The plaintiffs in this case sued a private company for their alleged cooperation with the US Government in both extraordinary rendition and torture. The Obama administration asserted that 'state secrets privilege' used previously by the Bush administration should be invoked and the case should

thus be dismissed. For details see; mohamed-v-jeppsen-extraordinary-rendition-and-state-secrets.html accessed 22 June 2010

13. http://supreme.justia.com/us/92/105/case.html Accessed 22 June 2010.
14. http://jurist.law.pitt.edu/forumy/2007/03/un-american-way-kafkaesque-case-of.php Accessed 22 June 2010
15. First referred to by former US Attorney General John Ashcroft.
16. *Harbury v Deutch* (2000) established that non-resident aliens in non-US territory are not protected by the Fifth Amendment from torture. In this case a Guatemalan citizen was allegedly tortured in Guatemala by CIA officials. The court held that even if the torture was planned in the US, 'the primary constitutionally relevant conduct at issue here – the torture – occurred outside the United States' and therefore fell outside of the protection of the Fifth Amendment.
17. http://www.statewatch.org/news/2002/feb/11freed.htm
18. The Mail on Sunday, 2006
19. http://www.opendemocracy.net/ourkingdom/2007/11/18/the-case-for-detention-without-trial-rebutted accessed 16 June 2010.
20. www.motherjones.com/news/feature/2004/05/04_403.html

6
Article 6 and Extraordinary Rendition

> Any discussion of civil liberties and restrictions upon people naturally at some point focuses on the fact that arguably certain restrictions upon individual freedom are sometimes necessary and are implemented for the safety and well being of the majority of people. However, the difficulty here of course is that who decides what is reasonable and for whom and in what circumstances?[1]

This chapter highlights contemporary deviations from Article 6 – the right to a fair trial – as illustrated by cases of extraordinary rendition. Subsequent to the previous UK Government's attempts in August 2008 to extend the maximum permitted duration of detention without trial in the UK to 42 days, which was discussed in the previous chapter, it assesses allegations of the use of British overseas territories as secret prisons and recent reports by leading media that individuals have been rendered to such locations and held there illegally. This chapter will also contain an analysis of judicial decisions in cases relating to the right to a fair trial in order to assess how far the European Convention on Human Rights and the UK Human Rights Act 1998 prevent contemporary abuses of the ideals of the rule of law and essential civil liberties.

Article 6: the right to a fair trial

Possibly the most oft-quoted article of the European Convention on Human Rights and subsequently embodied within the UK Human Rights Act 1998, Article 6 guarantees the right to a fair trial. Specifically it provides that:

> In the determination of his civil rights and obligations or of any criminal charge against him, everyone is entitled to a fair and public

hearing within a reasonable time by an independent and impartial tribunal established by law. Judgement shall be pronounced publicly but the press and public may be excluded from all or part of the trial in the interest of morals, public order or national security in a democratic society, where the interests of juveniles or the protection of the private life of the parties so require, or the extent strictly necessary in the opinion of the court in special circumstances where publicity would prejudice the interests of justice.

Everyone charged with a criminal offence shall be presumed innocent until proved guilty according to law.

Everyone charged with a criminal offence has the following minimum rights:

(a) to be informed promptly, in a language which he understands and in detail, of the nature and cause of the accusation against him;

(b) *to have adequate time and the facilities for the preparation of his defence;*

(c) *to defend himself in person or through legal assistance of his own choosing or, if he has not sufficient means to pay for legal assistance, to be given it free when the interests of justice so require;*

(d) *to examine or have examined witnesses against him and to obtain the attendance and examination of witnesses on his behalf under the same conditions as witnesses against him;*

(e) *to have the free assistance of an interpreter if he cannot understand or speak the language used in court.*

Essentially, therefore, Article 6 specifies that everyone shall be presumed innocent until proven guilty and outlines various other minimum rights. Its embodiment in the UK Human Rights Act 1998 has underscored one of the long-accepted fundamental freedoms in Britain, that an individual is protected from being detained unless he or she has been convicted of an offence in accordance with the law. As mentioned in previous chapters, the importance of not detaining people without a fair trial dates back to the ancient writ of habeas corpus embodied in the Magna Carta signed in 1215. This established that no one should be deprived of life, liberty or property without recourse to the due process of law. It represents an unparalleled symbol of freedom under the law. Historically the writ was a judicial mandate which established that any prison inmate should be brought before the court in order to determine whether that person was either guilty, and therefore whether they were imprisoned lawfully, or if not, that they should be released from custody. The right of habeas corpus has always been accepted as the most efficient safeguard of personal liberty. I have commented previously (2009: 132) that:

> The 'Great Writ' ended the King's power to kidnap people, lock them in dungeons and never bring them to court. The habeas story began in an English meadow at Runnymede on June 15, 1215, when dissident English nobles forced King John to sign the Magna Carta, a contract limiting the power of the king in exchange for his right to rule. John was an autocrat and an ineffectual war king. He had alienated the papacy, the aristocracy, the French and imposed ruinous taxes, all of which prompted a war. As a result, England's barons forced John at sword-point to sign the Magna Carta, which began the transformation of habeas from a tool to bring people to trial to a legal action allowing detainees to challenge the lawfulness of their detention.

Habeas corpus remains the cornerstone of what most democracies consider to be their core democratic principles. More specifically, the right of any individual, if arrested and detained, to be tried before a court of law in order to establish guilt or innocence. In any democratic society, therefore, habeas corpus ought to provide the basis upon which any state should justify its right to detain a person under law and if that detention cannot be so justified, then that person should be released. Prior to the enactment of the Human Rights Act 1998 the legal position in the UK regarding the civil liberties of the individual was premised on the notion of residual rights. Citizens were made aware of the things they were not allowed to do, as proscribed specifically by law, with the assumption that anything which lay outside of these restrictions was allowed. This interpretation seems to have been based on the attitude of British Judges that individuals should be free to do whatsoever they wish, without the fear of interference by, or sanction from, executive officials or others. Whether this would still be the likely judicial interpretation – in the light of more recent legislation – is debateable. Specifically, within the UK and since the events of both 9/11 and the terrorist bombings of the public transport system in London in July 2005, UK laws have been amended to tackle this threat to society. Initially, the Antiterrorism, Crime and Security Act, which was enacted on December 14, 2001 authorised the indefinite detention, without an indictment, of foreigners suspected of terrorist activities. Article 21 of this Act allows for indefinite incarceration based on a certificate issued by the Secretary of State for Home Affairs:

> The Secretary of State may issue a certificate under this section in respect of a person if the Secretary of State believes that (a) the person present in the United Kingdom is a risk to national security, and (b) suspects that the person is a terrorist

Any such certificate issued by the Home Secretary allows a person identified within the terms of the Immigration Act 1971 to be detained for the purposes of either expulsion or return to their country of origin. Subsequently in March 2005 the Prevention of Terrorism Act gave the Government powers to expand the emergency provisions to which foreigners are subjected – within the context of war on terror – to cover the whole population, and gave the Secretary of State for Home Affairs judicial prerogatives to detain suspects without trial on the basis not of what they have done, but according to what the Home Secretary thinks they could have done or might do in the future.

Recent legislation such as this, which represents the UK Government's response to the threat of terrorism since the atrocities of 9/11 in the US and July 2005 in the UK (and specifically the Anti-Terrorism, Crime and Security Act 2001; the Prevention of Terrorism Act 2005, together with a House of Commons vote in 2008 to move to 42-day detention (which was subsequently defeated in the House of Lords) are of significance not least because they all represent inroads into that fundamental British freedom. The question here is surely whether this can be justified – even in the face of threats such as terrorism. Could it be argued, for example, that current laws which are in place to facilitate the arrest, detention and questioning of suspects – whilst still respecting their rights under the Convention – are sufficient in most cases to be able to ascertain whether the suspect may be charged, without the need for authorising periods of extended detention for one particular alleged crime? This could be a matter of opinion. On one hand, it could be argued that in the light of the threat of terrorism and those events of September 11th and, closer to home, the July 7th bombings in London, this illustrates the devastating effects that terrorism can have on the wider public. In this sense, the Government tells us that terrorism constitutes a very real threat to the life of the nation. Clearly there are conflicting discourses about this. It is possible to contend that individuals are being made to feel they are more at risk, they therefore accept what the Government says about needing more legislative restraints on behaviour and movement and therefore the general acquiescence that is required to push more and more legislation through on the back of this is readily available and plays right into the hands of a Government which seeks to enforce the social control of the populace. One example of the results that this can have was demonstrated by the unusual situation which developed onboard a plane at Manchester airport in 2009. It was reported that some of the 150 passengers on the Malaga-bound flight overheard two men of Asian appearance talking Arabic. Passengers first told cabin crew they feared for their safety then demanded police action, whilst others disembarked minutes before the flight was due to leave.[2]

On the other hand, commentators such as Waddington,[3] whilst acknowledging that the phrase that could be applied to this is 'rule by fear', also comments:

> When was it otherwise? In the 19th century when the garrotting panic of the 1860s produced the Offences against the Person Act? Or may be at the turn of the 19th and 20th centuries when people feared German Imperialism? When Geoff Pearson wrote 'Hooligan' (charting moral panics over a century) he unwittingly undermined the argument that there was anything new in such panics. We live in a much more democratic age, because of de-alignment of the electorate. Fifty years ago politics was tribal, but affluence and changing patterns of work and life have liberated people from party loyalties. So, how does the politician mobilise the electorate? He does what Greenpeace do viz the environment, Liberty does with regard to erosion of rights, Macmillan Support does regarding the treatment of cancer patients, and every other campaigning organisation does regarding their pet concern – he or she highlights the problems and offers solutions. Now crime and disorder emerged as a political issue around the 1970 General Election, it is doubtful whether it was an invention of party politics. Lea and Young pointed to how crime disproportionately afflicted the working class; feminists scared women witless about the dangers of sex and violent crime; and as David Garland argues, crime actually started to affect the middle classes, if only by insurance requirements to install security devices.

Whilst I accept that Jim has a point, the idea that because it was ever thus signifies that it is neither a problem nor demands either attention or resolution, I do not accept. The increasing over-reach of the law demands attention, not only because the creeping power of the executive facilitates fear-driven law and practice but also because, as this book has sought to demonstrate, the widespread use of the Human Rights Act 1998 is flawed as a defence against the oppressive use of State power. If individuals are constantly subjected to ideas of heightened risk, as demonstrated by the Malaga-bound flight mentioned above, they are more likely to accept Government restrictions on this basis, without question. This blind acceptance is not necessarily either healthy or democratic and merely facilitates the potential for greater social control at the hands of the state. Striking a balance between protecting fundamental rights and freedoms and preserving security, law and order is always going to be difficult but the debate itself sensitises one to the issues. Obviously all states should have dual responsibilities to preserve *both* in the most consistent and lawful way possible. The freedom to speak, to express, to protest and to dissent are the forms of liberty which are essential to any democracy and must never be compromised, even if it means giving those with radical and unpalatable views the right to be heard. As long as that debate continues, we can be sure democracy survives and that certain points of view do not obscure the importance of human rights. It is also crucially important to remember the contention that:

> an anti-terrorism policy that ignores human rights is a gift to terrorism. It reaffirms the violent instrumentalism that breeds terrorism and undermines the public support needed to defeat it. A strong human rights policy cannot replace the actions of security forces, but it is an essential complement. A successful anti-terrorism policy must endeavour to build strong international norms and institutions on human rights, not provide a rationale for avoiding and undermining them.[4]

The intention of this chapter is to focus specifically on the practice of extraordinary rendition. This cannot easily be separated from the concept of detention without trial and therefore, as I have said in previous chapters, there is a certain blurring of these ideas. However, as before, I have attempted, in so far as it is possible, not to duplicate material unless it is to make a particular point of importance. The concept of extraordinary rendition not only negates the venerable principle of habeas corpus, to which I have already referred, but – if we accept it without question as a means of combating terrorism – it also represents a surrender of society's values about essential civil liberties and human rights. Let us begin therefore by establishing what extraordinary rendition is.

Extraordinary rendition

Extraordinary rendition is the Central Intelligence Agency's (CIA) programme of kidnapping individuals in one country and flying them to another country or countries – normally with the intention of having them tortured. It represents an example therefore of individuals being detained without trial but more than this, the process of individuals being unlawfully and covertly detained by Government agencies which is arguably in direct contravention of both the European Convention on Human Rights and the UK Human Rights Act 1998. In the US the CIA alleges that it is an intelligence-gathering exercise, yet the use of evidence obtained through torture is banned in most countries. Torture is banned completely under international law and is not allowed under any circumstance anywhere in the world. The CIA has admitted to 'rendering' over 30,000 men, women and children who have just disappeared. The actual number may be far higher. Countries all over the world, on all continents, have been involved in the programme, either through sharing intelligence used in the programme, allowing 'rendition' flights to stop over, refuel on or overfly their territories, assisting in torture directly or handing over individuals to be 'rendered'. Reprieve (2007: 4) the UK Human Rights Charity identifies rendition as having three distinct elements;

 (i) *Apprehension – This can be ad hoc, for example involving no semblance of a legal process, or it can resemble a legal process;*
 (ii) *Transfer – This can be entirely ad hoc and without process, for example, on a CIA plane, or it can involve elements of process, for example, a 'deportation' without the victim being given the chance to adequately challenge his transfer.*
 (iii) *End point – This is normally some form of incommunicado or semi incommunicado*

US detention, proxy detention by a third-party state, or some form of joint detention.

> 'Rendition' and 'secret detention' together amount to the crime against humanity of 'enforced disappearance,'[5] and usually involve other serious abuses of rights, for example torture and inhuman and degrading treatment, prolonged incommunicado detention and absence of access to due process.

According to a Report of the European Parliament in February 2007 it is alleged that the CIA has sanctioned over 1,000 such flights and as such has contravened Article 3 of the UN Convention against Torture which provides that;

1. No State Party shall expel, return or extradite a person to another State where there are substantial grounds for believing that he would be in danger of being subjected to torture.
2. For the purposes of determining whether there are such grounds, the competent authorities shall take into account all relevant considerations including, where applicable, the existence in the State concerned, of a consistent pattern of gross, flagrant or mass violations of human rights.

In spite of this, there have been a number of well-known cases of rendition. The previous chapter highlighted the case of Khalid el-Masri; however, in that chapter I discussed this case from the position it represents in relation to detention without trial. As noted previously, it is difficult to separate these issues entirely because most of these cases involve all of the issues I am attempting to address in this book. Whilst trying to avoid repetition it is pertinent to mention that El-Masri claimed that he was drugged and transferred to an American-run prison in Afghanistan where he was held for five months, beaten, kept in solitary confinement and interrogated before suddenly being released by being dumped on a road in Albania. In an effort to substantiate his story, El-Masri has had strands of his hair analysed in order to prove his whereabouts and the fact that he had been rendered illegally. Subsequently American agents admitted kidnapping him but said it was a case of mistaken identity. In this instance, it could be called a case of 'erroneous' or mistaken rendition. Such claims have not been restricted to foreign countries. A number of allegations that British airports have been used by the CIA for extraordinary rendition flights have also been made and in July 2007, the Government's Intelligence and Security Committee released its Rendition Report, detailing US and UK activities and policies. Reprieve's (2007) Report to the UK Foreign Affairs Select Committee's Inquiry into the Overseas Territories focused on human rights issues in the overseas territories of Diego Garcia[6] and Turks and Caicos.[7] Numerous allegations of rendition and secret detention at these locations have been made in recent years by credible organisations such as Human Rights Watch and the Bar Human Rights Committee.[8] More detail on this evidence will be provided later in this chapter. However, given that there is clear evidence that these practices persist, it is pertinent to establish the current legal position relating to the process of extraordinary rendition.

The law relating to extraordinary rendition

There is relatively little case law relating specifically to extraordinary rendition; however, that which does exist provides some insight into the legal precedents which should be highlighted. For example, in the case of *R v Secretary of State for the Home Department, ex parte Greenfield [2005] 4* the court held that when conducting disciplinary hearings in prison, the hearing should be conducted with all the features of the Convention's fair trial guarantees. The relevance of this ruling is that breaches of Article 6 have been alleged in situations where there has been a delay or a loss of procedural opportunity – that is, where the loss of that opportunity may have adversely affected the eventual outcome of the trial. In addition, cases have been brought where there has been incompetence on the part of the legal advisor to the point that the trial has been severely prejudiced. Another notable example is the case of *Cakici v Turkey (2001)* which involved multiple violations of Article 6. In this case the applicant's brother was in police custody where he was subjected to violence including beatings which inflicted a broken rib, having his head split open and suffering electric shocks. This treatment was also held to have violated Articles 3 and 5. It is not commonly known that the James Bulger murder case also gave rise to a further case which involved a violation of Article 6. The case of *T and V v United Kingdom (2000) 1* involved the trial of the two children who had tragically committed the murder of two-year-old James Bulger whilst being just ten years old themselves. The relevance of Article 6 here is that it requires that there be an equality of arms between the accused and the prosecution such that the accused is not at a disadvantage. The two juvenile defendants had been tried in court in the same way and with the same formality that an adult would have been, and there was evidence that the proceedings had been incomprehensible and frightening to the two defendants, who were unable to understand fully what was happening. The formality of the proceedings was described as something 'which must at times have seemed incomprehensible and intimidating for a child of 11'.

A question which is sometimes asked in relation to Article 6 is whether the right to the presumption of innocence as specified in Article 6 also implies a right to silence. The answer to this appears to be that the right to the presumption of innocence does not imply the right to silence. However, the court should not convict the accused on the basis of drawing a negative inference from his/her silence alone. This was established in the case of *Averill v United Kingdom (2001)* . The court should also be cautious to use the issue of the suspect's silence where there has been a good reason offered for that silence, as in the case of *Condron v United Kingdom (2001)*. In this case, the defendant had been advised to remain silent by his solicitor, who suspected that he was suffering from the effects of withdrawal from heroin. Article 6 specifies that a person has the right to defend themselves either by conducting their own defence or by using the legal assistance of his or her own choosing. If the defendant has no means to pay for that legal assistance, then his right to a fair trial means that such assistance should be provided free of charge if the interests of justice so demand. For example, in the case of *Granger v United Kingdom (1990) 9* the applicant was a man of limited intelligence, who had been charged with a criminal offence. He had applied for legal aid, but had been refused. In court, he read directly from notes which had been prepared by his solicitor, but it was clear that he did not understand the nature of what he was reading. The European Court held this to be a violation of Article 6. It was apparent that, given the applicant's limited intelligence and the complex nature of the case, a fair trial could not take place for the applicant without legal aid, which he should have been given. The scope of Article 6 means that a defendant should be given fair and unbiased treatment at every stage of his or her trial, and that the trial should be conducted in an open and transparent manner, free from discrimination or any other unfair disadvantage.

Perhaps the most well-known case concerning these issues in recent times is the case of *R v Abu Hamza [2006]1*. This case concerned a criminal law trial and a stay of proceedings. The question here was whether a delay in bringing the proceedings could give rise to adverse publicity and thus the likelihood of the defendant not having a fair trial. The subsequent case of *Babar Ahmad, Haroon Rashid Aswat, Syed Tahla Ahsan and Mustafa Kamal Mustafa (Abu Hamza) v United Kingdom (2010)* was brought in respect of the potential extradition of Abu Hamza[9] and three others accused of setting up an Islamist jihad training camp in the US. In response to this call for their extradition, the men claimed that extradition would subject them to harsh treatment and the possibility of extraordinary rendition under Articles 2, 3, 5, 6, 8 and 14 of the European Convention on Human Rights. To support their case the men provided what has been called a 'shopping list' of complaints against the US which Wagner (2010: 1)[10] says included arguments that:

1. The diplomatic assurances provided by the United States were not sufficient to remove the risk of their being designated as 'enemy combatants'

2. Those assurances were also insufficient to prevent their being subjected to extraordinary rendition.
3. Two alleged that designation as enemy combatants would place them at real risk of being subjected to the death penalty
4. There was a real risk that they would be subjected to 'special administrative measures'
5. There was a real risk they would be detained in a 'supermax' prison such as ADX Florence.
6. They would face sentences of life imprisonment without parole and/or extremely long sentences of determinate length
7. There was a real risk of a flagrant denial of justice due to the possible use at their trials of evidence obtained by treatment or threat of treatment of third parties
8. Three of the men claimed that the extensive publicity which the United States Government's counter-terrorism efforts had attracted would prejudice any jury, particularly when they were to stand trial in New York.
9. Abu Hamza alleged that any jury in his case would be prejudiced by the fact that he had been identified as an international terrorist by the United States Government.
10. The first three men alleged that the threat of a long sentence by United States prosecutors would lead to coercive plea bargaining amounting to a flagrant denial of justice.
11. Finally, the first and second applicants alleged that their detention by the United Kingdom authorities pending their extradition was in violation of Article 5 of the Convention as there was no requirement that the United States Government demonstrate a prima facie (at first sight) case against them in its extradition request.

Although the Court decided that almost all of the complaints were inadmissible and in relation to extraordinary rendition, the court said it was not convinced that the men were likely to be rendered, the main problem for the court was their possible imprisonment in ADX Florence, a prison in Colorado.[11] The men asserted that detention at this facility would result in the imposition of life sentences if they were convicted. Deciding that no extradition should take place for the time being, the court concluded that:

> If a sentence of fifty years' imprisonment were imposed, even with the 15% reduction which is available for compliance with institutional disciplinary regulations... the applicant would be nearly seventy-eight

years of age before he became eligible for release. In those circumstances, at this stage the Court is prepared to accept that, while he is at no real risk of a life sentence, the sentence the second applicant faces also raises an issue under Article 3.[12]

This case demonstrates that one of the ways of combating extradition can be the use of Article 6, the right to a fair trial. In the UK, the precedent that a person cannot be returned to a judicial system which is likely to breach their rights to a fair and public hearing has also been established in other cases such as *Dudko v The Government of the Russian Federation* [2010] where Lord Justice Thomas explained that in order for the claimant to succeed, it was necessary to show that *'the deficiencies in the process were such that the trial he would face on his return would be so fundamental as to amount to a nullification or destruction of the very essence of the rights [Article 6] guaranteed.'* The result of judgments such as these is that it is an increasingly difficult task for the courts to balance the protection of people within the UK's borders against breaches of their human rights, whilst also ensuring that if the State is to extradite or deport them, they will not be sent to other States which will not so protect them. This also means that courts are making difficult judgments on complex political and legal systems, often on the basis of incomplete evidence. This clearly places a strain upon the legal system and can generate unpopular decisions. However, it could also be argued that the alternative, where the courts would be causing serious human rights breaches effectively through omission, might be less desirable.

As a result of high-profile cases such as this, the debate about extraordinary rendition has been somewhat more transparent at least within the media in recent years; however, there has been little real political movement on the issue as highlighted by Reynolds (2006)[13] who says that although a 2006 report by the Council of Europe[14] signalled European suspicions about rendition – and more specifically about US involvement in it – the report itself did not contain any major revelations and thus could only be seen as a 'useful compendium' of public information. The report – carried out by a Swiss MP, Dick Marty – commented specifically on US policy in relation to allegations of rendition and suggested it was clearly in contravention of the Geneva Conventions, by 'outsourcing' torture in Eastern Europe. This report has been criticised for its reliance on secondary data concerning rendition and secret prisons in Europe. Reynolds (ibid.) also reported that [then] US Secretary of State Condoleezza Rice commented that the US [did] not 'permit, tolerate, or condone torture under any circumstances, [will] continue to respect the sovereignty of other countries, and does not transport, and has not transported, detainees from one country to another for the purpose of interrogation using torture' I have mentioned elsewhere (Moss 2009: 157) that:

> in spite of the fact that no jurisdiction has admitted to this wholly extra-legal conduct it has been suggested that this practice has increased since the terror attacks of 9/11. There have been a number of well known cases of rendition, some of which precede the attack on the twin towers in the US ... It has also apparently been used in the mid 1990's by the CIA in their attempts to track down Islamic militant organisations such as Al Qaeda. Since 9/11 further allegations have been made, mainly in the media, that the US had subjected hundreds of people who have been suspected of being terrorists, to extraordinary rendition.

It is relevant, therefore, to assess more recent allegations and evidence of the practice of extraordinary rendition.

Evidence of extraordinary rendition

There have been numerous allegations of rendition, particularly since the advent of the 'war on terror' in 2001 subsequent to the World Trade Centre terrorist attack. These allegations have been made both in the US and the UK. Despite claims and counter claims by both the US and UK Governments, there is no evidence to suggest that the process of rendition has ceased. The relevance of this chapter therefore speaks for itself. Although no contemporaneous evidence is yet in the public domain, we have little reason to believe that this process has indeed stopped or that evidence will not subsequently come to light.

Thus far, the evidence and discourse surrounding rendition includes the following examples. In February 2008, the foreign secretary, David Miliband, admitted that two flights carrying detainees en route to Guantánamo Bay stopped off to refuel at the military based on the British-administered island of Diego Garcia in the Indian Ocean.[15] Through a High Court case brought by lawyers acting on his behalf, allegations emerged in 2008 of the collusion between British and American Intelligence in the torture and rendition of British resident Binyam Mohamed in 2002–2004 in Pakistan, Morocco and Afghanistan. There is no longer any doubt that British agents were involved. This case was referred to the office of the Attorney General and then to the Director of Public Prosecutions. The Parliamentary Intelligence and Security Committee has also reopened its investigation. However, these are not independent inquiries. In February 2009, Defence Minister John Hutton admitted that the British Army in southern Iraq had illegally handed over two Pakistani suspects to the American authorities there in 2004, when Basra was under British administration. They were subsequently 'rendered' to Afghanistan where they were tortured.[16] Allegations of the British Army handing over to the US suspects who were then 'rendered' first emerged in early 2008 when former SAS soldier Ben Griffin spoke out. However, he quickly had a court order imposed on him by the Ministry of Defence to prevent him revealing what he knew. In 2006 the [then] transport secretary Alistair Darling commented that at least six US planes linked to extraordinary rendition (using their serial numbers) had indeed used UK airports in excess of 60 times but despite this he argued that there was no evidence that they had categorically been used for rendition. This type of comment follows a pattern of denial by the previous UK Labour Government in which politicians consistently either denied, or claimed that they were not aware of any cases of rendition, in spite of the fact that the National Air Traffic Service has previously said there were 200 flights through British airspace between 2001 and 2006, by the CIA planes associated by campaigners with rendition. Instrumental in asking crucial questions about this at the time was the [then] Liberal Democrat foreign affairs spokesman Michael Moore who asked Mr Darling specifically for details of landings by six jets with the registration numbers N2189M, N8183J, N970SJ, N129QS, N368CE and N85VM. In spite of the fact that Mr Darling confirmed that these planes has landed in the UK on a total of 63 times, he reiterated that this did not provide evidence of UK involvement in rendition. In a response to this Michael Moore commented that:

> We have a right to expect both the British and American governments to come clean. The disclosures raise serious questions about the number and purpose of CIA flights through the UK. Coming after the Council of Europe found major holes in the oversight of foreign security agencies, this compounds the case for a review of air traffic controls and a full inquiry into international rendition. A fundamental question remains unanswered. Has the UK government actually asked the United States how many individuals have been rendered through Britain? If this hasn't been asked, then why on earth not?[17]

There is also evidence that telegrams sent by the British security services concerning individuals in Gambia led to their arrest at Gatwick airport and subsequent rendition by US authorities. Apparently two men were originally suspected of carrying an explosive device, which turned out to be a battery charger. Following their journey to the Gambia, a further telegram was sent alleging their involvement with the radical Muslim cleric, Abu Qatada. As a result, the two individuals were apparently escorted in chains, to a jet which then flew them to a CIA facility in Afghanistan where they were subject to sleep deprivation techniques. They were then flown to Guantanamo Bay. Although this evidence emerged during a High Court trial to secure their release, the UK Foreign Office has consistently claimed that it did not request their detention in the Gambia and did not have any role in their transfer to Afghanistan and Guantanamo Bay. The problem with this, even if true, is that this type of action would constitute a clear breach of human rights under the ECHR and the HRA 1998 since the UK, in handing over individuals to the US, would have known that they might subsequently have been mistreated. European MP's have also questioned the extent of US involvement in rendition after admissions that some terror suspects had been flown overseas for interrogation, but denials that they had been tortured. A report by the Italian MEP Claudio Fava (2006)[18] also criticised other countries such as Italy and Sweden for overlooking CIA flights which may have used their airports and said that they should have taken the responsibility to check the purpose of such flights. Indeed, considering the existence of flight logs and flight plans, it is difficult to imagine that claims – that such landings by US planes were solely for refuelling – could not be substantiated. The case of Kahlid el-Masri, which has been mentioned in earlier chapters, is a case in point; whatever one believes about Mr Masri's account of events, it would be possible to trace the flights alleged to have transported him from Algeria via Majorca, Spain, Skopje, Macedonia and Kabul to Baghdad. So far, the CIA has decided not to comment on the findings of this report. More recently, although US President Barack Obama announced in 2009 that Guantanamo Bay would close, this has still not happened and does not change the position whereby the US administration insists that other detainees held by the US in Afghanistan have no constitutional rights. Connelly (2009)[19] reports that Human Rights lobbyists in particular have been disappointed with the President's somewhat pragmatic approach to human rights policy since his election, and it appears that President Obama's ambivalence towards detainees overseas has been fuelled by a fear of setting a precedent.

One of the most strenuous critics of this type of policy has been Human Rights Barrister Gareth Peirce who comments (2010: 20) that:

> In the white heat of 9/11, Cheney, Rumsfeld and Bush considered the concept of due process irrelevant as they ransacked the world in search of suspects. Seeking justification they conjured up new definitions. An 'enemy combatant' was any individual judged to be actively aligning himself against America; 'military commissions' were constructed to deal with combatants thus defined. In parallel, America's ambition to extend its jurisdiction grew. ....The concept of its own conformity with international legal principles being exposed to outside judgment is entirely alien to the US... [and] more than half a century after the nation-states of the world committed themselves to a significant chain of treaty obligations intended to permit external scrutiny of their internal compliance with those treaties, America continues to maintain a remarkable isolationism.

Peirce (ibid.) adds that although some commentators have given Obama credit for trying to demonstrate that it is possible for the executive to wage war whilst also respecting the limits imposed on presidential power by the rule of law, in reality she claims that this is not the case. Specifically she comments that in February 2009, Judges asked the Obama administration if it wanted to deviate from the position previously taken by the Bush administration – namely that of imprisoning people indefinitely without trial. The answer was unequivocally no.

As mentioned earlier in this chapter, two of the most infamous locations to have been associated with rendition and secret detention have been Diego Garcia and Turks and Caicos. A Council of Europe Report (2007: 17) stated that:

> We have received concurring confirmations that United States agencies have used the island territory of Diego Garcia, which is the international legal responsibility of the United Kingdom, in the 'processing' of high-value detainees. It is true that the UK Government has readily accepted 'assurances' from US authorities to the contrary, without ever independently or transparently inquiring into the allegations itself, or accounting to the public in a thorough manner.

It also described the term enhanced interrogation techniques as:

> essentially a euphemism for some kind of torture, and it is clear that under the various instruments binding the UK in this respect, the

interrogation regime admitted by the US as having been applied to the above prisoners, would amount to torture or cruel, inhuman and degrading treatment for the purposes of interpreting UK responsibility for events at Diego Garcia. (ibid.)

This was also verified – in a manner of speaking – by former UK Home Secretary Jack Straw who is quoted in Hansard (2004)[20] as saying that:

In the exercise of powers conferred on him by the Prisons Ordinance 1981 of the British Indian Ocean Territory, the Commissioner for the Territory has declared certain specified premises in Diego Garcia to be a prison.

To translate into plain English, this simply means that the Government at the time was well aware of the facilities which existed on Diego Garcia for holding people and the reasons that they might be held there. In addition to evidence of flights which have travelled via other countries en route to Diego Garcia, a number of ships have also been deployed there allegedly for use as floating prisons. These have included the USS Bataan and Peleliu and amongst others the USNS Watkins, Sisler, Charlton, Pomeroy, Watson, Red Cloud, Soderman and Dahl.[21] It would appear logical, therefore, that in the light of the evidence, if the UK is serious about its commitment to upholding the rights embodied in Article 6, it should perhaps undertake an investigation into this evidence. The fact that no such investigation is likely to take place poses the question of how effective is Article 6 in upholding the rights of those whose country might be a signatory to the European Convention on Human Rights, and might further have embodied those principles within its own Human Rights Act but which still appears able to sidestep the fundamental values which were not of European making at the outset, but which was, as this chapter highlighted earlier, significant for its origins in history and dates back to the ancient writ of habeas corpus embodied in the Magna Carta signed in 1215. I mentioned then that this established that no one should be deprived of life, liberty or property without recourse to the due process of law and thus represents an unparalleled symbol of freedom under the law. So what has happened to this right in the 21st century?

Achieving a balance between liberty and security

The quotation from Moss (2009) at the start of this chapter acknowledges the difficulty of realistically achieving any sort of balance between civil liberties and the restrictions upon individuals which might arguably sometimes be necessary to preserve the safety and well-being of the majority of people. It also, however, flags up the difficulty inherent in the question of who should decide what is reasonable, for whom and in what circumstances. In certain circumstances there may be principles which drive the kind of restrictions that might legitimately be imposed. However, the evidence suggests that in relation to issues of national security and perceived or real threats of terrorism, Governments continue to feel the need to be seen to be doing something in the face of a moral panic created by postulations about the war on terror. This paves the way for a greater levels of restriction based on decision motivation by political expediency and goes some way to explaining how the idea of extraordinary rendition has become not only possible but acceptable. But can we really argue, whatever the political landscape – and given our supposed commitments to Articles of the ECHR such as Article 6 – that this is a credible way of dealing with suspected terrorists? The movement towards this position has been facilitated by both US and UK responses to the so-called 'war on terror' the language of which has helped to provide justifications for the sidestepping of basic libertarian values which most people have taken for granted for centuries. The labelling of such suspects as 'enemy combatants' has facilitated the circumvention of aspects of criminal justice systems and has thus allowed those so labelled to be rendered and detained, without the need for indictment in a court of law and without the need to provide suspects with normal recourse to legal representation. I have commented that the justifications for the abandonment of due process such as that embodied in Article 6 has been the strongly held belief that the 'war on terror' is of such significance and poses so great a threat, that virtually any means of dealing with this threat has become viable, and any departure from human rights is a forfeit that the terrorist must be prepared to pay. I have also commented before (Moss 2009: 91) that a widely held belief appears to be that in relation to these situations:

> Criminal courts are cumbersome, too slow and unpredictable in their results, and because detained suspects are already deemed guilty, trials before a court of law would be an expensive waste of time. Those in favour of this position may also take the view that in some circumstances inhumane and degrading treatment of suspects and even torture may be justified in the name of the 'war on terror'. However, by abandoning due process under the rule of law and by violations of the human rights of suspects, are the United States administration

and British governments not betraying the values and principles of the foundation of democracies they seek to defend? Is it justice to deny captives who may have to suffer decades of imprisonment any opportunity to prove their innocence before a court of law?

However, surely even when a person's safety is threatened by terrorist activities, it remains of critical importance that these safeguards are able to protect the individual from unlawful actions by the Government. This position is a fundamental part of the rule of law. Kunschak (2006: 29) states that for detention to be considered non-arbitrary and legal under international law a number of conditions have to be satisfied.

> Firstly, detention must be objective in each individual case. In human rights law, such grounds must be stated in some prior legal basis and, in addition, comply with standards of basic justice, that is they must be reasonable, appropriate and proportional. Humanitarian law authorises the detention of combatants by reason of their status as POW's as well as the detention of civilians for imperative security reasons of absolute necessity. Secondly, detainees must be told why they have been arrested and detained ... And [any] administrative decision to detain must be reviewed by a neutral third authority, at least at the request of the detainee. This ... authority must be impartial and competent and rely on a fair procedure. Additionally, the prohibition of arbitrary detention also involves a temporal element. The basic principle is 'the longer the detention, the higher the probability of arbitrariness'. Although a specific time limit cannot be found in human rights law and jurisprudence, the permissible period of administrative detention without trial must be measured in hours or days as opposed to weeks, following which judicial review must commence. Indefinite detention without judicial review is prohibited.

Arguably the critical importance of human rights and essential civil liberties should not be obscured by the threat of terrorism, no matter how serious a danger to security that threat is considered to be. No matter how certain any Government is about terrorist suspects, the requirement to treat all suspects with the same equitable rules in respect of their detention and right to a fair trial, should surely not be compromised. This assumes in the first instance that intelligence relating to security is always correct and that concerns about security and human rights are always treated with equal importance. Many critics of the current UK policy on terrorism would argue – as I have – that this view is profoundly mistaken. I have made the point before Moss (2009: 93) that:

> An anti-terrorism policy that ignores human rights is a gift to terrorism. It reaffirms the violent instrumentalism that breeds terrorism and undermines the public support needed to defeat it. A strong human rights policy cannot replace the actions of security forces, but it is an essential complement. A successful anti-terrorism policy must endeavour to build strong international norms and institutions on human rights, not provide a new rationale for avoiding and undermining them.

One of the critical issues in relation to security is the manner in which any society assesses the extent to which its values are surrendered in order to increase protection from terrorist attacks. The difficulty here is the balance to be achieved between – on the one hand – the suspension of democracy in order to defend it and the avoidance of weakness in acting against it. Because every conflict is unique this necessarily complicates the formulation of a response. There is no 'off the peg' or 'one size fits all' model and therefore every administration the world over treads a fine line between being accused either of reacting in an overly harsh way, or of being overly tolerant. Thus, any administration imposing countermeasures against terrorism is likely to be in a no-win situation. As a result it is all the more important not to lose sight of what terrorism is all about. In the broadest sense it can be majorly indiscriminate and either can, or is designed specifically to, provoke panic or other reactions that the perpetrators can harness for their own purposes. In either sense it is a means to an end – whether it is for the purpose sustaining a 'jihad' or for inflaming public opinion against the West. As a result, whatever response occurs against the terrorist threat, the problem of balancing this against human rights and civil liberties is ever present and ever problematic. Nonetheless, however difficult this may be, arguably human rights and civil liberties should prevail. If they do not, this negates completely both the European Convention on Human Rights and international law, and would essentially advocate as a precedent the use of torture, detention without trial and extraordinary rendition as permissible as well as negating the principle of habeas corpus. Pertinently, Professor Ken Pease reminded me at this point of the 'dragons' teeth aspect of extraordinary rendition, and of the relevance of the Irish Republican Jeremiah O'Donovan Rossa[22] who relevantly was arrested and jailed in 1858 without trial for a year. His life as an Irish Fenian is well documented but he is perhaps best for the speech given at his funeral by Pádraig Pearse[23] which ended with the lines:

> They think that they have pacified Ireland. They think that they have purchased half of us and intimidated the other half. They think that they have foreseen everything, think that they have provided against everything; but, the fools, the fools, the fools! – they have left us our Fenian dead, and while Ireland holds these graves, Ireland unfree shall never be at peace.[24]

Simply put, making people martyrs is counterproductive; so, with regard to the situation in Iraq – this being the reason, we are told, for all of these extraordinary measures, such as rendition – one could perhaps ask whether the Americans and the British have learnt anything. For if anything was guaranteed to create a common focus for Iraqi nationalism it was this.

Of concern also is the fact that in spite of European law and the enactment of the same principles within domestic law – in the form of the Human Rights Act 1998 – it has still been possible for both the US and UK Governments to enact legislation which has facilitated behaviour in relation to terrorism which erodes civil liberties and undermines the basic principles of those essential rights which are supposed to be held so dear. All of this has been possible because of the argument that the risk of terrorism has increased. However, is this really the case or is it merely the *perception* of risk which has increased? The problem here is that whatever the case, once liberties have been eroded, the slippery slope to further erosion is facilitated.

Extraordinary rendition, like detention without trial, is the abomination of liberty in any country which claims to observe the rule of law and represents an infringement – even in the face of terrorism – of civil liberties. Clearly, realism dictates that in the globalised world countries cannot, and perhaps should not, tackle these problems alone. The sharing of data, information, experience and resources is important in successfully tackling and dealing with threats. However, we should not forget that we have many hard-fought rights such as the right to privacy, the right to property, the right to free speech and the right to life. If those rights are actively threatened by criminals, terrorists and even Governments there must be a duty and responsibility to help protect them through practical measures. The problem in achieving this is in achieving the right balance and a proportionate and effective result. Dershowitz (2006)[25] comments that:

> No democracy could be, or should be, willing to employ... tyrannical methods. But if mass-casualty terrorism were to become rampant, there would be demands by the public to take extraordinary preventive measures that would almost certainly violate moral and legal norms. Thankfully, neither Great Britain nor the United States has reached this point yet, and the measures taken to date – increased surveillance, border controls, intensity of interrogation, airport security – have not diminished the 'feel of freedom' for most citizens (at least for those who do not fit the 'terrorist profile'). But if either nation were to experience repeated 9/11s or 7/7s – especially if such mass-casualty terrorist attacks could have been thwarted by extraordinary measures that could have been taken but were not – the public outcry for adopting such measures would become deafening (to say nothing of the outcry for all-out war against any nation suspected of supporting the terrorists – recall Afghanistan). That is why effective prevention of terrorism, by means consistent with basic moral and legal norms, is so important for the preservation of civil liberties. Put another way, the greatest threat to civil liberties today may well be additional successful acts of mass-casualty terrorism. That is why those who love liberty must be at the forefront of efforts to prevent terrorism, even if such efforts require some compromises of the maximalist civil liberties paradigm. So, although it would be possible to prevent future acts of mass-casualty terrorists by taking extreme measures that would eviscerate the feel of freedom, we should not succumb to such tyrannical temptations. But we must begin to discuss other ways of achieving significant victories in the war on terrorism without replicating the immorality of our enemies.

Without doubt, the assertion would be made that in order to fulfil their function of providing security, law and order, States depend on the power to deprive persons of their individual liberty. Indeed I have already mentioned at the start of this chapter, circumstances such as quarantine, where this might be the case. The problem with this is that this power is likely to be abused particularly when it is used to counter emotive threats like terrorism. Deprivation of liberty is a serious consideration which has been of concern constitutionally for centuries and notably since the time of the Magna Carta 1215 and as subsequently amended and extended. In the present climate, restrictions on the deprivation of essential liberties can be found in both the international law of human rights and in humanitarian laws. The right of habeas corpus, or rather, the right to petition for the writ, has long been celebrated as the most efficient safeguard of the liberty of subjects. The 'Great Writ' ended the king's power to kidnap people, lock them in dungeons and never bring them to court. The habeas story began in an English meadow at Runnymede on June 15, 1215, when dissident English nobles forced King John to sign the Magna Carta, a contract limiting the power of the king in exchange for his right to rule. John was an autocrat and an ineffectual war king. He had alienated the papacy, the aristocracy and the French and imposed ruinous taxes, all of which prompted a war. As a result, England's barons forced John at sword-point to sign the Magna Carta, which began the transformation of habeas from a tool to bring people to trial to a legal action allowing detainees to challenge the lawfulness of their detention. Today, habeas is arguably the single most important legal lever to prevent unjust and indefinite imprisonment. Habeas corpus identifies what distinguishes authority under the law from authority that merely purports to be, but is not the law. It is a core democratic principle. If one is to view the US and UK as free and democratic societies, it is of cardinal importance that these principles be upheld. To threaten habeas corpus undermines the very fabric of the rights of the nation because when a person is arrested under false charges or without charge, or, in the case of rendition, kidnapped, that person has a right to petition a court to ask whether this is justified under law. Accordingly the state must justify its right to detain a person under law, or that person must be set free.

Notes

1. Moss, K. (2009) Security and Liberty: Restriction by Stealth. London: Palgrave Macmillan, pp 113.
2. For the full account, readers may wish to access; www.dailymail.co.uk/pages/live/articles/news/news.html?in_article_id=401419&in_page_id=1770
3. In a personal communication to the author, May 2010.
4. Moss (2009: 93).
5. According to the UN Human Rights Committee; 'The practice of enforced disappearance of persons infringes upon an entire range of human rights embodied in the Universal Declaration of Human Rights and set out in both International Covenants on Human Rights as well as in other major international human rights instruments.' For further on this see; http://www.unhchr.ch/html/menu6/2/fs6.htm#rig
6. This is the largest and only inhabited island in the Chagos Archipelago, in the Indian Ocean and has a military base which operates for the 'joint defence purposes' of the US and the UK.

7. Turks and Caicos are a British Overseas Territory consisting of two groups of tropical islands in the West Indies.
8. For further information see; www.hrw.org/press/2002/12/uk1230ltr.html and http://www.barhumanrights.org.uk/pdfs/Jack%20Straw%20DG.pdf
9. Abu Hamza is an Egyptian Sunni activist well known for his preaching of a violent and politicised interpretation of Islam, also known as militant Islamism or jihadism. Formerly the Imam of Finsbury Park Mosque, London, he is currently in Belmarsh prison in the United Kingdom awaiting possible extradition to the US where he has been accused of attempting to establish a terrorist training camp in Oregon and providing aid to al-Qaeda.
10. http://ukhumanrightsblog.com/2010/07/09/worries-over-us-justice-system-as-abu-hamza-extradition-delayed/
11. ADX Florence is a maximum-security prison located in Fremont County, Colorado, US. Unofficially known as *Supermax*, or *The Alcatraz of the Rockies*, it is operated by the Federal Bureau of Prisons, a division of the US federal Government and houses prisoners who are deemed the most dangerous and in need of the strictest control.
12. Babar Ahmad, Haroon Rashid Aswat, Syed Tahla Ahsan and Mustafa Kamal Mustafa (Abu Hamza) v United Kingdom – 24027/07 [2010] ECHR 1067 (6 July 2010)
13. http://news.bbc.co.uk/1/hi/world/europe/4644124.stm accessed 15th August 2010
14. http://assembly.coe.int/CommitteeDocs/2006/20060124_Jdoc032006_E.pdf accessed 15th August 2010
15. Readers may be interested to access the report by *News Night* which can be accessed at http://news.bbc.co.uk/1/hi/programmes/newsnight/7411076.stm
16. For further information see http://news.bbc.co.uk/1/hi/uk_politics/7914669.stm
17. http://news.bbc.co.uk/go/pr/fr/-/1/hi/uk_politics/4817374.stm
18. http://news.bbc.co.uk/1/hi/world/americas/4946668.stm
19. http://news.bbc.co.uk/today/hi/today/newsid_7903000/7903102.stm
20. Hansard, Column 1222W, 21st June 2004
21. Reprieve (2007: 13).
22. Jeremiah O'Donovan Rossa (September 1831–29 June 1915), was an Irish Fenian leader (an organisation dedicated to the establishment of an independent Irish Republic in the 19th and early 20th century) and prominent member of the Irish Republican Brotherhood who was convicted of treason and exiled to America.
23. An Irish Republican political activist who was one of the leaders of the Easter Rising in 1916 and was subsequently executed for his part in this at Kilmainham Jail, Dublin, Ireland in the same year, aged 36.
24. http://www.iol.ie/~dluby/quotes.htm
25. http://www.spectator.co.uk/essays/all/24876/how-to-protect-civil-liberties.thtml

7
Securing Rights – But Which?

Ah, but a man's reach should exceed his grasp, Or what's a heaven for?[1]

In conclusion, this chapter draws together all the evidence from the preceding chapters. It will raise issues of international norms and legal obligations emanating from them in order to address what tensions exist between national laws and international laws and conventions in situations where national security is seen to be at stake. It will consider the impact of the EU's new five-year strategy for justice and home affairs and security policy for 2009–2014. These proposals have been set out by the shadowy 'Future Group' set up by the Council of the European Union and include a range of highly controversial measures including new technologies of surveillance and enhanced cooperation with the United States of America. This development shows how European Governments and EU policy-makers are pursuing unfettered powers to access and gather masses of personal data on our everyday lives – on the grounds that we can thereby all be safe and secure from perceived 'threats'. This chapter will suggest that a meaningful and wide-ranging debate regarding the current situation is necessary in order to strengthen British commitments to democracy.

On the basis of the evidence that has been highlighted in previous chapters, the current situation with regard to the levels of protection for some of the most important rights of the individual is clearly not ideal. It has been suggested that current laws enshrined in the Human Right Act 1998, and which was based on the European Convention on Human Rights only go part of the way towards protecting those basic civil liberties. I have highlighted some of the problems inherent in this situation, with specific regard to Articles 3, 5 and 6 of the Human

Rights Act 1998, and have commented upon the difficulties and complexities of preserving civil liberties whilst at the same time mindful of security. It has not been my intention to state a maximalist paradigm of civil liberties but to suggest that the current balance is not right, to offer some explanations for this and ultimately to suggest an approach which may resolve some – clearly not all – of the problems that these contentious issues raise. I do not wish to over simplify or to trivialise any aspects that I have dealt with, rather to widen the debate about such issues in an attempt to raise the awareness of academics and other relevant individuals or organisation to these crucial philosophical, ethical, moral and legal issues. First, the question arises concerning our expectations of democracy. This seems highly relevant to me. Whilst asserting that the current system fails adequately to balance civil liberties and security, no democracy can ever be entirely without drawbacks or compromises. Nor should we expect this. What, therefore, can we realistically expect of a democracy? Democracy has historically been equated with Government through the people. This was perhaps most famously invoked by Abraham Lincoln in his Gettysburg Address:

> …this nation, under God shall have a new birth of freedom, and that the government of the people, by the people, for the people, shall not perish from the earth.

Because democracy has often been revered as an ideal worth striving for, virtually anything commendable is hailed as democratic (such as the fall of Fascism in Nazi Germany and Communism in Eastern Europe) whilst anything universally disapproved of (such as the recent boarding of the Rachel Corrie by Israeli forces)[2] is generally termed 'undemocratic'. Thus, democracy has become an aspiration, and one which even the least democratic of individuals can lay claim to by virtue of the fact that it is a symbol. Thus, the label 'democracy' has become synonymous with aspirational Government but can also be used by just about anyone to justify even the most undemocratic of actions. A famous quotation that has been attributed to former Prime Minister Winston Churchill is:

> No one pretends that democracy is perfect or all-wise. Indeed, it has been said that democracy is the worst form of government except all those other forms that have been tried from time to time

Pertinently this quotation focuses on the weakness of democracy in the sense that there is no such thing as the 'perfect form of government' but possibly other forms of Government can produces less desirable results than democracy. Churchill was thus of the opinion that there was no other form of Government that could regulate public affairs better.

A good example would be the so-called democratic election process in Zimbabwe in 2008. Despite Robert Mugabe's obvious defeat in the presidential election by the Movement for Democratic Change (MDC) (in which Mugabe was said to have polled just 36% of the vote compared with the MDC candidate Morgan Tsvangirai's 55%), Tsvangirai was warned not to declare himself president because in Zimbabwe this would be classed as a coup d'etat – and we all know how coups are handled. Independent monitors of the election said there was no real possibility that Mugabe could have won the election legitimately, but in spite of this the MDC was left in a position where it was trying to arrange a peaceful transfer of power in the face of Mugabe's overt blocking of the electoral commission from releasing official results and threatening to treat an opposition claim of victory as a coup. Robert Mugabe did not feel he had to defend his actions, rather the power sharing compromise which eventually resulted from this non-legitimate election was declared by him as democratically elected, thus defining it into the realm of the defensible. The difficulty of translating the popular vote into victory can, of course, affect countries who consider themselves to be democratic. Take, for example, the 2000 US election contest between [then] Vice President Al Gore and George W. Bush. On the night of the election, exit polling indicated that Gore had won in Florida, and several television networks aired this. Several hours later, however, after more votes had been counted, the prediction was retracted on the basis that it was 'too close to call' and a recount by hand was required. This culminated in controversy because of the issues of the 'hanging chad'[3] in which the ballot papers had a hole punched out for the preferred candidate. Whilst in many cases there was a clean hole, in others the small piece of paper was not cleanly punched out, leading to debate about whether the true choice of candidate could be discerned. The controversy made international headlines, and the 'hanging chad' has become synonymous with the potential breakdown of election procedures. One of the central difficulties of voting systems per se can also be summed up by Arrow's Impossibility Theorem[4], which suggests that no reasonably consistent voting system can ever result in truly sensible results. The theorem is based on putting preferences into a sensible order where they are known as 'transitive'.

Returning to the notion of democracy, perhaps one of the most important but rarely acknowledged facets of modern democracy is that it is not a static concept. It is not the same democracy that the ancient Greeks would have been familiar with; they debated issues openly and in Athens took turns in holding public office. Modern democracy is generally accepted as being defined by the electorate choosing whom they will elect to govern. This is significant because clearly the concepts of democracy and the ideal of 'rule by the people for the people' have changed with the passage of time and with advances in societies and cultures. Thus the application of the concept is not straightforward because as society changes over time, ideas of democracy, of what is good and bad, acceptable and unacceptable, also changes. I have referred to these processes previously, specifically in relation to the regulation of citizens by the law and the concept of crime which (Moss 2006: 2):

> ... comes into existence when a government legislates to make something a crime. This differs from jurisdiction to jurisdiction although there are, of course, some overlaps. Definitions of crime change over time alongside changes in society. Some acts which used to be crimes are no longer, such as consensual adult homosexual acts, whilst new crimes derive from new opportunities and ways of behaving afforded by advances in technology

The basic idea here seems to me to be the same since historically democracy was, according to Mendus (2008: 11), 'treated with great suspicion and was thought to be a foolish way to govern'. Over time, both democracy and attitudes to it have changed; it has been upheld both as a noble aspiration and, according to John Stuart Mill (1859), an ideal where political power lay with the uneducated, illiterate and poor and thus would achieve nothing but mediocrity. Only recently, therefore, has the term 'democracy' come to signify that which should be strived for at every opportunity. The question remains, however; is this realistic? Opponents of democracy have argued both historically and contemporaneously that democracy is not ideal because it is not an appropriate form of Government for underdeveloped countries and that it is unreasonable to suggest that immature societies should aspire to this. It has also been suggested that democracy gives too much social control to a small number of individuals who may not necessarily act in the best interests of the majority. Crucially, whatever debates exist, democracy does not have to be a static ideal; it is something which can, and has, evolved over time. For example, in the UK, we considered that we lived in a democracy even before the notion of universal adult suffrage was realised. Nowadays, to suggest that the British society was a true democracy at a time when women were denied the vote would be unthinkable. However, what this clearly demonstrates is that democracy is capable of progression and perhaps just for this reason it is an ideal worth pursuing.[5]

Democracies depend therefore to some extent on ideals however unattainable some of them may be. Perhaps the point is that to strive for the ideal is the goal rather than the attainment of it or, to quote Robert Browning (1855):

> Ah, but a man's reach should exceed his grasp, Or what's a heaven for?[6]

The basis of those ideals and their origins can also therefore be of importance. The Human Rights Act is based on continental European ideals, not British ones and, according to Robertson (2010: 11), thus represents a compromise which was based on the lowest common denominator resulting in weakly protected rights. Reminding us of the principle that justice must be seen to be done' he comments that:

> In 1913 in Scott v Scott the Law Lords declared that 'every court in the land is open to every subject of the King.' By 1950....only when justice could not be done at all was secrecy allowed – eg, to hide the identity of a blackmail victim. But the law in other countries was very different: the Nazis in Germany prosecuted homosexuals and 'moral defectives' in secret, and Scandinavian countries shielded defendants from publicity before – and sometimes after – their conviction. So the lowest common denominator compromise was chosen, hence the weasel words of Article 6 of the Euro Convention: 'the press and public may be excluded from all of part of a trial in the interest of morals, public order...or where the private life of the parties so requires. In 2005 the Law Lords disastrously decided the rule in Scott v Scott had been superseded by Article 6 and the result was an effervescence of anonymity orders, gag orders and secret proceedings. This is an example of how the Convention has damaged a freedom seen as fundamental and safe.

Robertson's view is that having based the most recent statement of our rights on a European ideal, we have effectively watered down rights of domestic origin which were established centuries ago by the Magna Carta 1215, the Petition of Right 1628 and the 1689 Bill of Rights. These symbols of liberty made clear statements about the standards to be met in terms of preserving liberty but have been emasculated by adherence to the principles of the European Convention and also subsequent UK legislation such as the Extradition Act 2003. One example which Robertson (ibid.) refers to in relation to this is that of the extradition of Gary McKinnon, who hacked into US Army computers. causing £350,000 worth of damage. McKinnon, an Asperger's sufferer, apparently did not realise the gravity of his actions, and Robertson argues that because of this, he would have been dealt with sympathetically in the UK. However, under the Extradition Act 2003 McKinnon still faces 'fast track extradition' to the US over seven years after his initial arrest and ultimately may face up to ten years imprisonment. This flies in the face of age-old principles like the ban on disproportionate punishment introduced in the Bill of Rights 1689; moreover, it cannot be stopped under any principles enshrined in the European Convention, because what McKinnon will face in a US prison will not amount to 'inhuman or degrading treatment or punishment'. Nonetheless, for someone suffering from a mental disorder, a prison sentence of up to ten years may well be cruel and is certainly unusual. It is for reasons such as this that a British Bill of Rights, which includes aspects such as the prerogative of mercy for cases just such as this, would be far preferable to the European Convention on Human Rights. Before I discuss the prospects for a move in this direction, I have a caveat to what I am writing.

Having read this chapter, Professor Ken Pease, to whom I am greatly indebted, commented that a look at the wider world would be appropriate. I make no apology for the fact that this book is mostly UK-based, since my point hinges on whether the European Convention on Human Rights is an appropriate basis by which to judge UK rights and thus whether its enactment into domestic law through the Human Rights Act 1998 was or remains appropriate. However, I accept that this point is well made. I have said before that it is not my intention to assert some maximalist paradigm of civil liberties. Neither is it my intention to ignore the merits of the democracy in which we currently live. Indeed, it is precisely because of our current political and cultural environment that I am able to write this book and to have it published. However, Ken (2010)[7] commented that:

> To me, agonising about databases and CCTV when for most of the developing world the notion of rights is foreign and personally unattainable strikes me (being Biblical) as straining at gnats and swallowing camels.

For this reason I want to make it clear that I do not want to dismiss some of the essential certainties with which we live. For example, whilst acknowledging that a person may be caught on CCTV with their lover, we know for certain that an unjust or outrageous punishment will not be the outcome. This cannot, of course, be said for other jurisdictions with whom we would not share the same ideologies or justice system. For example, the most recent case of individuals falling foul of very different laws in other countries can be demonstrated by the case of Ayman Najafi and Charlotte Adams, who were sentenced in Dubai to a month in prison, subsequent deportation and a £200 fine for drinking alcohol. The pair were arrested in Dubai in November 2009 for kissing in public at a hotel restaurant and is the latest in a series of incidents over recent years in which foreigners have broken Dubai's strict decency laws. Perhaps the most well-known case has been that of Michelle Palmer and Vince Acors, who were sentenced in 2008 to three months in jail, deportation and a £200 fine for having sexual intercourse out-side marriage (on a beach in Dubai) and offending public decency.[8] This case also symbolises the potential clash of cultures between Western values and conservative Arab laws. What would doubtless be consid-ered a fairly harmless act or misdemeanour in the UK can obviously be considered as much more serious elsewhere. We can also be fairly sure that in the UK we will not fall foul of the unjust rule of dictators such as Charles Taylor,[9] whose Revolutionary United Front fighters were notori-ous for hacking off the arms and legs of the civilian population with machetes, as well as killing, raping and robbing them.

In short, I want to stress that I agree that there should be a realisation that having this book published, saying what it does, puts our rights in the UK on a different planet to most people in the world. However, not taking what we have for granted is also crucial in trying to uphold and preserve democracy as we have come to know it. Without debate and discourse – even about seemingly small things – there remains poten-tial for the machinery of any Government to work far beyond its power. Keeping this debate alive and transparent may have helped to put us in this position. To be certain, we are better off than many countries in the world, but this does not mean we should rest on our laurels. We should continue to strive for justice and fairness and we should not turn a blind eye to small issues or to big ones – such as torture, detention with-out trial and rendition. This debate should now include a discussion of whether our Human Rights Act 1998, based as it is on a European model, continues to be the most appropriate way in which to preserve some of our essential rights and liberties. Is it time for a change to a more bespoke version of this legislation, and is a move in this direction feasible or even likely?

Human Rights or a Bill of Rights?

Before the May 2010 General Election, the Conservative party promised that if elected, it would, in its first term in office, repeal the Human Rights Act 1998 in favour of the introduction of a British Bill of Rights. I will deal with this specifically later in this chapter. Subsequent to the resultant hung Parliament and the Conservative coalition with the Liberal Democrats this might be much more difficult, if not impossible. But the questions are, why would they want to, and what effect would this have? Tory euro sceptics have long disliked aspects of the Human Rights Act (including the absolute prohibition on torture). They seem to have forgotten that the original ideas behind it were initially backed by the Churchill Government in the face of the threat of Communism and Fascism and on the basis that the promotion of ideals such as the right to a fair trial, the preservation of human dignity and free speech were worth protecting. The most recent Conservative manifesto policy did not entail Britain repealing the European Convention on Human Rights, thus ensuring that British citizens would keep the right to appeal to Strasbourg, but this has merely been another factor for the Tory euro sceptics to baulk about. The Government seems to be able to get away with this because, although the Human Rights Act 1998 made the European Convention on Human Rights part of UK law, most people do not know the difference between them. The Tories have argued that the idea behind enacting a new British Bill of Rights would be to protect the Convention's rights in British law and to prevent British citizens having to go to Strasbourg to protect those rights – but isn't this what the Human Rights Act has already sought to do? Prior to the election, the Conservative party suggested that either a Bill of Rights could be newly drafted or alternatively the European Convention could be used as its basis but with added sections compatible with the Convention. They did not say that there was anything that they specifically wanted to repeal – so one question which could be asked is: what is the point?

There are a number of problems with the Human Rights Act, some of which have been mentioned in previous chapters specifically in relation to the levels of protection afforded by the Act regarding Articles 3, 5 and 6. More generally, one of the problems with the Act is precisely that it was based on a continental European model and, as such, only codifies rights that can be classed as European. It gives no protection against knee-jerk laws passed by the domestic Government, not does it take into consideration the long British history of civil rights first enshrined in the Bill of Rights 1689 and which guaranteed free speech in Parliament. It gives no protection within the UK criminal justice system, for example, concerning trial by jury, demonstrated by the recent move to Judge-only trials for offences such as armed robbery. There are clearly inadequacies within the current legislation which arguably could be remedied by enacting a better system, more suited to current needs and based on UK specific, rather than European ideals. This may not be easy as there appears to be political reticence in some quarters about implementing such an idea. Why are some politicians afraid of enshrining these rights into a more appropriate document for the UK? The sceptic might say that it is because politicians like to have the flexibility to do what they like, and a new Declaration of Rights may stifle this flexibility, particularly if measures to entrench it were included – but since the General Election of May 2010, we have been promised real change to secure civil liberties, so surely the time has come to do something concrete about this?

There are many rights which are historically fundamental to our specific notions of democracy which a euro-based document can never enshrine and about which we should not be prepared to compromise – as we have in recent years. A further reason why we should act on this now is not just because these rights are poorly protected, but also because the furiously fast pace at which civil liberties are being degraded both by new laws and by a previous UK Government influenced to a huge extent by the US in relation to the post-9/11 perceived threat of terrorism and espionage. More time now appears to be spent on assessing threats and potential risk – which arguably cannot easily be quantified – than thinking about protecting civil liberties. This seems to be a particular problem within the UK, perhaps even more so than the US, where civil liberties advocates managed to oppose the plan for a Total Information Awareness system – but which we are introducing by the backdoor. One thing which appears to differentiate us in this sense from certain other jurisdictions is that we can almost always rely on the great British public not to be bothered. Perhaps this is a result of our domestic history and puts one in mind of a debate aired recently on BBC Radio 4 concerning the end of the Berlin Wall. One academic commented that the Germans were far more concerned about things exactly like the example given, because of the legacy of the Stasi – a legacy which we do not specifically share.[10] The result is that within the UK, there are few critical voices; inevitably, the fewer critics there are, the less pressure there is on the Government to alter course. This silence assists the drift towards authoritarianism and seems all the more odd if we touch on some examples of the rarely commented-upon moves against civil liberties that have occurred very recently.

Furedi (2005) comments ably on what he perceives as a lack of healthy debate regarding issues of civil liberties and more specifically the lack of overt dissent within the UK. He also comments that it often appears that we miss the point of crucial issues – one prime example being the 'war on terror'. He asserts that there is so much focus on the potential for literal threats from terrorism that any other issues, such as the threat posed by the *ideology* of what he calls 'jihadi militancy', have been forgotten. The reaction to the threat by the US and the UK, as an unsustainable, unjustified 'atavistic nihilism' perpetrated by a minority of people who have failed to move into the 21st century, has effectively clouded other important issues. This has prevented real debates about the origins of this problem, its possible links with Western values and modernity, and the potential solutions which could be based on both a better understanding of the ideologies of the adversary, and also a clearer picture of the principles, ethics and morals of our own civilisations. The confusion which surrounds issues such as thus is not unique. Within the UK we are arguably quite adept at 'getting the wrong end of the stick' ably assisted by the British media. In so doing, we often miss the real point of issues or focus intensely on certain issues to the exclusion of others that are just as, if not more, important. One recent example is demonstrated by the debate over the differing interpretations by British courts as to what kind of behaviour amounts to what type of offence. This debate has been particularly widely discussed in relation to the complex issue of assisted suicide which, for the time being, remains a criminal offence. However, interim guidelines issued in September 2009 by the Director of Public Prosecutions set out the factors which weigh in favour of and against prosecution in different cases in England and Wales. The public debate focused specifically on three examples of assisted suicide. First was the case relating to Kay Gilderdale, who had administered lethal drugs to end her severely ill 31-year-old daughter's life after the young woman's own attempts at suicide failed. The mother was cleared of attempted murder. Second was the case of Frances Inglis, who was jailed for nine years for murder after she injected her brain-damaged son Thomas, with a lethal dose of heroin. Finally there was the case of broadcaster Ray Gosling, who was being investigated by police after admitting on the BBC's Inside Out programme that he had smothered his dying lover with a pillow in hospital.[11] It is interesting that the subsequent debate concerning these three cases did not particularly hinge on what the crucially important differences might be between assisted suicide and intentional killing or murder, or how the criminal justice system ought to respond to these, but on the illnesses of the deceased individuals in question and the backgrounds and personalities of those who had been involved at the time of their deaths. The minutiae of sensational aspects of these cases effectively obscured the real debate that should have occurred.

What else are we getting wrong? Current debates about privacy, the availability of information and how it might potentially be used, do not appear to turn on critical issues of civil liberties but on peripheral matters such as personal indiscretions. James (2008) cites the case of the 'Ken Aide' – the former Mayor of London's assistant who was under scrutiny after questions were raised about two specific issues. The first concerned money that had been entrusted to him by British tax payers. Second was the fact that he had been sending romantic emails to a friend. The focus on 'Ken Aide' was not on his alleged financial malpractice, but on his love life, since the London Evening Standard decided to print his emails word for word. James (ibid.) addresses himself in the main to the debate about privacy. Of equal importance is the fact that only the personally sensational aspect in this case was a matter for public discourse. This being aided by the media, of less concern was the small matter of the public purse and what constitutes efficacy in matters of the use of the taxpayers' money. This over emphasis on the sensational, rather than the important aspects of cases, has been facilitated by the erosion of the right to privacy, largely uncontested. Public interest only appears to focus on what salacious information can be obtained about public figures, and currently it only requires that you have a mobile phone, or you use email, Facebook or Twitter for you to forget about having secrets or a private life. The demand for superficial titbits about the rich and famous has obliterated the debate about what should remain private and why. No one is particularly interested in the fact that the right to privacy was something basic to all civilisations but which totalitarian states have consistently tried to rid themselves of. The debate focuses not on the principles of what is acceptable, but disappointingly only on the nature of what can be obtained. James (2008) comments that:

> Pinching private phone calls and e-mails ought to be a crime, but somehow it isn't. And it probably won't be. There are too many laws as it is; too many of the new laws are useless; and a law against printing anything you can find would probably be seen as an infringement

of free speech, even though the unrestricted theft of private messages amounts to an infringement of free speech anyway. After the Ken Aide e-mail incident hit the headlines, some commentators were quick to note that if you really want to speak freely in private, the thing to do is write an old-fashioned letter.

Moran (2008) has commented that we appear to be carrying ever larger loads of invisible data on our backs for the Government to pick through as and when it pleases. Added to this the Regulation of Investigatory Powers Act 2000 – perhaps unsurprisingly ignored by the press at the time – has the potential to facilitate an army of snoopers checking up on our correctness. The Government stated that its official purpose was:

> to make provision for and about the interception of communications, the acquisition and disclosure of data relating to communications, the carrying out of surveillance, the use of covert human intelligence sources and the acquisition of the means by which electronic data protected by encryption or passwords may be decrypted or accessed; to provide for commissioners and a tribunal with functions and jurisdiction in relation to those matters, to entries on and interference s with property or with wireless telegraphy and to the carrying out of their functions by the Security Service, the Secret Intelligence Service and the Government Communications Headquarters; and for connected purposes.[12]

No one has seen fit in the last decade to ask what 'connected purposes' means but it certainly sounds Orwellian. The over-preoccupation with data and what ills they can solve or indeed how they can and should be used is another issue which is not discussed widely enough. Many individuals hold the view that it does not matter what information is kept about people; if you are innocent, you have nothing to fear. This does not, however, take account of the fact that mistakes with data can be, and have been made, nor does it seek to engage in the wider (and arguably more important) philosophical debate about whether certain types of data on ordinary law-abiding citizens *should* be kept, and if so, for what purposes they might be used. Take, for example, the revelations in 2009 concerning the development by the police of covert mechanisms for monitoring individuals labelled as 'domestic extremists' – a term which does not appear to have any accepted definition nor any legal basis. According to the Office of the Information Commissioner, these mechanisms have included the collection of photographs and personal details of thousands of activists who attend demonstrations, rallies and political meetings and which are being stored on police databases. Officers attending such meetings are also apparently given 'spotter cards' to identify individuals who may instigate offences or disorder at demonstrations. Three specific police units apparently have the ability to monitor 'domestic extremists'. These are overseen by the Association of Chief Police Officers and include the National Public Order Intelligence Unit (NPOIU), which has a large database of individuals that have been termed political activists. When asked what was meant by the term 'domestic extremism' former Home Secretary Alan Johnson is cited by Evans & Lewis (2009) as commenting that supporting animal rights was:

> just one form of domestic extremism. If the police want to use that as a term, I certainly wouldn't fall to the floor clutching my box of Kleenex.[13]

The problem with this approach is that it is surely undemocratic to place just about anyone in the UK who has a strong view about anything, on a list of suspects. The legality of recording the details of thousands of law-abiding protesters on secret nationwide databases should be a cause for serious discourse, not least because of the potential for this type of creeping oppression – if not transparently debated – to become over-whelming and to go beyond what any Government suggests they might first have intended as the objects of their scrutiny. The extent of this type of data collection is demonstrated by the case of Linda Catt, who was told that footage of her protesting at the 2008 Labour Party con-ference had been placed on the NPOIU database and that her car was being tracked by a network of automatic number plate–reading cameras at the roadside. Aside from examples such as this, there have also been revelations that much of this type of data has already been gained and stored unlawfully. For example, in May 2009 the Court of Appeal found that the Metropolitan Police had unlawfully retained photographs of individuals on its public order unit (CO11) database. Originally having over 2,000 images, the database has since been reduced in size follow-ing an audit which revealed that over 40% of the images were held outside the guidelines laid down by the Court of Appeal. Evans & Lewis (ibid.)[14] cite a spokesperson from the Association of Chief Police Officers (ACPO) as commenting that:

> People on the database should not be worried. There are lots of rea-sons why people might be on the database. Not everyone on there is a criminal and not everyone on there is a domestic extremist but

we have got to build up a picture of what is happening. Those people may be able to help us in the future. It's an intelligence database, not an evidence database. Protesting is not a criminal offence but there is occasionally a line that is crossed when people commit offences.

There are clearly many unresolved civil liberties questions about the way images can be taken and stored in the modern surveillance society. It is therefore crucial, with the increasing amount of information that can be collected and stored, that any agency capable of doing so should only be allowed to undertake this for the proper reasons and in accordance with the Data Protection Act 1994. It should also be made clear to people that should they find that their personal information is kept on a database, that they have the right to request information about why it is being kept, where and for how long. There is clearly a need for the police to maintain law and order, but the question remains, how significantly intrusive does the apparatus of surveillance have to be to facilitate this?

The lack of transparent discourse surrounding such issues – although not a source of much public or academic comment – was recently also commented on by children's author Philip Pullman, whom Taher (2009) cites as accusing Government ministers of creating a surveillance society based on 'institutional paranoia and furtive hatred' and commenting that:

'We must fight to defend, to restore and sustain what the virtue of not now, but what could be the natural behaviour of state. We are better people than our government think.'[15]

These comments, made at a civil liberties conference at the Institute of Education in central London, were provoked by revelations at the time concerning the Government's failure to disclose Cabinet minutes prior to the war in Iraq dating back to 2003. Although at the time of writing the Chilcot Inquiry into the war in Iraq is ongoing, the lack of interest in some of the crucial issues therein is both pertinent and palpable. This lack of interest appears to pervade whole spheres in relation to difficult issues, not least the secrecy which surrounds much Government action not just in relation to foreign affairs but also domestically. The debate about oppressive laws that potentially erode civil liberties has come and gone with little comment in spite of the fact that the number of imprisonable criminal offences created by secondary legislation and not debated by Parliament reached record levels. More than 400 new offences were created without direct parliamentary approval in the last Labour Governments' period in office. Of these, 98 offences which would result in custodial sentences were created by regulations in 2007 alone. Lack of debate and therefore lack of scrutiny have effectively meant that significant tranches of legislation have gone unchallenged, resulting in many laws being used beyond their intended purpose and numerous changes of principle being smuggled through by technicalities.

Within the last few years there has been a series of reports on intelligence and security both within the European Union and also specific to the UK. Most recently, for example, the Intelligence and Security Committee Annual Report 2008–2009; Pursue Prevent Protect Prepare: The UK's Strategy for Countering International Terrorism Annual Report 2010; the National Risk Register of Civil Emergencies 2010 edition; the UK Statement on National Security Strategy 2010 and the National Security Strategy: Memorandum from the Cabinet Office 2010.[16] Principal amongst these has been the 'Action Plan implementing the Stockholm Programme' from the European Commission, which has followed the deliberations of the Future Group, set up by the Council of the European Union to consider the impact of the EU's new five-year strategy for justice, home affairs and security policy from 2009 to 2014. Bunyan (2010)[17] comments that the recommendations and plans of the Stockholm programme could be seen as akin to the *'harnessing of [a] digital tsunami'* and that whilst the plan talks about the protection of values, interests and rights, he counters that the record of the European Union revolves significantly more around security than rights or liberties. The Action Plan includes proposals to track what it describes as 'troublemakers and travelling violent offenders' (although what the plan defines into these categories is not mentioned in the document) who will be recorded on a database. The report also mentions that agencies should exchange information on travelling violent offenders, including those attending sporting events or large public gatherings. Bunyan (2010)[18] comments that:

> The EU already has in place questionable procedures for the bilateral exchange of information and intelligence (which may be 'hard' or 'soft', ie: suspicions/allegations) for cross-border protests. The idea of creating a permanent EU-wide database of suspected 'troublemakers' or alleged 'violent troublemakers' on the SIS offends against the right of free movement. Only two Member States out of 27 have national laws on the issue and to 'harmonise' the collection of such personal information and intelligence onto a central database is utterly dis-

proportionate. Since the onset of the EU's response to the 'war on terrorism' the prime targets have been Muslim and migrant communities together with refugees and asylum seekers. Now there is an emerging picture across the EU that demonstrations and the democratic right to protest are among the next to be targeted to enforce 'internal security'.

Statewatch has voiced its concerns that over 80% of decisions regarding security issues made by the European Parliament were actually agreed in secret, 'first readings'[19] and that this is neither a representative nor a democratic way of responding to security generally and border management specifically.

The transparency of the debate

Thus there is arguably an overarching lack of transparency about many of these issues and a lack of informed debate as a result. This is not to say that it is always possible to have total transparency about all decisions, and nor is it possible to consider all views all of the time or to give every belief legal protection. Distinctions must be made, and this point puts one in mind of the recent case of Tim Nicholson, the climate change activist who was made redundant by his employers but took them to a tribunal alleging that he had been dismissed because the company did not like his views on the environment. In particular, Nicholson cited an occasion when he had been at odds with the chief executive of the firm who had left his BlackBerry in London whilst on a business trip to Ireland, and who then asked one of his staff to get on the next plane and take it to him. Nicholson's view was that this was not just self-indulgent and environmentally unfriendly, but that it was an overt show of contempt for his beliefs about climate change by his boss. In a ruling which established that Nicholson *was* entitled to protection for his beliefs and that his claim over dismissal should be heard by a tribunal, a Judge said that Nicholson's views on the environment were so deeply held that they were entitled to the same protection as religious convictions, and that there were five tests which could be applied to determine whether such a belief would be covered by employment regulations on religious discrimination;

(i) The belief must be genuinely held.
(ii) It must be a belief and not an opinion or view based on the present state of information available.

(iii) It must be a belief as to a weighty and substantial aspect of human life.

(iv) It must attain a certain level of cogency, seriousness, cohesion and importance.

(v) It must be worthy of respect in a democratic society, not incompatible with human dignity and not in conflict with the fundamental rights of others.

This is a classic example of individuals having views which are odds and demonstrates the difficulty of balancing beliefs, views or even rights. On the one hand it could be argued that if individuals have a strong philosophical belief it may merit protection from discrimination. The problem is, how one distinguishes between worthy and unworthy beliefs, or between beliefs and 'lifestyle choices'. Added to this is the problem of opening up 'floodgate' claims to everyone who asserts that they have a deeply held view about something and have thus been victimised if those views are not protected in the workplace. There are those who would assert that *any* deeply held belief should be protected. Presumably this could extend to belief systems like humanism or vegetarianism. Whether such a belief would qualify for protection is an interesting point. Nicholson himself argued that his views on climate change were moral and ethical and thus were similar to religious views. He claimed that the company had claimed to be green when in fact it was not. It may have been less than honest of them to hire Nicholson in the first place, in which case this would have been a basis for seeking recourse at an industrial tribunal to determine whether his sacking amounted to constructive dismissal. It is also possible to imagine, however, that Mr Nicholson may have made himself unpopular if his approach was somewhat self-righteous or sanctimonious. Whatever point of view one takes, however, surely the real point is that the company was dishonest about its policies. However, dishonesty does not mean that every belief should be given legal protection. Freedom to hold a view and to speak out about it does not necessarily equate with the need for more legal restriction.

The need for greater transparency of debate about sensitive or contentious issues is of importance. A wider debate does not necessarily have to result in more restrictions or laws but if a democracy is to work properly then more individuals need to be aware of the important issues facing society. Perhaps the time for that debate, in view of the hung

Parliament of May 2010 and the resulting Coalition Government, has come. Indeed Robertson (2010: 11) suggests that:

> David Cameron's offer of...a Bill [of Rights] was left out of the coalition compromise and has now been referred to a committee....If they can put together a credible and inspiring draft, the Prime Minister should summon a national convention to debate it followed by a referendum in which the people of this country could decide to entrench it as the first building block of a written constitution – unalterable except by a referendum or by a two thirds vote in the Commons.

If we take the position that there has been an erosion of civil liberties – a point which I have argued before (Moss 2009) – it follows that a more informed and transparent approach to these issues should be adopted to raise awareness amongst the general public about what might be termed a crisis of fundamental rights and freedoms. One of the few moments when such issues have taken centre stage can be demonstrated by the resignation of David Davies, the Conservative MP, over the vote to extend detention times in the UK. In his resignation statement, Davis said that he feared the move to 42-day detention was just the beginning of an 'insidious, surreptitious and relentless erosion of fundamental British freedoms'.[20] His concerns have also focused on moves to what he has termed a 'database state' as well as the previous Labour Government's commitment to ID cards and the erosion of jury trials. The transparency of the debate could be furthered by greater opportunities for people to become more aware of and involved in discussions about global human rights abuses; the balance between the need for security and liberty post-9/11; legal versus political protection for human rights and the monitoring of new legislation for human rights infringements. Some views might be unpalatable but it remains important in a democratic society for all views to be heard. In relation to the transparency of the debate, Lippman (1939: 190) has commented that:

> the creative principle of freedom of speech...is a system for finding the truth. It may not produce the truth or the whole truth all the time, or often, or in some cases ever. But if the truth can be found, there is no other system which will normally and habitually find so much truth.

Lippman (ibid.) argues that the idea of upholding the right to speak freely should not be deemed to be a magnanimous, noble or unselfish course of action, but must be protected simply because we should be forced to hear what our opponents have to say since it may result in improvement of opinions. This is not, he claims, something we are unfamiliar with; for example, when we consult a doctor, we may not like what s/he has to say to us, but we listen because we recognise there may be some benefit in the doctor's diagnosis. Not stifling opposition is also important because it can combat evil. According to Lippman (ibid.):

> [only] totalitarian rulers think they do not need the freedom of an opposition; they exile, imprison, or shoot their opponents.

So freedom to speak, and thus to have a transparent and informed debate, is arguably a system for better elucidating the truth, and that is why we need to value our liberty and to continue to protect and develop it. However, it is clear that Rawls (1971) would not agree on the basis of his idea of the veil of ignorance mentioned earlier. This is not the only important issue, however; talking is one thing, listening is the other. It is not necessarily the uttering of the opinions that matters. Of much more importance is the necessity of listening and thus appreciating and confronting the debate. Within the UK – as elsewhere – it is this we are less than good at and Governments in particular are rarely good listeners because such failure helps them to sidestep uncomfortable or difficult issues.

Governmental sidestepping

There is a fairly long history within the UK of successive Governments being able to evade or sidestep certain legal or moral principles. This is facilitated by the UK's flexible constitutional system, has occurred on numerous occasions and is normally justified on the basis of defence, national security or, more recently, as a result of the threat of terrorism. Law and the social structures in which it operates are variables which by necessity must interact. Neither can be understood in isolation from the other, and most legal systems are both discretionary and idiosyncratic in relation to the particular society in which they operate. The discretionary element of legal systems has often been criticised for a number of reasons, not least the possibility of unfairness and inconsistency in judicial decision making. There are also those who have emphasised the advantages that a discretionary legal system offers. For example,

Hay (1975) argued that such discretion was an essential expression of the power of paternalism and that it could affect issues such as the ability to grant or deny mercy. Whilst there are those who would both agree and disagree with these sentiments, the long, often impassioned and certainly unconcluded debate about the balance between law and human rights has continued. Whether one agrees or disagrees with Hay it is certain that no one interested in the relationship between law and morality can dismiss three of Hay's particular insights, namely that;

- law enforcement can only be understood by placing it within an historically specific social and political context;
- an understanding of the functions of legal authority is necessary to any evaluation of the legal system and;
- legal power and particularly the power of discretionary authority can be routinely manipulated to support those privileged by position.

Weber (1964) regarded the political systems of modern Western societies as forms of 'legal domination' with their legitimacy based upon a belief in the legality of their exercise of political power. Weber's was a positivistic concept of law – meaning that law is precisely what the political legislator (whether democratic or undemocratic) enacts as law as long as it accords with legally institutionalised procedures. As such, Weber suggested that the law cannot legitimise itself by claiming that it has an alliance between law and morality. Rather, he suggested that law possesses its own rationality, independent of morality and that any assimilation of law and morality threatens the rationality of law and thus the legitimate basis of legal domination.

One of the more interesting and unique factors which facilitates this process is the exercise of the prerogative. Prerogative powers are unique to the Crown and recognised by the common law. They refer to a period in our constitutional history when the Monarch exercised very significant discretionary powers in respect of Parliament and the courts. Gradually as an independent Parliament began to evolve, with Government responsible to and reliant on Parliament for its authority to act, statutes are now the basis of that authority but some sovereign rights remain. Dicey (1915) expressed this constitutional position as:

> the residue of discretionary or arbitrary authority, which at any time is left in the hands of the Crown...Every act which the executive government can lawfully do without the authority of an Act of Parliament is done in virtue of this prerogative.

In reality, and with the exception of certain prerogative powers that involve the Monarch personally, such as the appointment of a Prime Minister, the dissolution of Parliament and the grant of honours, prerogative powers are exercised in the name of the Crown by and on the advice of ministers. In the context of the current so-called unwritten constitution there is no definitive and comprehensive list of prerogative powers. Many authors separate powers into two categories; those relating to foreign affairs and those relating to domestic affairs. A further division can be made between those exercised by the Government of the day, and examples here would encompass foreign and security policy, and those personal to the monarch such as the Royal Assent. In reality, powers are either exercised by Government, or convention dictates the manner in which powers are used.

Conventional imperatives allow the Monarch to continue to perform traditional functions within the constitution whilst at the same time maintaining independence from the political process. The Royal Assent, the dissolution of Parliament, the appointment of ministers and the appointment of the Prime Minister are personal prerogatives which no longer recognise any discretion. There remains the theoretical possibility that the Crown will refuse to assent to a Bill which, for example, sought to prolong the life of Parliament beyond the five years stipulated in the Parliament Act 1911 or may refuse a request for dissolution where, in the event of a hung Parliament, an alternative party leader might be approached to form a Government. It is more likely that the major political players would resolve such issues for the Monarch to endorse as has most recently occurred in the May 2010 general election.

Although the personal prerogatives of the Crown are constrained by convention there are still circumstances in which a real exercise of power could occur. For example, the Sovereign is Commander in Chief of the armed forces, and their control, organisation and disposition are governed by the prerogative. In *Chandler v DPP (1964)* a challenge to the siting of American nuclear air bases in the UK on the grounds that is was not 'in the interests of the State' predictably failed. Lord Reid observed '…the disposition and armament of the armed forces are, and for centuries have been, within the exclusive discretion of the Crown and no one can seek a legal remedy on the ground that such discretion had been wrongly exercised'.

The prerogative has also allowed the Ministry of Defence in the case of *R v Ministry of Defence, ex parte Smith (1996)* to prohibit homosexuals from serving in the armed forces, although this decision was subsequently found to be in violation of the ECHR. A further example is the case of *Burmah Oil v Lord Advocate (1965)* where the court linked reliance on the prerogative to deal with emergencies which threaten the State, in this case the conduct of war, to the prerogative right to control the armed forces. The destruction of the appellant's oil installation to prevent them from falling into enemy hands was held to be a lawful act under the prerogative.

Traditionally the courts have adjudicated on whether a prerogative power existed but were unwilling to go further and consider the legality of the exercise of that power. The turning point came in the case of *Council of Civil Service Unions (CCSU) v Minister for the Civil Service (1985)*. The Minister for the Civil Service was empowered to make regulations and issue instructions relating to the terms and conditions of civil service employees. The legal basis of this resided in the prerogative, civil servants being Crown employees. In 1982 an Order in Council was made banning employees at GCHQ from being members of a trade union on the grounds that industrial action could jeopardise national security. There was no consultation, an established practice when terms and conditions had been renegotiated in the past. The House of Lords held that the exercise of powers was reviewable but in the instant case, although there did exist a legitimate expectation to be consulted, this was defeated by the overriding interests of national security. Such has been the concern over this exercise of discretionary power in relation to serious issues such as defence and national security that the Public Administration Select Committee published a report entitled 'Taming the Prerogative: Strengthening Ministerial Accountability to Parliament' (2003/2004 Session).[21] The report urged the Government to list prerogative powers exercised by ministers with a view to framing appropriate legislation to ensure proper ministerial accountability and commented that:

> ...the Government should initiate before the end of the current session a public consultation exercise on Ministerial prerogative powers. This should contain proposals for legislation to provide greater parliamentary control over all the executive powers enjoyed by Ministers under the royal prerogative. This exercise should also include specific proposals for ensuring full parliamentary scrutiny of the following Ministerial prerogative actions: decisions on armed conflict; the conclusion and ratification of treaties; the issue and revocation of passports.

There is thus a complex interaction between the impact of socio-economic changes and the categorisation of illegal actions. This clearly makes issues of law and civil liberties difficult to reconcile, particularly in sensitive cases where issues of human rights are pitted against those of defence and national security. Added to this are the difficulties which emanate from domestic politics in the UK and how the competing issues of security and civil liberties have been traded off, one against the other. Tracing this from the start of the previous Government's victory at the 1997 general election, the Labour Party manifesto at that time stated that citizens should have statutory rights to enforce their human rights in the UK Courts; that the new Government would incorporate the European Convention on Human Rights into UK law to allow our people access to them in the domestic courts, and that the incorporation of the European Convention would, they said, establish a floor, not a ceiling, for human rights. Some eight years later, Tony Blair commented that:

> Should legal obstacles arise we will legislate further, including, if necessary, amending the Human Rights Act in respect of the interpretation of the European Convention on Human Rights.[22]

The question is, were those promises kept, and if not, why not? I have sought to argue in the preceding chapters that promises to uphold essential human rights and civil liberties, which have been enshrined in history for centuries, have not been upheld and that abuses of the most basic concepts of, for example, habeas corpus, have been sidestepped. I have sought to establish that principle underpinning any explanation for this systematic erosion has been Government policy which has put the need to ensure greater security in the so-called 'war on terror' higher on the political agenda of the last decade than the continued commitment to civil liberties. I have also commented in previous chapters that this is not new; in fact this approach is one which has developed over decades, not least in relation to the conflict in Northern Ireland. However, most recently this approach has been underlined by the terrorist attacks in the US on 11 September 2001 and, of course, the London bombing of July 2005. Whilst not wishing either to diminish the tragedy of these events, or to suggest that some Governmental response was not necessary, the response could arguably be seen as being disproportionate. The [then] Labour Government subsequently passed a series of new laws containing broad provisions, in spite of the fact that the UK had already legislated to produce some of the strictest anti-terrorism laws in Europe. This has included five specific pieces of legislation passed in less than ten years; the Criminal Justice (Terrorism and Conspiracy) Act 1998, the Terrorism Act 2000, the Anti-Terrorism, Crime and Security Act 2001 the Prevention of Terrorism Act 2005 and the Terrorism Act 2006. Whether or not one agrees with the need for greater security in the face of a heightened terrorist threat, five new Acts, all terrorism-based, within the space of only nine years, surely represents a dramatic response, and unsurprisingly aspects of these laws are arguably incompatible with human rights law. For example, Amnesty International (2006: 11) has commented on:

> the breadth of the definition of 'terrorism', which leaves scope for political bias in making a decision to bring a prosecution. The definition is open to subjective interpretation. In addition, such a broad and vague definition easily lends itself to abusive police practices. In the UK peaceful protestors have been stopped, searched and items have been seized from them on the basis of the broad powers that are granted under anti-terrorism legislation to the police.

It is precisely the inordinate breadth of such legislation that has allowed the Government to sidestep criticisms surrounding the UK's involvement in the Iraq war. Issues such as torture, detention without trial and extraordinary rendition, which have been highlighted in previous chapters, go some way to establishing the limitations of the current Human Rights Act 1998 and emphasise the need for reform. Added to this, issues currently (at the time of writing) being raised by the Chilcot Inquiry in relation to national security, defence and terrorism all appear to have provided the Government with justifications to behave in unaccountable ways. Barder (2010)[23] comments that:

> There's a more general lesson to be learned from this ingrained habit of over-reacting to risk. It has been characteristic of New Labour under Blair and Brown to be pathologically risk-averse. The reaction to even the most limited threats of terrorism has been to rush into legislation, much of it designed to permit the imprisonment or house arrest of people who have not committed any offence but who the security authorities think might commit some terrorism-connected offence in the future: hence the indefinite detention of terrorist suspects without charge, trial or conviction for any crime, under the vile régime of Control Orders and the attempted deportation of foreigners who have lived blameless lives in our country, sometimes for years, on mere unproven suspicion of some indirect involvement with terrorism or other terrorist suspects. The government has

tried to legislate to permit the sectioning and indefinite detention of people suffering from indefinable and untreatable forms of mental illness – not because they have done anything to harm others or themselves, but because some committee of men in suits thinks they might do so in future. The same government has introduced the even more vicious system of Indeterminate Sentences for Public Protection, under which those who have committed any of a huge number of offences, some inherently trivial, may be given a tariff or minimum sentence of imprisonment representing the punitive element in the sentence (for retribution, deterrence and rehabilitation) but who will not be released after serving the minimum sentence – sometimes just a few weeks – but will be kept indefinitely in prison until they can prove to another body of men (and women) in suits that they won't re-offend if released.

Like many other Government critics, Barder (ibid.) is not alone in the opinion that the Governments' preoccupation with risk is irrational and based on the fear of being blamed should something go wrong, rather than on a sound assimilation of the real implications. Better perhaps to react disproportionately to a perceived risk, however unquantifiable and whatever infringement of human rights this might incur, than to be found wanting and thus to blame for some possible future event – however unlikely. Thus, the emphasis on risk enabled the previous Government to pass numerous laws allowing for every possible risk, but which at the same time does nothing to uphold the long-established values of liberty. In 2006, Amnesty International recommended that the [then] Government should;

- *abandon policies and measures involving punishment of a criminal nature unless imposed by an independent judiciary upon conviction for a recognizably criminal offence following a trial fully compliant with international fair trial standards;*
- *stop the use of 'control orders'; ensure instead that when there exists a reasonable suspicion that someone has committed a crime, he or she is charged promptly with a recognizably criminal offence, and tried within a reasonable time in proceedings which fully comply with international fair trial standards;*
- *repeal all legislative measures, including in particular the Prevention of Terrorism Act 2005, that curtail the independence of the judiciary and thereby undermine the rule of law;*

- *stop undermining the prohibition of torture or other ill-treatment at home and abroad, for example, by attempting to persuade the European Court of Human Rights to reconsider its jurisprudence establishing that the prohibition of torture or other ill treatment encompasses an absolute prohibition against sending a person to a country where there is a real risk that they would be subjected to such a treatment.*
- *ensure instead that effective redress is provided in domestic law for human rights violations caused by the implementation of legislation found to be incompatible with ECHR rights.*[24]

More recently, other developments to combat terrorism have included very different approaches to those with which we have become familiar. Casciani (2010b) recently reported on a summer camp with a difference held at Warwick University by Dr Muhammad Tahir ul-Qadri, whom he describes a 'an Islamic scholar with a gift for rhetorical flourishes and a message of love for mankind'. Dr ul-Qadri's message hinges on the fact that, contrary to popular belief, extremist Muslims are actually in the minority but thus far have been far more vocal than the silent majority of peace-loving Muslims. His solution is the integration of Muslims into British society and the issuing of a *fatwa* (religious ruling) against terrorism. The weekend camp is called 'The Guidance' and accepts that the time has come to respond to extremist voices who so far have taken centre stage in trying to convince young people in particular about the truth behind the teachings of Islam. Describing the current problem as one of policy, Casciani (ibid.) points out that:

> Dr Qadri is talking about the cancer of terrorism that develops from an infection. He sees the infection as the various strands of hard line Islamist thinking that subscribe to belief in a clash of civilisations. Governments have tried banning some of the groups...But the problem for policymakers is that they find it hard to prove that hard line organisations are part of a 'conveyor belt' towards terrorism.

The problem is not, however, straightforward. Although the Muslim Council of Britain says it wishes to offer real solutions to these social issues, critics say its leadership is weak when it comes to extremism. This compounds the problem for the UK Government in deciding to whom to offer its support. Indeed, with a new Coalition Government elected in May 2010, their approach to these issues, in comparison to the previous Government, is of critical importance. Will this Government's approach differ in respect of the balance between security and civil liberties, and what are the signs of this so far?

Recent developments in human rights and civil liberties

Two major criticism in relation to the UK Government have been its relatively unfettered sovereignty which allows it to legislate on any matter whatsoever and its authoritarian stance in relation to crucial issues such as civil liberties. These criticisms have been extended to many areas including the flexibility of the life of a given Parliament and the possibility for each Government to call an election at a time it considers is most advantageous to the incumbent. Encouragingly, the new Coalition has recently undertaken to deliver a number of Parliamentary reforms including the introduction of the Fixed Term Parliaments Bill. This Bill (which reached the Lords stage on 1st June 2011 and is set to become law by July 2011) stipulates that general elections should henceforth occur every five years on the first Thursday in May, thus removing the power of the Prime Minister to call an election only when expedient for the current Government. This represents an encouraging and equitable restriction on the UK Government's capacity for flexibility. Further reforms will include a reduction in the size of the House of Commons from 650 to 600 MP's and draft legislation for a wholly or mainly elected House of Lords. This is likely to occur very gradually, however, as the proposal is for a 'grandfathering system' which would change the composition of the Lords over a number of years. More specifically in relation to civil liberties the Coalition has launched a public consultation called 'Your Freedom' with the intention of collecting views as to laws and regulations which should be repealed. Following the consultation, some of these laws and regulations may be repealed in what they have termed the Freedom Bill. This would also adopt the safeguards currently found in the Scottish model for the DNA database; would outlaw fingerprinting of children at school without parental permission; would further regulate CCTV and would also restore rights to non-violent protest. An Identity Documents Bill has also been suggested which would remove any possibility of ID cards and the National ID Register. The Coalition have also established their commitment to reviewing the Extradition Act 2003; the US/UK extradition treaty; current counter-terrorism legislation, including Control Orders, and the Regulation of Investigatory Powers Act 2000; the decommissioning the controversial children's database ContactPoint and the amendment of the Freedom of Information Act 2000 to cover more organisations and support cross-Government measures to provide greater transparency. They have also stated their intention to establish a Commission to investigate the creation of a UK Bill of Rights. Conservative MP for Kettering, Philip Hollobone, has already introduced a Private Members Bill of Rights which, if passed, would repeal the Human Rights Act 1998. The Second Reading of the Bill is likely to take place in May 2011.

Earlier in this chapter I commented that before the May 2010 General Election, the Conservative party promised that, if elected, it would repeal the Human Rights Act 1998 in favour of the introduction of a new British Bill of Rights. Such pre-election promises are not uncommon, of course; but the 'proof of the pudding', as they say, is in the eating. Most Governments have made promises to reduce regulation and bolster private enterprise but few have been successful. We have only to remind ourselves of Harold Wilson's promises in his 1947 'bonfire of controls'.[25] From time to time, politicians claim to be – and probably are – sincere about reducing the regulatory burden when it is clear that this has spiralled out of control; there is also clear opportunity to cut down on the deluge of legislation that has reached the statute book under New Labour since 1997 – and about which I have written before.[26] The problem is, can the Government really do something about its own inevitable compulsion to regulate? The Coalition has stated that it wants to address the erosion of civil liberties caused by the previous Government's propensity for over-legislating and certainly the plans mentioned above go some way to facilitating this. My opinion, that the last decade has not been a good example of UK civil libertarian tradition, lends itself to such a review. However, these promises are in their early stages, and time will tell if promises such as the 'Your Freedom' referendum actually come to fruition. We are told that a Commission to look into a UK Bill of Rights will be established but the truth of the matter is that should the UK remain a signatory to that Convention, repealing the Human Rights Act would be a pointless and retrograde step unless the new Government come up with a viable alternative.

Clearly, the law should be viewed as a 'living instrument', its interpretation moving in parallel with the passage of time and in keeping with accepted social practices and norms. Given the limitations of the articles of the Human Rights Act, and which have come directly from those originally enshrined within the European Convention on Human Rights, what is the ideal solution? How can we secure our future against further encroachments into our civil liberties, preserve democracy in the particular ways we want to in Britain and in ways which are designed specifically for the needs of our citizens, at the same time ensuring that rights fundamental to our concept of democracy are protected? We can do this precisely by enacting our own Bill of Rights, not a hand-me-down from Europe that has been 'made to fit' but a bespoke declaration which, according to Robertson (2010: 11):

> 'proudly recites our heritage and history of liberty which will be immutable and enforceable'.

Even critics of my general views appear to endorse the view regarding the shortcomings of such close legal relations with Europe, about whom Waddington (2010: 1) comments:

> I'm afraid I don't hold the United Nations in high regard. In my view, it is absurd to take seriously an assembly of the world's dictatorships that issues decrees about human rights. By my count, there are barely 30 of the 192 member states of the United Nations that qualify as democratic. Duplicity is piled upon hypocrisy when one casts one's eye over the signatories to this high-sounding Convention Against Torture; not only does it include such paragons of virtue as Nigeria and Yemen; it includes amongst its number the very countries to whom the United States is alleged to have sent detainees under 'extraordinary rendition', namely Morocco and Pakistan; not to mention Jordan to which the European Court of Human Rights has prevented the UK Government extraditing Abu Qatada. So, we are left in the extraordinarily ridiculous position that it is a breach of the convention to deport people to other signatory states of that very same convention! To misquote Ian Hislop, editor of Private Eye: if this isn't lunacy on stilts, then I'm a banana

There has been a systematic erosion of civil liberties over the past two decades, more recently insidiously defended by the threat of terrorism. More laws have criminalised more people, more surveillance takes place and yet we are weakly protected in our own country by unsuitable laws which, like children's hand-me-downs, don't fit us very well and out of which we will soon grow even further. Justifications that have been used are defence, national security, the public interest, the war on terror, fighting extremism, preventive detention, the preventive paradigm, the veil of ignorance and upholding democracy. But giving everyone the right to fair trial, within a reasonable time, is democratic. Not torturing people is generally democratic – perhaps with the exception of the ticking bomb scenario. Not kidnapping people and transporting them to foreign countries is democratic. So how can doing all of these things – in spite of universal prohibitions – be done in the name of democracy? Perhaps the most shocking indictment of the 'war on terror' which appears in large part to have justified most of these developments was US President Barack Obama's recent address to troops at Andrews Air Force Base in the US on Tuesday 16th August 2010. The Onion (2010: 1)[27] reports Obama as saying:

> For nearly a decade, our mission in Iraq has been to root out those who would choose violence over peace, to create a stable Iraqi government, and to transfer power to an incorruptible civilian police force, and, in a manner of speaking, we sort of did some of that, right? More or less? Granted this is not the definitive World War 2-like victory most of us expected, but there's a military triumph in there somewhere I swear. You just have to look at it from the right angles.

It is less than heartening to hear the President of a country which has spent $750 billion on this operation, and which has cost the lives of 4,400 US and over 300 British troops, describe it in such definitive terms. This is the war that has provided the justification for detention without trial, for extraordinary rendition and for the proliferation of torture – all in the name of security, justice and democracy. It is the reason we have been told such measures were required – that democracy required it in the so-called 'war on terror'. The problem remains, however, that the debate continues to be lacking in transparency, and the majority of people still do not feel that either their liberty or the liberty of others (about whom they are probably unconcerned anyway) is threatened by any of these measures. What also seems to be missing is a sense of moral leadership. Let us not be in any doubt that this is important; we only have to remind ourselves of the catastrophic impact of leaders lacking a higher moral purpose such as Hitler, Mussolini and, of course, Saddam Hussein. Of course, there is a further debate to be had here – and one which I do not intend to pursue in this book – namely that although most people would dispute this, leaders such as these would have argued that what they were doing *was* morally purposeful. To reiterate an earlier point, I am not suggesting that we succumb to a paradigm of maximalist civil liberties, but that rather than accepting without question extreme ways of confronting the current problems of crime – including terrorism – we should start and continue an informed debate about how to combat these problems without succumbing to the same immorality as those we seek to castigate. Aptly, McTeer (1995: 903) comments that:

> Failure to engage in this kind of debate may lead to a situation where the public discussion of the fundamental issues involved would stagnate at the level of slogans...we must now find new processes and contexts for the resolution of issues which profoundly affect society. Otherwise, we will be faced with ad hoc public policy and legislation in an area of extreme importance to the integrity and freedom of both society and the individual.

Karl Popper (2002) claimed that democracy was not necessarily a good of itself but was still the best system for combating tyranny and evil. Whilst it is not possible to assume that all claims to the moral high ground are either totally good or totally bad, perhaps realism dictates that what we *should* be seeking is a commitment to a global democracy which, whilst not perfect, might be the best way to ensure greater transparency of Government. Perhaps it was always and will always be the case that the newly possible strains moral precepts but this makes it all the more crucial that our interests should continue to focus on how the law responds to this and if it does so in an appropriate and socially or morally acceptable way. Is it not time to redress the balance by putting in place something which is designed for us, which suits our needs, our legal system and our particular security issues and which really gives some realistic protection for the rights which are generally considered inalienable in any true democracy? One size really doesn't fit all.

Notes

1. From the poem 'Andrea del Sarto' (The Faultless Painter) by Robert Browning (1812–1889), published in 1855.
2. The Rachel Corrie, an Irish-owned ship was boarded on 5 June 2010 by Israeli naval forces whilst carrying 20 passengers, crew and humanitarian aid to Gaza. Israeli forces took control of the vessel and took it to the southern Israeli port of Ashdod. The action received wide condemnation throughout the world with protests in Syria, Greece, Mauritania, Bahrain and Malaysia, where some demonstrators burned Israeli flags. In Norway, a military seminar in which a lecture was to be given by an Israeli army officer was cancelled. The Israeli Foreign Minister countered criticism by saying that their policies had not changed and they had already made it clear to the Irish and others, that no ship would reach Gaza without a security inspection. For further details see http://www.timesonline.co.uk/tol/news/world/middle_east/article7144671.ece?token=null&offset=12&page=2 (accessed 16 June 2010). At the time of writing, an inquiry is taking place into these events.

3. 'Hanging chad' refers to a small piece of paper which is punched from a larger sheet of paper, but still remains attached. During the 2000 US presidential election, controversy surrounded the eligibility of ballots that had a hanging chad instead of a cleanly punched hole, to indicate the voter's choice of candidate. The term has remained in popular use with political commentators.

4. Named after the Nobel Prize–winning economist Kenneth Arrow, it establishes method of aggregating individuals' preferences into group preferences. For example, if an individual likes apples best, then oranges, then bananas, that means they prefer apples to oranges and to bananas, and oranges to bananas. However, if a preference cannot be put in best-to-least order the preferences are known as 'cyclic' or 'intransitive'. Arrow was trying to create a voting system that was consistent and fair and would lead to transitive group preferences over more than two options, but he proved that this was impossible.

5. It is worth noting of course that by the same token, evil is also capable of progression.

6. From the poem 'Andrea del Sarto' (The Faultless Painter) by Robert Browning (1812–1889), published in 1855.

7. In a personal communication to the author 26th August 2010.

8. http://www.timesonline.co.uk/tol/news/uk/article4953188.ece

9. Former Liberian President Charles Taylor is currently on trial in The Hague. His trial represents the culmination of a lengthy campaign for him to be brought before an international court for allegedly funding Sierra Leone's former rebels, the Revolutionary United Front, by selling diamonds on their behalf and buying weapons for them. He has been charged with Crimes against Humanity, violation of Article 3 of the Geneva Conventions and of war crimes. Other serious violations of international humanitarian law with which he has been charged include sexual slavery, rape, use of child soldiers and enslavement.

10. Note that the Stasi were only in East Germany.

11. Gosling was later charged with wasting police time 'by knowingly making a false report tending to show that an offence had been committed, contrary to sec 5 (2) of the Criminal Law Act 1967'. For more on this see; http://www.bbc.co.uk/news/uk-england-nottinghamshire-11035402 accessed 20th August 2010.

12. Introduction to the Regulatory Investigatory Powers Act 2000.

13. http://www.guardian.co.uk/uk/2009/oct/26/police-challenged-protest-files

14. http://www.guardian.co.uk/uk/2009/oct/26/police-challenged-protest-files

15. http://www.timesonline.co.uk/tol/news/uk/article5660293.ece

16. All of which can be accessed at the following links; http://www.statewatch.org/news/2010/apr/uk-isc-annual-report-08–09.pdf
    http://www.statewatch.org/news/2010/apr/uk-nss-contest-annual-report-2010.pdf http://www.statewatch.org/news/2010/apr/uk-national-risk-register-2010.pdf http://www.statewatch.org/news/2010/apr/uk-nss-statement-2010.pdf http://www.statewatch.org/news/2010/apr/uk-jt-nat-security-cttee-note.pdf

17. http://www.statewatch.org/analyses/no-95-stockholm-action-plan.pdf

18. http://www.statewatch.org/analyses/no-93-troublemakers-apr-10.pdf

19. http://www.statewatch.org/analyses/no-84-ep-first-reading-deals.pdf
20. http://news.bbc.co.uk/go/pr/fr/-/1/hi/uk_politics/7450627.stm
21. http://www.publications.parliament.uk/pa/cm200304/cmselect/cmpubadm/422/42202.htm
22. Cited in; Amnesty International (2006) *United Kingdom: Human Rights: A Broken Promise.* February 2006
    AI Index: EUR 45/004/2006, International Secretariat, 1 Easton Street, London Wc1x 0dw, United Kingdom, p. 4.
23. http://www.barder.com/2369
24. Amnesty International (2006: 80).
25. Former British Prime Minister Harold Wilson is remembered for his 'Bonfire of Controls'. Between November 1948 and February 1949 he removed hundreds of controls covering consumer goods, industrial equipment and the purchase of foreign supplies. This delighted the press and the public but was not popular with many of his own MP's.
26. See for example Moss (2009) *Security and Liberty: Restriction by Stealth.* London: Palgrave Macmillan.
27. The Onion (2010) *Obama Declares Victory, Sort of, Depending on how you Look at it, in Iraq.* August 18, Issue 46–33, p. 1. http://www.theonion.com/articles/obama-declares-victory-sort-of-depending-on-how-yo,17916/ accessed 18 August 2010.

References

Allan, T.R.S. (2001) *Constitutional Justice: A Liberal Theory of the Rule of Law*. Oxford: Oxford University Press.

Allhoff, F. (2006) 'A Defense of Torture: Separation of Cases, Ticking Time-Bombs, and Moral Justification', *International Journal of Applied Philosophy* 19(2), 243–264.

Amnesty International (2008) *To Be Taken on Trust? Extraditions and Diplomatic Assurances in the War on Terror*. New York: Amnesty International, 10th March 2008, AI Index: AMR 51/009/2008. Accessed 18th August 2010 at; http://www.amnestyusa.org/document.php?lang=e&id=ENGAMR510092008

Amnesty International (2006) *United Kingdom: Human Rights: A Broken Promise*. February 2006, AI Index: EUR 45/004/2006, International Secretariat: London.

Amnesty International (2001) *Stopping the Torture Trade*. London: Amnesty International.

Amnesty International (1973) *Report on Torture*. London: Duckworth.

Amnesty International (2002) *Memorandum to the US Government on the Rights of People in US Custody in Afghanistan and Guantánamo Bay*. London: Amnesty International.

Barder, B. (2010) *The Blair Defence: Never Take a Risk*. Accessed 16 Feb 2010 at http://www.barder.com/2369.

Barnett, H. (2010) *Constitutional and Administrative Law*, 8th edition. London: Routledge.

Bell, J. (2008) 'Behind this Mortal Bone: The (In)effectiveness of Torture', *Indiana Law Journal* 83(1), available at http://papers.ssrn.com/sol3/papers.cfm?abstract_id=1171369 accessed 27 July 2010.

Blair, T. (2010) *Evidence to the Chilcot Inquiry on the Iraq War*; Friday 29 January 2010 http://www.iraqinquiry.org.uk/transcripts/oralevidence-bydate/100129.aspx accessed 17 February 2010.

Boyle, K. (1982) 'Human Rights and the Northern Ireland Emergency', in John A. Andrews (ed.) *Human Rights in Criminal Procedure*, Norwell, MA: Kluwer Academic Publishers, 1982, 144–160.

Bunyan, T. (2010) *A Bit more Freedom and Justice and a lot more Security*. European Commission: Stockholm Programme: Statewatch Analysis: Commission: Action Plan on the Stockholm Programme http://www.statewatch.org/analyses/no-95-stockholm-action-plan.pdf

Campbell, D. and Evans, R. (2006) 'Surveillance on Drivers may be Increased.' *The Guardian* Tuesday 7 March, at http://www.guardian.co.uk/uk/2006/mar/07/transport.freedomofinformation

Casciani, D. (2010a) *Al-Qaeda Ring Leader Wins Appeal against Deportation*. BBC News, 18 May, 2010, accessed 18 May 2010 at http://news.bbc.co.uk/go/pr/fr/-/1/hi/uk/8688501.stm

Casciani, D. (2010b) *Muslim Summer Camp Preaches Anti-Terror Message*. BBC News, 8th August 2010, accessed 16th August 2010 at http://www.bbc.co.uk/news/uk-10905070

Cendrowicz, L. (2010) 'Is the European Union Exporting Torture Devices?' *Time Magazine*, March 31, 2010. Accessed 12 May 2010 at http://www.time.com/time/world/article/0,8599,1976495,00.html

Chilcot Inquiry (2010) accessed 27 July 2010 at; http://www.iraqinquiry.org.uk/

Cobain, I. (2009) 'The Truth about Torture'. *The Guardian*, 8 July 2009. Accessed 14 May 2010 at; http://www.guardian.co.uk/politics/2009/jul/08/mi5-mi6-acccused-of-torture/print

Cohen, S. (2002) *States of Denial: Knowing about Atrocities and Suffering*. London: Polity Press.

Copeland (2008) 'Academic Freedom: Are there Limits?' *University and Colleges Union Magazine*, April, 2008, 26.

Cory, P. (2003) *The Cory Collusion Inquiry Report*. London: HMSO.

Council of Europe (2007) *Council of Europe Parliamentary Assembly Committee on Legal Affairs: Secret detentions and illegal transfers of detainees involving Council of Europe member states*. Switzerland: Council of Europe.

D'Ancona, M. (2007) 'Gordon Brown's Strategy Has Fallen to Pieces'. *The Telegraph*, 18 November 2007, Accessed 16 June 2010 at http://www.telegraph.co.uk/comment/columnists/matthewd_ancona/3644087/Gordon-Browns-strategy-has-fallen-to-pieces.html

Davis, B. (2007) The Un-American Way: The Kafkaesque Case of Khalid el-Masri. *Jurist,* March 5th 2007. http://jurist.law.pitt.edu/forumy/2007/03/un-american-way-kafkaesque-case-of.php accessed 22 June 2010.

Dershowitz, A. (2003) *Why Terrorism Works: Understanding the Threat, Responding to the Challenge*. New York: Yale University Press.

Dershowitz, A. (2006) *Preemption: A Knife That Cuts Both Ways*. Issues of Our Time: W.W. London: Norton & Co.

Dershowitz, A. (2006) 'How to Protect Civil Liberties'. *The Spectator* 2nd September 2006 at http://www.spectator.co.uk/essays/all/24876/how-to-protect-civil-liberties.thtml accessed 23 August 2010.

Devlin, Lord Patrick. (1965) *The Enforcement of Morals*. London: Oxford University Press.

Dicey, A.V. (1915) *Introduction to the Study of the Law of the Constitution*. History of Economic Thought Books. McMaster University Archive for the History of Economic Thought, edition 8.

Dorward, J. (2010) 'Giant Schengen Database Hold a Host of Personal Details That Could Be of Use to Criminal Gangs.' *The Observer*, 7 Feb 2010.

Dworkin, R. (1986) *A Matter of Principle*. Oxford: Oxford University Press.

EU Committee on Legal Affairs and Human Rights (2006) *'Alleged Secret Detentions in Council of Europe Member States' available at* http://assembly.coe.int/CommitteeDocs/2006/20060124_Jdoc032006_E.pdf

Evans, R. and Lewis, P. (2009) 'Police Forces Challenged Over Files Held on Law-Abiding Protesters'. *Guardian.co.uk,* Monday 26 October 2009. Accessed 3 June 2010 at; http://www.guardian.co.uk/uk/2009/oct/26/police-challenged-protest-files

Furedi, F. (2010) *Rescuing Adult Authority in the Twenty-first Century*. Accessed 17 February 2010 at; http://www.frankfuredi.com/index.php/site/article/375/

Furedi, F. (2009) 'Unspeakable: Why the West Strains to Name Its Enemy'. *The American Interest,* Sept-Oct 2009 issue 5(1).

Furedi, F. (2005) 'Dissent? Not Today, Thank You'. *Times Higher Education Supplement*, 9 September 2005 available at http://www.frankfuredi.com/index. php/site/article/66/ accessed 31 August 2010.

Ford, A. (2009) 'Alan Johnson Announces Plans to Curb Excessive Council Surveillance'. *Times Online*. 4 November ; accessed January 15 2010 at http:// www.timesonline.co.uk/tol/news/politics/article6902047.ece

Foucault, M. (1975) *Discipline and Punish*. London: Penguin Social Sciences.

Frick, A. (2008) 'Cheney Defends Torture: It "Would Have Been Unethical or Immoral" For Us Not To Torture'. *Think Progress*. 18 December 2009. Accessed 18 May 2010 at http://thinkprogress.org/2008/12/18/cheney-morality-of-torture/

Garland, D. (2001) *The Culture of Control: Crime and Social Order in Contemporary Society*. Oxford: Oxford University Press.

Garner, M. (2007) 'Are Academics Being Put at Risk by Anti-Terrorist Measures?' *The Independent Education*, Thursday, 14 June 2007. Accessed 31 August 2010 at http://www.independent.co.uk/news/education/higher/are-academics-being-put-at-risk-by-antiterrorist-measures-452977.html

George, R.P. (1990) 'Social Cohesion and the Legal Enforcement of Morals: A Reconsideration of the Hart-Devlin Debate.' *American Journal of Jurisprudence* 35(15), 8.

Gibbard, A. (1984) 'Utilitarianism and Human Rights.' *Social Philosophy and Policy* 1: 92–102, Cambridge University Press.

Green, P. and Ward, T. (eds) (2005) *State Crime: Governments, Violence and Corruption*. London: Pluto Press.

Hart, H.L.A. (1971) *Law, Liberty and Morality*. Stanford University Press.

Hay, D. (1975) *Albion's Fatal Tree: Crime and Society in Eighteenth Century England*. New York: Pantheon.

Hirsch, A. (2009) 'Davis Warns Mps of Erosion of Civil Liberties'. *The Guardian*, Friday 20 February 2009.

Hittinger, R. (1990) 'The Hart-Devlin Debate Revisited.' *American Journal of Jurisprudence* 35(47), 49.

Home Office (2007) *Securing the UK Border: Our Vision and Strategy for the Future*. London: HMSO.

Home Office Report (2008) *'Tackling Violence Action Plan'* London: HMSO.

House of Lords & House of Commons Joint Committee on Human Rights (2009) *Legislative Scrutiny: Digital Economy Bill Fifth Report of Session 2009–10* HL Paper 44 HC 327 Published on 5 February 2010. London: The Stationery Office Limited.

ICRC (2004) *Report of the International Committee of the Red Cross (ICRC) on the treatment by the Coalition Forces of Prisoners of War and other Protected Persons by the Geneva Conventions in Iraq during arrest, internment and interrogation*. ICRC: February 2004.

Jackson, J.D. and Doran, S. (1995a) *Judge without Jury: Diplock Trials in the Adversary System*. Oxford: Clarendon Press. Reviewed by Virginia E. Hench (William S. Richardson School of Law, University of Hawai'i, Manoa) Published on H-Law (April, 1997). Accessed 4 March 2010 at http://www.hnet.org/reviews/show-rev.php?id=959

Jackson, J.D. and Doran. S. (1995b) 'Diplock Courts: A Model for British Justice? Northern Ireland's System of Trial by Judge Is Widely Hated', *The Guardian Independent Finance and Law section*, September 13, 1995, p. 12.

James, C. (2008) 'Someone's Watching You' 14th March 2008, accessed 9th November 2009 at http://news.bbc.co.uk/go/pr/fr/-/1/hi/magazine/7296856.stm

Jaworowski, K. (2010) 'Polish Priest Checks Fingerprints for Mass Attendance.' *Reuters (Warsaw)* Friday 29 January 2010, accessed 15th Feb 2010 at http://af.reuters.com/article/oddlyEnoughNews/idAFTRE60S1PJ20100129?sp=true

Jenkins, S. (2006) 'These Cartoon don't Defend Free Speech, They Threaten It.' *The Sunday Times* 5 February 2006 accessed 29 July 2010 at http://www.times-online.co.uk/tol/comment/columnists/guest_contributors/article727080.ece

Koppelman, A. (2009) *'2002 Military Memo: CIA Tactics 'Torture,' Ineffective.'* http://www.salon.com/news/politics/war_room/2009/04/24/jpra_memo accessed 27th July 2010.

Kunschak, M. (2006) *Creating Legal Black Holes? Terrorism and Detention without Trial: Towards a Changing Rule in International Law.* Unpublished M.Phil dissertation, University of Cape Town, School of Advanced Legal Studies.

Landau, M. (1987) *The 'Commission of Inquiry into the Methods of Investigation of the General Security Service Regarding Hostile Terrorist Activity'* (The Landau Commission), 30 October 1987.

Langbein, J.H. (1977) *Torture and the Law of Proof: Europe and England in the Ancient Regime.* Chicago: Chicago University Press.

Leigh, D. (2004) 'uk Forces Taught Torture Methods'. *The Guardian*, Saturday 8 May 2004, accessed 14 May 2010 at http://www.guardian.co.uk/uk/2004/may/08/iraq.iraq

Levant, E. (2009) *Shakedown: How Our Government is Undermining Democracy in the Name of Human Rights.* New York: McClelland & Stewart.

Lippman W. (1939) 'The Indispensable Opposition'. *Atlantic Monthly,* 164, 189–90.

Locke, J. (1690) *Second Treatise of Government* accessed 28 July 2010 at http://www. htconstitution.org/jl/2ndtreat.htm

Locke, J. (1988) *Two Treatises of Government.* Edited by Peter Laslett. Cambridge: Cambridge University Press (Original published 1689).

Lombroso, C. (2006) Criminal Man. New York: Duke University Press (First published in 1876).

Lords Select Committee Report (2009) *Surveillance: Citizens and the State.* London: HMSO.

Luban, D. (2005) *Rhode and Luban's Legal Ethics Stories.* London: Foundation Press.

Machan, T. (1990) *Liberty and Culture: Essays on the Idea of a Free Society.* London: Prometheus Books.

Mendus, S. (2008) *Democracy: A Nightmare or a Noble Dream?* The Tampere Lecture 2008 can be accessed at http://www.tampereclub.org/epublications/vol3_mendus.pdf

McBarnet, D. & Whelan (1991) 'The Elusive Spirit of the Law: Formalism and the Struggle for Legal Control', *Modern Law Review,* November, 848–873.

McBarnet, D. (2004) *Crime, Compliance and Control.* Aldershot: Ashgate.

McTeer, M.A. (1995) A Role for Law in Matters of Morality. *McGill Law Journal,* 40, 893–903.

Mill, J.S. (1859) *On Liberty,* reprinted (1998) London: Longman.

Moran, J. (2010) 'Panic or Panacea? Border Security in the UK', in J. Winterdyk and K. Sundberg (eds) *Transforming Borders in the Al Qaeda Era*. London: Taylor and Francis.

Moran, J. (2008) *'Crime Control and Civil Liberties'* Talk given to the Association of British Insurers, London.

Moss, K. (2006) 'The Future of Crime Reduction', in Moss, K. and Stephens, M. (eds) *Crime Reduction and the Law*. London: Routledge.

Moss, K. (2009) *Security and Liberty: Restriction by Stealth*. London: Palgrave Macmillan.

Munro, C. (2005) *Studies in Constitutional Law*. 2nd edition. Oxford University Press: Norton-Taylor, R. and Dyer, C. (2007) 'Government Arguments on Iraq Death Dismissed'. *The Guardian*, Thursday 14 June 2007, 4.

Norton- Taylor, R. (2010) 'High Court challenge over UK government's Torture Guidance', *guardian.co.uk*, Tuesday 23 February 2010.

O'Connor, D. (2006) The Commission of Inquiry into the Actions of Canadian Officials in Relation to Maher Arar. Canadian Government Publishing.

Paine, T. (2010) *Common Sense*. New York: Createspace. (originally published 1776).

Parton (2008) 'The Change for Children Programme in England: Towards the Preventive Surveillance State', *Journal of Law and Society* 35(1), 166–187.

Patton, G.W. (1993) *A Textbook of Jurisprudence*. Oxford: Clarendon Press.

Pease, K. (2009) Preface to Moss, K. *Security and Liberty: Restriction by Stealth*. London: Palgrave Macmillan.

Peirce, G. (2003) *Internment: the Truth behind the War on Terror*. Lecture for Liberty at the LSE, 15th December 2003. Accessed 16th June 2010 at http://www.liberty-human-rights.org.uk/issues/pdfs/internment-lecture.PDF

Peirce, G. (2008) 'Was it Like this for the Irish?' *London Review of Books* 30(7), 10 April 2008, 3–8.

Peirce, G. (2010) 'America's Non-Compliance'. *London Review of Books* 32(9), 13 May 2010, 18–22.

Popper, K. (2002*)* *The Open Society and its Enemies, Volume 1*. London: Routledge.

Public Administration Select Committee (2004) *'Taming the Prerogative: Strengthening Ministerial Accountability to Parliament'* (2003/2004 Session) at http://www.publications.parliament.uk/pa/cm200304/cmselect/cmpubadm/422/42202.htm

Rawls (1971) *A Theory of Justice*. New York: Harvard Publishing.

Raz, J. (1977) 'The Rule of Law and its Virtue', *The Law Quarterly Review*, 93(195), 209.

Reprieve (2007) *Enforced Disappearance, Illegal Interstate Transfer and other Human Rights Abuses Involving the UK Overseas Territories*. London: Reprieve.

Reynolds, P. (2006) 'Rendition Report Adds to Terror Debate', *BBC News 24* January 2006, http://news.bbc.co.uk/1/hi/world/europe/4644124.stm accessed 15th August 2010

Roberts, Lord (c1915) *On Conscription* cited at http://www.historylearningsite.co.uk/conscientious_objectors.htm

Robertson, G. (2010) 'The Case for a Bill of Rights'. *The Independent*, 1st June pp. 10–11.

Shamsi, H. and Pearlstein, D. (2006) 'Command's Responsibility Detainee Deaths in U.S. Custody in Iraq and Afghanistan'. *Human Rights First Report*,

February 2006. Accessed 14 May 2010 at http://www.humanrightsfirst.info/pdf/06221-etn-hrf-dic-rep-web.pdf

Steel, K. (2007) 'What Really Happened to Maher Arar?' *The Western Standard* 26 Feb 2007. Accessed 3 June 2010 at http://www.westernstandard.ca/website/article.php?id=2333&start=0

Steyn, Lord Johan. (2003) Lecture to the British Institute of International and Comparative Law, November 2003. Cited in Lewis, A. (2004) *Are we Better off? One Liberty at a Time.* www.motherjones.com/news/feature/2004/05/04_403.html

Stone, G. R. et al. (2006 *Constitutional Law, 2007 Case Supplement*, fifth edition. Aspen Publishers: Walters Kluwer Law and Business.

Sussman, D. (2005) 'What's Wrong with Torture?' *Philosophy and Public Affairs* 33(1), Blackwell Publishing Inc.

Surveillance Studies Network (2006) *The Surveillance Society*. Report for the Information Commissioners Office.

Swain, H. (2009) 'Teach Yourself Human Rights'. *The Guardian,* 24 February 2009.

Taguba, A. (2004) 'Article 15–6 Investigation of the 800th Military Police Brigade.' Investigative report on alleged abuses at US military prisons in Abu Ghraib and Camp Bucca. Accessed 29 July 2010 at *www.npr.org/iraq/2004/prison_abuse_report.pdf*

Taher, A. (2009) 'Philip Pullman Attacks Labour for Eroding Civil Liberties'. *The Sunday Times*, 1 March, 2009. Accessed 4 June 2010 at http://www.timesonline.co.uk/tol/news/uk/article5660293.ece

The Onion (2010) *Obama Declares Victory, Sort Of, Depending On How You Look At It, In Iraq.* August 18, Issue 46–33, p. 1. http://www.theonion.com/articles/obama-declares-victory-sort-of-depending-on-how-yo,17916/ accessed 18 August 2010.

The Times Online (2008) 'Civil Liberties Violated by Electronic Interception.' July 11, 2008. http://business.timesonline.co.uk/tol/business/law/reports/article4312594.ece

The Times Online (2007),'Home Secretary's Control Orders Made Unlawfully.' November 5, 2007. Accessed 3 June 2010 at http://business.timesonline.co.uk/tol/business/law/reports/article2806534.ece?token=null&offset=0&page=1

Thomas, R. and Walport, M. (2008) *Data Sharing Review*. Information Commissioners Office. Accessed 17 February 2010 at http://www.justice.gov.uk/reviews/docs/data-sharing-review-report.pdf

Wade, H.W.R. (2004) *Administrative Law,* 9th edition. Oxford: Oxford University Press.

Waddington, P.A.J. (2005) 'Slippery Slopes and Civil Libertarian Pessimism'. *Policing and Society* 15(3), September, 353–375.

Waddington, P.A.J. (2010) 'a Personal Communication to the Author Regarding Views on Torture' 18 May 2010.

Wagner, A. (2010) 'Worries Over us Justice System as Abu Hamza Extradition Delayed'. Accessed 19 August 2010 at http://ukhumanrightsblog.com/2010/07/09/worries-over-us-justice-system-as-abu-hamza-extradition-delayed/ UK human rights blog

Waldron, J. (2010) *Princeton Readings in the Rule of Law*. Princeton University Press.

Weber, M. (1978) *On Economy and Society.* University of California Press: Berkley and Los Angeles, California.

Wolfenden, Sir John (1957) *Report of the Committee on Homosexual Offences and Prostitution.* Cmnd 247, London: HMSO.

Zimbardo, P. (2007) *The Lucifer Effect: Understanding How Good People Turn Evil.* New York: Random House.

Index

Index of Cases

Index of Statutes